THE VAUDOIS
LAST FAITH STANDING

THE VAUDOIS
LAST FAITH STANDING

*An Incredible Story of Faith,
Survival and Endurance*

STEPHEN G. BEUS

HARMONY STREET PUBLISHERS
PITTSBURGH, PENNSYLVANIA

Copyright @ 2018 by Harmony Street Publishers.
All rights reserved.

No part of this publication may be reproduced or transmitted in any form or by any means, electronic or mechanical, including photocopying, recording or by any information storage and retrieval system, without written permission of the publisher.

Harmony Street Publishers,
192 South 17th Street, Pittsburgh, Pennsylvania 15203
Harmony.Street.Publishers@gmail.com

ISBN-13: 978-0-9983996-4-5
Library of Congress Control Number 2018954975

Design of Cover and Text by Hue Creative, Megan Katsanevakis

To Pat, for her unconditional love and support.

For Michel and Marianne Beux

CONTENTS

Preface	ix
CHAPTER I. Origins - to 1250 AD	1
Foundation and Progress of the Primitive Church	2
The Vaudois and Possible Beginnings	17
Turmoil within the Roman Church	37
Vita Apostolica	44
Emergence of the Vaudois	55
Persecution, Extermination and Exodus	69
Conclusions	76
CHAPTER II. Bridge to the Reformation (1250-1550 AD)	83
European Life in the late Middle Ages	86
Consolidation, Expansion and Regrouping	97
The Organization of the Vaudois in Medieval Times	115
Persecution	123
Encounter of the Vaudois with the Reformation	139
CHAPTER III. Survival (1550-1686 AD)	157
General Impact of the Protestant Reformation	158
Impact of the Protestant Reformation on the Vaudois	164
Survival	171
In Conclusion	195
CHAPTER IV. Expulsion, Exile and Return (1686-1690 AD)	199
Political-Religious Developments	201
The Expulsion of the Vaudois	210
Exile and Return	226

CHAPTER V. FREE AT LAST (1690-1848 AD)   247
   THE TIMES   249
   THE VAUDOIS HOMELAND   257
   THE BENEFACTORS   262
   FREE AT LAST   268

BIBLIOGRAPHY   273

ACKNOWLEDGEMENTS   287

PREFACE

1992. Leaving the city of Pinerollo some 35 km south and west of Turin this fine spring morning in Italy, we head west on highway S23 toward the mountains in the direction of Grenoble on the French side of the Alps. We pass through the small unremarkable village of Porte and leaving the highway we turn west across the Chisone River into San Germano at the very foot of the Cottian Alps. The name San Germano is familiar from the records of our people. The village lies about 22 km from the French border, and has long since grown into a city and become predominantly Catholic though as for that, the Vaudois or Waldensian names remain in many of the local businesses: Malan, Bertalot and Boudrandi.

Extending on west and leaving behind the winding, narrow streets of San Germano, the road begins to climb into the mountains. After seven or eight kilometers and a few hundred meters in elevation we come to a sign indicating the beginning of the village of Pramollo, the home of our ancestors. In view beyond the sign are only a few small houses and a Catholic church; no one in the streets this morning. We follow the road as it leaves the small cluster of houses and ascends through a series of switchbacks in a serious climb up the mountainside. Often the curve of the road is protected by a bricked-in retaining wall and here and there is a simple roadside shrine where a traveler by foot may pause to worship. From time to time we come to an intersection where lonely side roads branch off in various directions, some going on up the mountain and some angling down. At the intersections are posted signs indicating the names and directions to little hamlets that together form the sprawling network which is the village of Pramollo.

Some ten kilometers more up the mountainside and we come to the village center. It sits on a plateau the size of several football fields containing, in addition to the cluster of houses, a Catholic church, the Waldensian temple, a school and a pastor's home. The temple is the meetinghouse or gathering place of the Pramollian Waldenses. There are no businesses to be seen. In front of the temple is a memorial to the dead of the village from two world wars. All of the surnames are right out of our ancestral records including the recorded sacrifice of a Beux for each war (Ernesto and Giacomo for Wars I and II respectively). On this site stood the old round temple "La Rotunda" constructed beginning in 1699, whose facade bore the inscription, "C'est la Maison de Dieu" or "The House of God." The round temple became structurally unsound in the late 1800s and its successor, the current building, was constructed in 1886.

The floor plan of the current temple is a simple 12x17 meter rectangle and the building has few frills inside or out. Inside, the walls are bare, the floor stone and the rude benches for function only. On each side of the room and halfway forward there are wood stoves with stacks of firewood and flues rising up and angling over to the wall. Center front features a raised round pulpit with a modest canopy, displaying in the mahogany woodwork of its dual spiral staircases, the only concession to the glitz and glamor commonly associated with medieval worship. We are struck by the stark contrast between this and the ornate cathedrals of Europe.

At the far side of the village center is a cluster of signs, one reading "Bosi," the Italian version of our original family name, Beux, and pointing on up the mountainside. We take the narrow road indicated and follow it up. In another five kilometers we arrive at what appears to be the highest of the hamlets, the small group of houses they call Bosi, clinging to the eastern slopes of the mountain named Gran Truc. Bosi consists of maybe a dozen homes, all rough-hewn using as brick the shale-like stone prevalent in the area, and imbedded into the mountainside in terraced fashion. We stop beside the community laundry, a crude stone water trough about two meters long, under roof, with mountain water piped in. An old woman bends over the front of the trough doing her morning wash by hand in the icy water. She is dressed warmly against the crisp spring morning with a sweater over her working dress. Years of hard labor and doing for herself are etched into her tough, durable face and have lent a permanent stoop to the shoulders.

We introduce ourselves to the old woman in English; she answers in Italian. She is friendly, demonstrative and vocal and she evidently wants very much to be helpful. We talk at some length with little communication. She tells us her name and that she lives in Bosi di Pramollo. Presently she goes away and returns with her daughter-in-law, Nellie, and a granddaughter. Nellie was evidently drawn from some household chore for she still wears a colorful apron over her gray skirt. She is of darker complexion with a radiant face that finds reason to smile in every circumstance. The granddaughter appears to be about eight years of age and is the image of her mother. Mother and daughter immediately drop everything they are doing and become our guides.

The peculiar construction employed in almost all of the buildings and walls throughout the area catches our eye and interest. Small, near-flat, natural stones are collected from the surrounding area and fitted and mortared into a brick-like construction. Many of the older buildings feature large flat stones overlaid on each other for the roof. The result is a sturdy, durable building with a singularly coarse and primitive appearance. Except where the narrow roadway passes between them, the houses of Bosi are bunched together within a few feet of each other in no apparent pattern, with foot paths in between. They show evidence of tight communal living and give new meaning to the term, "small town." There are no livestock in view and the surrounding terrain shows evidence of terraced farming and grape culture. We notice a middle-aged couple working with hoe and rake on the mountainside about 100 meters above us. One wonders how in years past the people were able to extract a living from this beautiful, forbidding land before it was possible, as it is now, to supplement their subsistence with income from employment in the industry below.

Back at the village center we are introduced to the pastor's wife who speaks very good English. She is a tall thin woman with a worried look and a great deal to accomplish before her day is done. She produces a treasure of hand-written records reaching back into the 1700s. We scan them briefly: minutes of meetings, lists of members, the business of the town, all faithfully recorded in French. She trusts us implicitly and says we can look at them all we want, just lay them on the desk when we leave. Meanwhile she has a class in town she must teach. She notes that her husband isn't Waldensian, but is of another Protestant denomination, and was hired by the local community to be their pastor. Of the village and church school, which has been in operation for centuries, she tells us, this is to be their last year. There are too few students and next year they will have to go down to San Germano to school. Lots of things are changing. Whereas a hundred years ago all their given names were French, today they are all Italian.

Nellie brings the local postmistress, Alma, whose maiden name is Beux, a truly prospective cousin, and her 15-year old son, Loris. Alma is gray-haired and middle-aged and her stern and skeptical expression belies the kindness that lurks beneath, for she too is available to assist in every way. The son is friendly and cooperative, and though he is bashful about it, he can muster a little English in a pinch, which is what we are decidedly in. They pronounce the name, Beux, as we would say the word "burrs," and indicate that there are several families with that name still living in the village of Pramollo. All of the people we meet are friendly, gracious, thrilled to see us and trusting to a fault. They appear to be happy people, never tired of smiling and they make us feel like family.

We ask about the cemetery and they lead us a few hundred meters down a narrow, winding roadway to a lonely spot of level ground where lies a small, square, walled-in cemetery plot where the Waldenses of Pramollo have buried their dead for centuries. The stone walls and adjoining stone cottage appear to be of ancient construction and are moldering in general decay. We look at each of the headstones, photographing many. Alma shows us the grave sites of her parents and other relatives, explaining many of the relationships. We shall not soon forget the feeling that the cemetery brings. The fog has settled in until we can see little except the wooded mountainside angling up and nothing but fog dropping off below. It is like something out of Brigadoon, and yet there is no strangeness nor spookiness, not a bit of the eerie about the place. It feels more like a country home than a burial ground. We sense a warmth and tenderness, a welcoming, as if the very stones were pleased with our visit, much after the manner of the people who have accompanied us here.

It is here that we part with our distant relatives and new-found friends with many fond expressions of farewell, both we and they reluctant to say "a riverderci." Back in the village center we see a sign indicating the "Pramollo Museo," but cannot determine how to get there. Being instructed of another villager, we eventually follow a path winding in and out among the houses to the lower edge of the village center there we find a simple museum housed in the old one-room schoolhouse, "Scuola Elementari," constructed of the standard brick covered with stucco. The room is about five by eight meters with a table in front for the teacher and several rows of benches with desks for the students. The desks and benches are of rude construction and deeply worn from use. On display are clothes the people wore, a large abacus, old books and other artifacts. On the walls are a map of the scattered village of Pramollo, pictures of graduating classes, a chart of the number of students over the last hundred years and other displays. Odd that a small one-room school should become the town museum, as if it displays the principal product of the community. We ponder the enduring commitment of these impoverished people to the education of their youngsters. We stand long and snap many a picture in this ancient schoolhouse where our second-great grandparents likely studied as children back in the 1820s, and their parents before them, and their parents before them.

A storm is gathering and the fog has settled in, limiting visibility to about 50 meters, and we hurry to the car and begin our descent. As we glide down the mountainside in our modern automobile, returning to the comfortable world in which we live, our thoughts turn circles around our

Waldensian ancestors. What awful experiences and terrible fear drove them here to this obscure place, this extremity of human habitation? What stroke of luck or fate permitted them to find a place and circumstances where, against all odds, they could successfully defend themselves and outlast their tormentors? What was the nature of their love of God and devotion to duty which kept them true to their faith and allowed them to perpetuate their race and religion as the vanguard of the Reformation? How did they survive over the centuries from the 1100s to the 1800s when, at last, world opinion brought an end to their mindless persecution? We return to the mainstream of Italian life in the flatland this Tuesday afternoon in April, while high above us the unseen mountain people cling to their faith, their families and their mountainside, striving to keep their ancient traditions, their religion and their way of life from slipping away.

The sudden summer hailstorm drove us from the mountains earlier than we had hoped, but not before the mystique of this unique religious group and their tragic, courageous history entangled us inextricably in its web, launching me on a decades-long quest to discover the origin of the Vaudois, their tortuous history and the secret of their survival. Throughout my subsequent odyssey, what intrigued me most was how the small thread of their story could possibly have maintained its continuity through eight centuries of the vicissitudes and tremors of European history as civilizations ebbed and flowed, kingdoms rose and fell, and wars raged round about them. How did they survive when countless contemporary dissident Christian groups were harassed, persecuted and exterminated? Searching for answers has taken me on a journey of surprising discovery, growing appreciation and utter amazement.

I found their history to be a remarkable roller-coaster ride, but not one with the excitement and thrills we usually imagine. It was a roller-coaster ride from hell. For the first 200 years their rediscovery of the ancient truths of the New Testament separated them from the mother church and launched them onto a prolonged frenzy of proselytizing that spread their belief system throughout much of Europe. Countered by the relentless power of the Roman church combined with the absolute authority of secular princes, during the next 200 years, the Vaudois hunkered down and learned the art of obfuscation, a tiny irritating glimmer of light in a continent of darkness. The next 300 years they emerged from obscurity to greet the Protestant Reformation, only to be beaten back again and persecuted to near extinction, situated as they were amid the Catholic hegemony of southern Europe. Finally, the integrity of their life style, their incredible resilience and powerful unseen forces succeeded in producing true and lasting religious freedom, not only for themselves, but for the entire kingdom of Italy.

The reader must interpret the history of this valiant people according to his or her own lights, but the more it is understood and pondered, the harder it becomes to deny something very like divine intervention. There comes to mind a statement made by a delegate to the American Continental Congress in 1776, faced as they were by the daunting power of Great Britain. Said he, "During the Protestant Reformation, the Catholics enjoyed the support of the pope and all the monarchs of Europe; but as to them poor devils, the Protestants, they had nothing on their side but God Almighty."[1]

CHAPTER 1
Origins - to 1250 AD

Of the two most formidable heretical sects of the central middle ages, those of the Cathari and the Waldensians [Vaudois], it was only the Waldensians who survived in considerable numbers, constituting a pervasive but shadowy religious presence in the later middle ages. They alone provided a link between the movements of the vita apostolica of the late 12th century, in which they were an important and eventually distracting element, and the Reformation of the early 16th century, when remnants of the Cottian Alps still survived.[2]

The Waldenses were the strictly biblical sect of the Middle Ages ... [and] present a rare spectacle of the survival of a body of believers which has come up out of great tribulation.[3]

We have only limited knowledge concerning events of the early Middle Ages a millennium ago. Out of the obscurity of those times appeared a French-Italian religious group with amazing tenacity, the Vaudois or the Waldenses.[1] It is the beginnings and emergence of this early Protestant people that is the subject of this chapter. The origin of the Vaudois as a religious group can only be examined in the context of the Christianity out of which they emerged. Whereas a comprehensive discussion of Christian ecclesiastical history is beyond the scope of the present study, a brief review of that history will form a foundation for examining the origin and emergence of the Vaudois.

1. THE FORMATION AND PROGRESS OF THE PRIMITIVE CHRISTIAN CHURCH.

Beginnings. In a conversation between Jesus and his disciples, Peter declared his testimony, "Thou art the Christ, the Son the Living God" (Matt. 16:16).[2] Whereupon Jesus informed Peter that such a testimony could not have come to him in the normal way we learn things, but rather by revelation directly from his Father in Heaven. According to

---

1 The English *Waldenses* and the French *Vaudois* designations are used interchangeably.
2 Biblical references are taken from the King James Version and given in the conventional form at the reference site rather than in footnotes.

Matthew, Jesus then stated that upon this rock he would build his church and that the gates of hell would not prevail against it (Matt. 16:18).

Jesus chose and then ordained twelve of his disciples as apostles "that they should be with him, and that he might send them forth to preach, and to have power to heal sicknesses, and to cast out devils" (Mark 3:14 - 15). And further, he said to them "Ye have not chosen me, but I have chosen you" (John 15:16). Thus chosen the apostles became the leaders of the church of Christ. The establishment of his church was an important milestone of Jesus' ministry, for it would be the vehicle that would perpetuate his teachings following his mortal life. Said he to them, "Go ye into all the world, and preach the gospel to every creature" (Mark 16:15).

What of this institution which Jesus founded, the primitive Christian church? It appears that even after his resurrection and ascension; he intended to remain its head. The Book of Acts records instances of the resurrected Christ's guidance to the church by revelation from the choosing of Mathias to fill a vacancy in the twelve apostles left by the death of Judas Iscariot (Acts 2:24-26) to the instructions directed to the seven branches of the Church in Asia given through the apostle John (Rev. 1:4). The pattern of governance in the primitive Christian church was for his anointed servants, the apostles, to receive divine guidance by revelation through the Holy Spirit, hence Paul's metaphor wherein he speaks of the church being built upon the foundation of apostles and prophets with Jesus Christ himself as the chief cornerstone (Eph 2:19).

To the apostles were given the keys to lead the church and to make binding in eternity the covenants entered into by Christians in mortality, and much of the four gospels is devoted to Jesus' instruction to his apostles as he prepared them for their ministry. Under his guidance and their leadership, the primitive Christian church conducted the worship services, taught the principles, and administered the ordinances of the gospel as Jesus had introduced them.

Beyond the apostles and prophets as the foundation, we have a limited view of the organization of the primitive Christian church. Evidently bishops presided over congregations, assisted by deacons and with the help of a council of elders or presbyters. Writing of the 2nd century, Mosheim observes:

> The form of ecclesiastical government, whose commencement we have seen in the last century, was brought in this [2nd century] to a greater degree of stability and consistence. One inspector, or bishop, presided over each Christian assembly to which office he was elected by the voice of the people. To assist him in this laborious province, he formed a council of presbyters. A bishop, during the first and second centuries, was a person who had the care of one Christian assembly.[4]

To his church Jesus gave a mission and a charter. It was

to witness of him, that is to take the gospel he taught to the uttermost parts of the earth (Matt 24:14), baptizing those who believed and dispensing the gift of the Holy Ghost. Those who converted were baptized and received the remission of their sins. Only thus could they merit entrance to his Father's kingdom (Matt 16:16). His Messianic message was unequivocal. "Neither is there salvation in any other, for there is none other name given among men whereby we must be saved" (Acts 4:12). The gospel was not to be spread by the sword, for no one would be compelled to embrace the Christian doctrine or practice, but the principles were to be made known and available to all, and those gathered to the church were to become the household of God, and be brought unto "a unity of the faith and the knowledge of the Son of God, unto a perfect man" (Acts 1:8, Eph. 4:13).

As the apostles, leaders of the primitive Christian church, with keys in hand, embarked on this great, daunting adventure, what were the prospects for their success? The New Testament chronicles the intrepid efforts of Peter, John, Paul and other missionaries of the first century of Christianity. Following the manifestation of the Spirit at the day of Pentecost, Peter taught the gospel with new-found power, declaring that the prophecy of Joel was then fulfilled and the Spirit of God was being poured out upon all flesh (Joel 2:28). Ever at the center of the message was the Christ. "Let the house of Israel know assuredly that God made of this Jesus whom ye have crucified, both Lord and God" (Acts 2:36).

There followed then quite rapidly a substantial influx of

converts. Luke records that after Peter's inaugural missionary sermon, on the same day of Pentecost, 3000 souls were baptized. The apostles were arrested by Jewish authorities for their preaching, and they were threatened and forbidden to continue. But the prisons could not hold them and in defiance of authority, they persisted in declaring the Christian doctrine. As their ministry proceeded, the little church prospered as "the Lord added to the church daily such as should be saved" (Acts 2:47).

Volumes have been written and legends abound as to the spread of early Christianity. Reference is made to the ministry of the apostles unto the Britons, Celts, Gauls, and Germans, reaching such places as India, Spain, Syria, and North Africa. Contemporary writers believed that the message of Christ had soon penetrated the known, civilized world. Paul claimed in his time that the truth of the gospel "was preached to every creature which is under heaven" (Col. 1:23). Referring to the 1st century, Eusibius wrote some 250 years later:

> Thus, then under a celestial influence and cooperation, the doctrine of the Savior, like the rays of the sun, quickly irradiated the whole world. Presently, in accordance with divine prophecy, the sound of his inspired evangelists and apostles had gone throughout all the earth and their words to the ends of the world. Throughout every city and village, churches were rapidly abounding and filled with members from every people.[5]

And elsewhere, speaking of his time, the end of the 3rd century, Eusebius wrote:

> Like brilliant lamps, the churches were now shining throughout the world, and faith in our Savior and Lord Jesus Christ was flourishing among all mankind.[6]

The early years of Christianity, except for some short-lived Gnostic deviations, witnessed a relatively undisturbed belief system devoid of the contention and division that characterized its later history. Milner reports that during the first two centuries, the various Christian congregations

> were all one body, one church of one mind and actually loved one another as brethren. The attention to fundamentals, to real Christianity, was not dissipated by schismatic peculiarities, nor was the body of Christ rent in pieces by factions. There were indeed heretics, but real Christians admitted them not into their communities.[7]

By the end of the 3rd century AD it appeared that the Christian gospel had penetrated everywhere within the bounds of the Roman Empire, though embraced by a relatively small number. After the initial bow wave of conversion, proselytizing became hard-scrabble work with limited success. Severe pressures of persecution from the Jews and the

Romans thinned the ranks of the true believers and warned others away. Conversion *en masse* was to come much later with the support of the Roman Empire and the consent of the princes of the world. Meanwhile, the fruits of the first three centuries of missionary work were reflected by 1800 bishops of the church, each presiding over a congregation, with a total estimated membership in excess of 3,000,000.[8][3]

Inroads in the Church. Historians have written of the ultimate triumph of Christianity, meaning that in time it graduated from a small persecuted sect to a grand state-supported religion and finally to the largest belief system in the history of the world. Christians generally take comfort in the inexorable blossoming forth of Christianity as a validation that the author of the work was what he claimed to be. However, it is clear that the church which eventually filled much of the world was a very different religious organization from that established by the Christ.

It is not known how long the church lasted in its primitive form, but we hear no more of apostles beyond Matthias, Paul, Barnabas and perhaps Silas and Timothy. With the passing of the apostles not only was the central authority of the church lost, but also the divine connection with its head, Jesus Christ. As Gibbon has observed, "Since every friend to revelation is persuaded of the reality, and every reasonable man is convinced of the cessation of miraculous powers, it is evident that there must have been *some period* in which

---

3 The absence of verifiable statistics leaves us with conjecture, and an estimated range of from 1-10 million. See also Schaff, II:22.

they were either suddenly or gradually withdrawn from the Christian church."⁹

The last known divine revelation, the Book of Revelations as found in the New Testament, was received and recorded by John during his exile to the isle of Patmos in about 100 AD, and we read no more of his ministry after about 115 AD. Evidently, thereafter church affairs were no longer conducted under the Christ's direction, and as a consequence, in the centuries that followed, many basic elements of the original church were lost or altered. The first genuine Christian historian, Hegesippus, wrote in 150 AD that

> Until [approximately 100 AD] the church remained a pure and uncorrupted virgin, for those who attempted to corrupt the . . . Savior's preaching, if they existed at all, lurked in obscure darkness. But when the sacred band of the Apostles and the generation of those to whom it had been vouchsafed to hear with their own ears the divine wisdom had reached the several ends of their lives, then the federation of godless error took its beginnings through the deceit of false teachers, who seeing none of the Apostles still remained, barefacedly tried against the preaching of the truth the counter proclamation of knowledge - falsely so called.¹⁰

The historian Milner, writing of the 3rd century, records that "Here terminated, or nearly so, as far as appears, that great first effusion of the Spirit of God, which began at the day of Pentecost. Human depravity effected throughout a general decay of godliness; and one generation of men elapsed with very slender proofs of the spiritual presence of Christ in the church." [11]

Historians report a marked decline in the devotion and righteousness of church leaders as well as the membership, especially during the relative persecution-free era in the first portion of the 3rd century, 200-275 AD.[12] Increasingly the church hierarchy abandoned their initial unpretentious bearing as they graduated from simple fishermen or tentmakers, walking the dusty streets in sandaled feet, to superior prelates and dignitaries, bespeaking more the role of powerful and wealthy landholders, issuing orders and receiving funds. Cyprian, bishop of Carthage (249-258 AD) witnesses that

> believers were brooding over the arts of amassing wealth, the pastors and deacons each forgot their duty, works of mercy were neglected, and discipline was at its lowest ebb. Frauds and deceit were practiced among brethren. Even many bishops, neglecting the duties of their stations, gave themselves up to secular pursuits: They deserted their flocks, gave no assistance to the needy and were insatiable in their thirst for money; they possessed estates by fraud and multiplied usury.[13]

There was considerable uncertainty in the early church

as to the propriety of change. Could a church established and initially guided by the Lord be appropriately adjusted or modified by mere human hands? In the 3rd century, Eusebius, bishop of Ceaseria and church historian, was at pains to declare the ideal of immutability for the Christian Church. Professor Lake in his Introduction to Eusebius' Ecclesiastical History argues that the

> object of the whole book was to present the Christian *Succession*, which did not merely mean, though it certainly included, the apostolic succession of the bishops, but rather the whole intellectual, spiritual and institutional life of the church. Eusebius, like all other early church historians, can be understood only if it be recognized that whereas modern writers try to trace the development, growth and change of doctrines and institutions, their predecessors were trying to prove that nothing of the kind ever happened. According to them the church had had one and only one teaching from the beginning; and it had been preserved by the "Succession" and heresy was the attempt of the devil to change it.[14]

Athanasius, later of fame as a principal belligerent in the Niceane controversy over the nature of Christ, was a proponent of succession. Wrote he: "The Catholic faith is that which the Lord gave, the apostles preached, and the fathers preserved; upon this the church was founded, and he who departs from this faith can no longer be called a Christian."[15]

In contrast to this ideal of succession, beginning in the 2nd century of the Christian era there commenced a period of theological jousting and controversy as the faithful learned sought to interpret the writings of the New Testament and surviving Christian traditions. Most of the early doctrinal disputations arose through attempts to reconcile Christian teachings and practice with Gnosticism, the prevailing philosophy of the era. Mosheim wrote:

> An opinion has prevailed, derived from the authority of Clemens of Alexandria, that the first rise of the Gnostic sect is to be dated after the death of the Apostles, and placed under the reign of the Emperor Adrian [Hadrian (117–138 AD)]; and it is also alleged, that before this time, the church enjoyed a perfect tranquility, undisturbed by dissensions or sects of any kind.[16]

Disputation arose about a multitude of doctrinal and procedural matters ranging in importance from the ordinary (When should Easter be celebrated?) to the sublime (What is the nature of God and Christ?). The central authority of the apostles had not yet been replaced by the preeminence of the bishops of Rome. The vacuum created by the absence of the apostles drew the bishops of the various Christian congregations together into synods or councils to achieve consensus, render judgment and establish orthodoxy. Early Christian synods were regional in nature, dealing with local controversies or parochial heresies. Gradually peripheral teachings and opinions were spun off and a semblance of orthodoxy in doctrine and practice emerged. Those deviating from the norm and sufficiently robust and popular warranted synodal attention and were dealt with through censure or excommunication. The establishment of orthodoxy often involved compromise in doctrine or practice or both as chronicled by Mosheim

> In this [2nd] century many unnecessary rites and ceremonies were added to the Christian worship. The bishops thought it necessary to increase the number of rites and ceremonies, to accommodate the prejudices of both Jews and heathens, and to render the public worship striking to the outward senses.[17]

Additionally, Mosheim describes some

> intestine divisions, occasioned sometimes by a point of doctrine, at others by a variety of sentiments about certain rites and ceremonies. The principal authors of these divisions have been stigmatized with the title of *heretics*, and their peculiar opinions of consequence distinguished by the appellation *heresies*. [Thus a heretic is] a person who, either directly or indirectly, has

been the occasion of exciting divisions and dissensions among Christians.[18]

In the early centuries of the Christian era, heretics were accosted for their deviation from the scriptural foundations of the church and from the doctrines and practices based thereon. Many were widely divergent, so much so that their connection to Christianity is hard to discern. Curiously, in the course of time, the roles of church and heretic became reversed. By the 12th century, heretics were accusing the Christian clergy of deviation from the scriptural foundation and seeking to return the church to that standard.

The Embrace of the Roman Empire. Near the beginning of the 4th century occurred the famous events leading to the *Constantine Intervention*, the momentous and historic embracing of Christianity as the state religion of the Roman Empire. Constantine the Great, though evidently neither converted nor baptized himself, made it his business to bring the primitive Christian church under the protective wing of the Roman government. Thus, in a Paul-like reversal, the dominant state of the western world ceased its relentless persecution of Christians and commenced to protect and nurture them. With that embrace, came also a degree of control and direction, for Constantine soon progressed from mentor and friend of the church, to instigator and conductor of church affairs.

The attention of nascent church theologians in the time of Constantine the Great was consumed with a lengthy and contentious argument about the nature of Christ and his relationship to God, the Father. At the beginning of the 4th century, the dispute had settled into a choice between the two schools of thought emanating from the Alexandrian theological school of North Africa. Alexander, bishop of Alexandria, contended that the Father and Son were in all respects coequal and coeternal, and in fact of the same substance or essence (homoousios). Arius, a senior presbyter in Alexandria, extended the earlier logic of Origen by viewing the Son as created by and therefore subordinate to the Father, a creation superior to all others, but not coeternal with the Father and not fully divine. Some church officials felt, as did Eusebius, that the issue was of little importance, "for he who believes in Christ has eternal life, not he who knows precisely how the Father begat the Son."[19] Others recognized in this issue a fundamental doctrinal question of Christianity addressing the divinity of its founder.

Constantine, having little interest in theology but wanting unity, called all bishops of the primitive Christian church together in an ecumenical council, the first of its kind, to decide this as well as several other minor issues. In a letter addressing the combatants (said to have been ghost-written by Eusebius), Constantine urged them to lay aside their contest over an unimportant doctrinal matter, especially one most lay members could never understand.[20] The council convened in 325 AD at Nicaea of Asia Minor (the modern day Iznik, Turkey) and upwards of 318 of the estimated 1800 existing bishops attended.

The council rejected the Arian position and banished

the unrepentant Arius from the Empire. In the end, only two bishops, both Egyptian, stood with Arius and were banished along with him. The writings of Arius were burned and his followers branded enemies of Christianity. The council accepted instead a position, the expression of which became one of the fundamental doctrinal statements of the Christian church, known as the Nicene Creed. Subsequent councils produced further drafts of the creed expanded to include reference to Jesus' birth by the Virgin Mary, one baptism for the remission of sins and the one holy catholic and apostolic church. By 380 AD the basic creed was established largely as known today.

> We believe in one God, the Father Almighty, Maker of all things visible and invisible. And in one Lord, Jesus Christ, the Son of God, Begotten of the Father; that is, of the essence with the Father, God of God, Light of Light, very God of very God, begotten, not made, being of one substance with the Father by Whom all things were made both in heaven and on earth; Who for us men and for our salvation came and was incarnate and was made man; he suffered and was buried; And the third day He rose again; from thence he shall come to judge the quick and the dead. And in the Holy Ghost. [21]

For most Christians, the Nicene Council of 325 AD and the creed it produced constituted an evolutionary milestone, an important defining moment in the history of organized Christian faith. For Roman Catholics, it marked a coming-of-age, the maturing and graduation of the primitive Christian church into a centrally-organized institution with established doctrine and liturgy, the standard to which all Christians should flock for all time. Not that the doctrine and practices were fixed and unchanging, but that there was a mechanism in place, the ecumenical council and the combined authority of the emperor and the bishops, to define and establish the same. For many Christian denominations arising in years to come, the Nicene Council marked the apex, the summit of the primitive Christian church, after which the church experienced a gradual but steady decline, leading finally to an apostate religion devoid of the pure doctrines and ordinances essential to salvation. To others, it marked the usurpation of authority by the bishops of Rome and the compromising of that authority by uniting with secular power.

In addition, future dissenters would claim that the Constantine Intervention marked the end of the church as an independent entity and the beginning of its slide into dependent existence, intertwined in varying degrees with secular institutions, sometimes dominating and sometimes dominated by, but always greatly influenced by such institutions.

2. THE VAUDOIS AND POSSIBLE BEGINNINGS.

Intimations of Vaudois Origins. The proliferation of religious organizations among Christians is troubling and confusing. Every denomination would fain be the only true one, the sole repository of the oracles of the Christian God. The Vaudois have made this claim more persistently than most and perhaps with better justification. Vaudois pastors and historians have frequently proclaimed their denomination to be the original church of Christ, true to the faith as established by the Lord in the meridian of time and maintained in its purity since the apostolic era. Muston expressed it best:

> The Vaudois of the Alps, are, in our view, primitive Christians, or inheritors of the primitive Church, who have been preserved in these valleys from the alterations successively introduced by the church of Rome into the evangelical worship. It is not they who separated from Catholicism, but Catholicism which separated from them, in modifying the primitive worship. Hence the impossibility of assigning a precise date to the origin. The church of Rome, which in its commencement also formed part of the primitive church, did not modify itself all at once, but as it became powerful, it assumed, together with the scepter of rule, the display, the pride, and the spirit of domination which ordinarily accompany power; whilst amid the Vaudois valleys, the primitive church, existing in comparative obscurity, remained in isolation, free, and without tendency to abandon the simplicity of its infancy.[22]

Such, with minor variations, was the opinion of a long line of Vaudois historians, including Leger, Peyran, Perrin, Allix, Worsford, Wylie, Bresse and Faber as well as the British benefactors, Morland and Gilly. Clearly their historical justifications fed upon each other, but there also seemed to be a genuine conviction among them that the efficacy of the Vaudois religious movement depended upon its ancient origins.

There is no simple consensus on the origin of the name Vaudois[4] or Waldenses. Most contend that it derives from Pierre de Vaud (or Peter Waldo), a reformer coming from the village Vaud, near to Lyons, France in the 12th century. However, citing Leger, Robinson argues that "From the Latin word Vallis came the English word valley, the French and Spanish valle, the Italian valdesi, the low Dutch valleye, the Provençal vaux, Vaudois, the ecclesiastical Waldenses. The words simply signify valleys, or inhabitants of valleys and no more."[23] The universally-acknowledged Vaudois home, stretching over eight centuries and into the modern era, is in the Alpine valleys along the French-Italian border, the Cottian Alps. It is not so much viewed as their point of origin as it is their traditional residence.

Robinson further states that "a rich merchant of Lyons, who was named Valdus because he received his religious notions from the inhabitants of the vallies (sic), openly dis-

---

4 By the 15th Century in France, Vaudois had become the designation of all deviations from the faith, and was especially applied to sorcery. Hence is derived the word Voodooism, descriptive of the sorcery of the French colonies." See Lea (B), 819

avowed the Roman religion, supported many to teach the doctrines believed in the vallies, and became the instrument of the conversion of great numbers."[24] Schaff contends that the Vaudois used none of these names, but referred to themselves simply as the *Poor of Christ*.[25]

Waddington wrote that though

> their origin is not ascertained by any authentic record . . . yet among their traditions there is one which agrees well with their original and favorite tenet, which objects to the possession of property by ecclesiastics. It is this – that their earliest fathers, offended at the liberality with which Constantine endowed the Church of Rome, and at the worldliness at which Pope Silvester accepted these endowments, seceded into Alpine solitudes; that they there lay concealed and secure for so many ages through their insignificance and innocence.[26]

Even the conservative Neander suggests "It is not without some foundation of truth that the Waldenses of this period asserted the high antiquity of their sect, and maintained that from the time of the secularization of the church – that is, as they believed from the time of Constantine's gift to the Roman bishop Silvester – such an opposition as finally broke forth in them, had been existing all along." [27] The claim was buttressed in the medieval period by a document entitled the *Donation of Constantine*, purported to reflect a deal struck between the church (as represented by Silvester[5]) and the state (Constantine the Great) granting the popes political control in perpetuity over the entire western portion of the Roman Empire. Though the document itself was later (1440 AD) proven to be a forgery from the 8th century, the Constantine Intervention still stands as a significant turning point in Christian history. Indeed, the Noble Lesson, the foundational document of the Vaudois, refers to the Constantine-Silvester transaction as the moment in history when the Catholic Church ceased to be what it claimed to be, after which

> All the Popes which have been from Silvester to this present,
> And all Cardinals, Bishops, Abbots, and the like,
> Have no power to absolve or pardon,
> Any creature so much as one mortal sin.[28]

According to Comba, initially the Vaudois claimed, not so much direct descent from the apostolic church, but rather they "appealed to apostolic tradition, unpracticed but unforgotten, they cherished the thought of reviving it again. They plead this antiquity for the sole purpose of reconnecting the truth of their faith and principles with its true source."[29] Over time, then it was not so much of a stretch to "call themselves successors of the apostles, and say that they are in possession of apostolic authority, and of the keys

---
[5] Bishop of Rome from 314 to 335 AD, later designated as pope.

to bind and unbind."[30]

Clearly it was the changes in ritual, worship and doctrine of the main-stream church, the deviation from scripture and apostolic traditions, which drove the Vaudois to a parting of ways. As to the actual separation of the Vaudois from the Roman Catholic Church, when and under what circumstances it occurred, about this, historians had varied opinions. The claim to ancient apostolic origins was supported by no proof, no convincing documentation, or at least none that survived the long night, the hundreds of years of persecution. Vaudois apologists offered instead circumstantial evidence, various scenarios in the form of strategically-placed dissenters or dissident movements, which might have generated a persistent following, which might have become the Vaudois.

The Vaudois and their Religion. The puzzle regarding the origin of the Vaudois rests partially upon a definition of their faith and the areas where they took exception to Catholic doctrine and practice. Over the centuries the Vaudois espoused a relatively consistent, unsophisticated theology and practice, though not entirely an unchanging one. Their earliest known documents included the *Noble Lesson* (Nobla Leçon), and a *Confession of Faith*, to which few Protestant denominations of today would take exception. The earliest available copies of these and other documents were retrieved by Samuel Morland, the special envoy Oliver Cromwell sent to the Vaudois of the Piedmont in 1655 AD to investigate reports of their persecution. The documents were written in the language of the ancient inhabitants of the Valleys, the Romaunt language, and ostensibly date from the year 1100 AD. Subsequent analysis of these documents, which reside in the library at Cambridge University, suggests that the dates may not be authentic and that the documents were first produced in 1400 AD.[31] Other historians construe their similarity to main stream Protestantism as evidence that the documents may have been produced even later, in the 16th or 17th Centuries, and thus reflect the form the Vaudois theology and practice took after encountering the Reformation. A similar collection of foundational Vaudois documents was assembled by Archbishop Ussher about the same time, and placed in the Library of Trinity College in Dublin. There is an additional Vaudois document called *Liber Electorum*, (Book of the Elect) authentically dated before 1400 AD, which corroborates much of that given in the Noble Lesson and the Confession of Faith.[32]

These documents confirm the Vaudois faith. They confess:

> that God is one . . . a most perfect being . . . that in that simple essence, there are three persons . . . the Father, the Son and the Holy Spirit . . . that the same God has manifest himself unto men by his works . . . and word . . . written in the Holy Scriptures, which we receive . . . as the rule of our faith and conduct . . . that God made all things . . . that he is neither the author nor the cause of the evil which men practice . . . but that

man deprives himself of happiness by listening to the devil . . . that man by his transgression lost the holiness he received and incurred [physical] death and is in a fallen condition, dead in sins, and [we] are not able of ourselves, to cherish a good thought . . . that Jesus Christ effected the complete expiation of our sins by his perfect sacrifice . . . that without him we cannot be saved . . . that Jesus Christ is our mediator . . . that through his mediation we may have access to the Father, to call upon him with confidence that we shall be heard . . . that we who are united with him in faith ought strenuously to perform good works . . . that the Lord will reward those who do with eternal life . . . that God gathers together a church in the world for the salvation of men, that this church has one leader and founder, namely Jesus Christ . . . that this church consists of the union of believers who were chosen of God before the foundation of the world . . . that the church of God teaches us his word . . . and institutes the sacraments, namely baptism and the Lord's supper.[33]

Reduced to fundamentals, the five principal and consistent objections of the Vaudois, which they also held in common with most of their contemporary dissident groups, compelling reasons for their disassociation with the Roman church, were

1. the New Testament is the sole valid basis of a genuine Christian belief system and should be available to the laity for study,
2. the church should not accumulate riches or power, rather the clergy if not the laity, should live lives of poverty,
3. Christian church ritual and practice should be restricted to basic sacraments, namely baptism and the Lord's Supper,
4. the use of icons, relics, invocation of the saints and the doctrine of transubstantiation are rejected as forms of idol worship, and
5. the Roman pontiff has no unique authority to govern Christianity nor to speak for all Christians.

Theology was not a principal concern of the Vaudois. They were neither a community of intellectuals nor a denomination of theologians. Rather than doctrine, sacerdotal issues and the form of worship were their concern. Hence when surrounded by a variety of dissident groups, they shared with them a common theology. When they encountered the Reformation in all its glory, they veered toward the Calvinist doctrine. Their doctrinal indifference enabled them to state in their Confession of Faith: "We cheerily accede to the sound doctrine taught in the reformed churches of England, the Netherlands, Germany, Prussia, Switzerland, Poland, Hungary, etc., and we humbly entreat all of these churches, and others settled in America, to regard ours, though few and destitute, as members of the mystical body of Christ."[34]

The progression of Roman Catholic doctrine and practice and the timeline when these elements took permanent root in the Catholic Church as compared with the relatively unwavering fundamentals of Vaudois theology and practice provides some hint as to the point in history, or rather the era, during which the two parted company. From earliest evidence, the Vaudois espoused the Apostles' Creed, the doctrine regarding the nature of Christ and God which grew out of the Nicene Council of 325 AD, and the first four ecumenical councils of the church confirming that their departure, and hence their origin, did not precede the 6th century.[6]

The Holy Scriptures. The foremost theological objection of the Vaudois had to do with the Holy Scriptures. To them these documents formed the sole standard for their faith. Anything deviating from scripture or adding to it was summarily rejected as man-made and without divine authority. They could not conceive of a Christian church whose members did not have access to the New Testament and whose clergy forbade its possession and availability.

What was the role of the Bible in the primitive Christian church and how did that role evolve in the Catholic Church over the centuries? In the absence of living apostles

---

[6] Protestants commonly accepted the first four ecumenical councils of the Roman Church as authoritative in clarifying the nature of Christ and God, namely: Nicaea (315 AD), Constantinople (381 AD), Ephesus (427 AD) and Chalcedon (451 AD).

and ongoing revelation, the various writings of the apostles became the *lingua franca* of the early Christian era. By the end of the 2nd century, the primitive Christian church adopted the core documents of the New Testament much as we know them today as the standard scriptures of the Christian religion. Collections of these documents were held by the widely-scattered Christian congregations and they formed the basis of the doctrines and practices of the church. Writing in the 3rd century, Eusibius defined the scope of the scriptures as they existed in the 2nd century.

> At this point it seems reasonable to summarize the writings of the New Testament which have been quoted. In the first place should be put the holy tetrad of the gospels. To them follow the writings of the Acts of the Apostles. After this should be reckoned the Epistles of Paul. Following then the epistle of John called the first, and in the same way should be recognized the epistle of Peter. In addition to these should be put the Revelation of John. . .these belong to the recognized books. Of the disputed books which are nonetheless known to most are the Epistle of James, that of Jude, the second Epistle of Peter and the so-called second and third epistles of John which may be the work of the Evangelist or by some other of the same name. Among the works which are not genuine must be reckoned the Acts of Paul, the work entitled the Shep-

herd, the Apocalypse of Peter. . .the letter called Barnabas and the so-called Teachings of the Apostles.[35]

In the 3rd century, church fathers took steps to formalize the canon of scripture then in common use. By the end of the 4th century the New Testament, largely as it is used today, was codified by the orthodox councils of the church. Early church leaders thought it highly desirable that the New Testament thus defined, be made available to all of the faithful. Mosheim writes:

> The apostles and their disciples took all possible care, and that in the earliest times of the church, that these sacred books might be in the hands of all Christians, that they might be read and explained in the assemblies of the faithful, and thus contribute both in private and in public to excite and nourish in the minds of Christians a fervent zeal for the truth and a fine attachment to the ways of piety and virtue. It is proper to mention the useful labors of those who manifested their zeal for the Holy Scriptures by the care they took to have accurate copies of them multiplied everywhere, and that at such moderate prices as rendered them of easy purchase, as also to have them translated into various languages, and published in correct editions. [36]

Further, Neander writes:

> It was desired that every Christian be acquainted with the Holy Scripture. Because of the expense and scarcity of written material and because of the poverty of most Christians, reading aloud in congregations became very important. For this reason and also because of widespread illiteracy, it wasn't efficacious to place a Bible in everyone's hands. Regular reading aloud and public exposition of the Bible were made available in lieu of personal study. . . . Because the Greek and Latin languages were only spoken by a portion of the congregation, only by the learned, and the rest only understood the vernacular language, as in many Egyptian and Syrian churches, church translators were provided like those in the Jewish synagogues, who simultaneously translated into the vulgar language so that everyone could understand. A basic principle of Christian upbringing for both men and women was that, early in life, one should become acquainted with the Holy Scriptures. Augustine and other church leaders admonished members to read the scriptures. "Let temporal concerns not be so compelling that you will say, 'I have no time to read God's word.'" [37]

McCracken and Canabiss state that, "up until the 9th century, The Bible was no closed book, at least not to the learned, and if the common people could not read God's word for themselves, this was because literacy itself was relatively rare, and not that the reading of the scriptures was deemed dangerous or forbidden to them. The Bible was read deeply and profoundly, and, what is more, it was remembered."[38]

It is not entirely clear when or for what reason this adherence to scripture became unacceptable to the Roman Church leaders, but in time there was a complete reversal of the well-established policies and practices of the primitive Christian church to make scriptures available. Sometime near the close of the first millennium, "The clergy asserted an exclusive. . ., custodial right to the Bible and there were frequent instances of the [church] forbidding not only vernacular translations of the Bible, but any reading at all by laymen."[39] Mosheim confirms the new policy:

> The Church of Rome persisted obstinately in affirming that the Holy Scriptures were not composed for the use of the multitude, but only for that of their spiritual teachers; and of consequence, ordered these divine records to be taken from the people.[40]

The council of Toulouse (1229 AD) presented the first instance of direct canonical prohibition of the books of scripture to the laity. Milner writes that "The laity were not allowed to have the Old or New Testaments in the vulgar language and forbidden to translate the scriptures." [41]

The unavailability of scripture became a *cause celebre* of dissidents and splinter groups. Activists from Peter Waldo to Martin Luther were only too eager to remedy the situation by translating the Bible into the vernacular tongue and making it available to the lay membership. The Vaudois claimed liberty of conscience and layman's right to have access to the scriptures and to preach the gospel, and refused to submit to the authority of the pope and the prelates. They embraced the supreme authority of scripture. Because of papal prohibitions and their enforcement by secular authority, the Vaudois were only able to maintain a few clandestine copies of the Holy Scriptures. Faithful Vaudois youth were expected to memorize whole books of scripture to be called forth when needed for the instruction of the faithful. Passau Annonymous wrote that he had seen laymen among the Vaudois ". . .who knew almost the entire gospels of Mark and Luke by heart, so that is was hardly possible to quote a word without their being able to confirm the text by memory."[42]

Possible Scenarios. There was a 4th century presbyter of the church, Vigilantus, living in the south of Gaul, who rose in opposition to certain church practices. The veneration of relics, the worship of images, celibacy of the clergy, vigils and the keeping of night-watches in the basilicas of the martyrs and other alleged corruptions of Christian worship drew his ire. Many of these issues were to lie at the heart of the Vaudois dissent. Opposed by the church fathers, Vigilantus' influence nonetheless waxed strong in Gaul and Spain. Jerome, writing in the next century, refutes his claims, and deplores that Vigilantus was able to establish a following among several bishops in the region, in time retreating for refuge to the Cottian Alps,[43] much later to be known as the traditional home of the Vaudois.

Also in the 4th century arose a movement that came to be called *Semi-arianism*, under the leadership of Aurentius, bishop of Milan. Embracing the Arian doctrine of the deity, the movement was made up of simple people who desired to adhere closely to Bible teachings, rejected the worship of relics and idols, and were opposed to complicated dialectics. They "would not abide anything not finding literal witness in the Bible."[44] With the death of Aurentius, the new bishop Ambrose moved quickly and effectively to suppress the movement, driving persistent adherents underground.

Pope Zachary, writing to Boniface (missionary to the Frankish Empire in the 8th century) complained of an heretical movement among the Gallic bishops. The bishops' dissent had to do with a variety of issues relevant to the faith of the future Vaudois, namely: opposition to the celibacy of priests, worship of relics, adoration of images, supremacy of the popes, purgatory, and masses for the dead.[45]

Under Pope Pascal I, a certain Claudius or Claude, chaplain to the Gallic king was appointed archbishop of Turin where he served for 17 years until his death in 824 AD. Claudius had many objections in common with the Vaudois. His regime was remarkable for its uncompromising opposition to the use of images, which he banned from all churches in his realm. He firmly espoused reliance on scripture and objected to the supremacy of the Roman See and the intercession of saints. Claude's opposition was within the church "I do not preach a new sect," he writes, "I who hold the unity of faith and proclaim its truth. I have checked, restrained and fought and subdued sects, schisms etc. in so far as I am able, I will not cease."[46] But his 17-year tenure in office even while opposing the papal endorsement of images speaks to the probability that his was not an isolated posture. "His position was sufficiently strong and appealing so that a faction remained for a decade or two and copies of his works were multiplied and studied, and ultimately his type of thought came to be deemed heretical."[47] Rorence, Prior of St. Roche, in 1640, while employed to investigate the heresy of the Vaudois, was convinced of the Vaudois-Claude connection, for he wrote that they were "not a new sect in the 9th or 10th centuries and that Claude of Turin must have detached them from the church in the 9th century."[48]

Throughout the first millennium, the power of the Roman pontiff was not yet universal in the church, and in particular the arch-diocese of Milan, including Turin and the Alpine valleys, was largely autonomous, subject to the rule of its own archbishop rather than the Roman pontiff. Its independence was characterized by the persistent opposition of Claudius to the use of relics and icons, the concept of transubstantiation and the primacy of the Roman bishop. Upon Claudius' death the diocese was gradually absorbed into the Roman sphere of influence, but the outlying areas, such as the Alpine valleys of Piedmont, continued to maintain their long-standing traditions of independence of doctrine and practice.[49]

Some 200 years after Claudius, the Patarenes or Patarelli were dissidents of the 11th century centered in Milan, whose principal objection against the church was the Simony and concubinage practiced by the clergy, the very elements being addressed at the time by the reforms of Pope Leo IX. By mid-century (1056 AD) the dissidents had gained sufficient traction to cause considerable civil unrest throughout the area, reopening the gap between Rome and Milan. Robinson contends that the Patarenes, as well as other dissidents of like mind, may have persisted in northern Italy until the time of the Reformation.[50]

St. Bernard's description could have been applicable to any number of dissident groups of the 12th century: "There is a sect which calls itself after no man's name, which pretends to be in direct line of apostolic succession; and which, rustic and unlearned though it is, contends that the church is wrong, and that itself alone is right. It must derive its origin from the devil, since there is no other extraction which we can assign to it."[51]

Most striking as evidence of an early dissident movement indistinguishable from the Vaudois is the account given by Eberwin of Steinfeld in 1143, describing a group of heretics calling themselves the Poor of Christ discovered in the Rhineland.[52] Everinius attributes to this group beliefs and practices compellingly similar to those of the Vaudois: imitation of apostolic life, disciples having no possessions, worthy members permitted to administer the Eucharist, rejecting the pope as having corrupted the apostolic dignity by engaging in secular activity, rejecting infant baptism, intercession of the saints, or any practice or belief not justified in the New Testament.

What distinguishes these dissidents and their movements as candidate originators of the Vaudois is geographic proximity, similarity of doctrine, rejection of papal authority, and strict adherence to scripture. In no case is there concrete, direct evidence to establish an historical connection. But to the Vaudois pastor-historians, the circumstantial evidence was enough, and certainly, neither can their historical connection be disproven. Yet who could deny that the Vaudois, in some sense, inherited a legacy of dissidence, if not connecting them back to the primitive church, at least establishing a persistent theme, carried from generation to generation? Historians want to require of the Vaudois apologists, physical evidence, yet what physical evidence could possibly survive centuries of persecution, expulsion and destruction?

It is said that history is written by the winners. Though winners in a sense (surviving 700 years of persecution at the hands of powerful enemies is a form of winning), the Vaudois were decimated and terrified by the loss of many a battle along the way. A people, subject to centuries of persecution and repression, leave only wisps and hints of a documentary trail. Most of what we know of the Vaudois history before 1600 AD comes from records written by their enemies, mostly composed in justification of their ill treatment, describing what dangerous, pernicious people these Vaudois were, deserving of the persecution they received; describing their teachings and practices and contrasting them with the established faith. Early Christian history provides some clues as possible origin scenarios for the Vaudois, but it offers no incontrovertible evidence of what precisely those origins were.

One of the Vaudois' greatest foes and a former coreligionist, Reynerius, an Inquisitor of the 13th century, referred to the alleged antiquity of the Vaudois and identified them as the "most dangerous of the heretics, because the most ancient."[53] The source of this statement in the literature is ambiguous. Comba attributed an expanded form of this quotation to an anonymous inquisitor of Passau writing about 1300 AD:

> Among all the sects, there is none more pernicious to the church than that of the Leonists,[7] and for three reasons: In the first place because it is one of the most ancient, for some say that it dates back to the time of Sylvester, others to the time of the apostles. In the second place because it is the most wide spread. There is hardly

---

[7] Leonists is one of the many terms employed for the Vaudois. Its origin may have been due to Peter Waldo's association with the city of Lyon, written anciently as Leon, or some think it comes from Leo of Ravenna who protested against the papal authority in the time of Charlemagne. (See Mosheim, III, Century XII:123.) Still others attribute the name to two cities inhabited by the early dissidents of the 9th Century, both called Leon and located on either side of the Pyrenees.

a country where it does not exist. In the third place, because if other sects strike with horror those who listen to them, the Leonists, on the contrary, possess a great outward appearance of piety. As a matter of fact they lead irreproachable lives before men, and as regards their faith and the articles of their creed, they are orthodox. Their one conspicuous fault is, that they blaspheme against the church and the clergy, points on which laymen are known to be too easily led away.[54]

Mosheim's translator, Maclaine, wrote that Reynerius referred to "the Leonists as being synonymous with the Waldenses as a sect that had flourished for above 500 years [that is, from before 750 AD]."[55] Reynerius (known elsewhere as Rainer Saccho and evidently one and the same as the Inquisitor known as Passau Anonymous [8]) did not directly support the apostolic antiquity of the Vaudois but only repeated their claims.

3. TURMOIL WITHIN THE ROMAN CHURCH.

Veneration of the Saints and Icons. Between the 4th and 10th centuries the doctrines and practices eventually rejected by the Vaudois were gradually incorporated into the Catholic

---

8 Robinson discusses the authorship of the Reynerius documents and notes the use of German terms suggesting the connection to Passau Anonymous; see Robinson, 446.

Church, setting the stage for, if not precipitating dissension and separation. The practice of venerating images of the saints was justified by Jerome as early as the 5th century: "We do not worship, we do not adore, for fear that we should bow down to the creature rather than to the creator, but we venerate the relics of the martyrs in order the better to adore him whose martyrs they are."[56] The practice was especially prevalent in the Greek Church during the 5th and 7th centuries.

The issue of icons, relics and images came to a head in the 8th century when the eastern church suffered the "Persecution of the Iconoclasts," led by secular princes and perhaps occasioned by the Muslim influence. The mounting pressure for reform in this matter led to a pseudo-ecumenical council convened by the Byzantine Emperor Constantine V at Constantinople in 764 AD, which not only rejected all worship of sacred images, public or private, but also denounced the use of religious paintings and sculptures and branded those who worship such as heretics and blasphemers. As an illustration of the absurdity of imperial control of the church, a scant 33 years later, the next generation of Byzantine rulers took action to reverse the ruling on icons. The second council of Nicaea was convened at the behest of the Empress-Regent Irene and her son Constantine VI in 787 AD. Mosheim reports the results of this council:

> The imperial laws concerning idolatry were abrogated, the decrees of Constantinople reversed, the worship of images and the cross restored,

and severe punishments pronounced against such as maintained that God was the only object of religious adoration.[57]

Infusion of Wealth and Political Power. At the dawn of the 2nd millennium, Christianity in the European world presented a weak and dissolute façade, providing opportunity and motivation for thinking people to veer away from the faith of their fathers. Wakefield describes: ". . .a papacy which sometimes seemed more intent on political programmes than spiritual leadership; bishops who loved pomp, prerogative and power; priests who were careless, ignorant, incelibate."[58] An additional ingredient was the unrest among the literate of the day as well as a quickening of spiritual hunger among the masses.[59] Numerous questionable practices of the church were firmly established leading what few students of scripture there were outside of the clergy to openly question and then directly oppose. Little wonder the Catholic hierarchy restricted availability of the Bible because the church had adopted many practices and doctrines that failed to meet the New Testament standard and thus were vulnerable to the claim of being invented by mere mortals to subvert the purity of the primitive church.

By the 10th century, the leadership of the church had sunk to its lowest level, somewhere near the 8th circle of hell, which Dante reserved for the practitioners of Simony. The papacy as well as episcopal offices of the church were routinely bought and sold in a manner worthy of Simon Magus himself. Successions of popes were elected, appointed, disgraced and deposed willy-nilly over a period of hundreds of years. Palace intrigues involving murder and mayhem, reminiscent of the waning years of the Roman Empire, played themselves out in the papal offices making a farce of church leadership. The division of the Christian churches, the great Rome-Byzantine schism of 1064 AD, was as much the East's rejecting the decadence of the West as it was a result of doctrinal or procedural disputes. "To the Greeks of this age, the Germans, Franks, and Anglo-Saxons of the contemporary West seemed crude barbarians, an illiterate and violent laity led by a worldly and corrupt episcopate."[60]

Mosheim dates the beginning of the material ascendancy of the church from a timely and providential invention early in the 8th century, when:

> A new and ingenious method was found out of acquiring much greater riches to the church, and of increasing its wealth through succeeding ages. An opinion prevailed universally at this time . . . that the punishment . . . reserved for the transgressions of the wicked, was to be prevented and annulled, by liberal donations . . . . In consequence of this notion, the great and opulent offered out of the abundance which they had received by inheritance or gained by rapine, rich donations to departed saints, their ministers upon earth . . . in order to avoid the sufferings and penalties . . . for transgression in this life, and to escape the misery pronounced against the

wicked in a future state. This new and commodious method of making atonement for iniquity, was the principal source of those immense treasures, which from this period, began to flow in upon the clergy, the churches and monasteries and continued to enrich them through succeeding ages down to the present time [1755 AD].[61]

Lay investiture, the evil twin of Simony, was perhaps equally influential in laying waste to effective leadership in the church. By this practice, bishops and prelates were appointed by kings and princes, most often as payback for extralegal benefits or prerogatives. Over time kings and nobles enriched bishops and abbots with gifts of land and feudal revenues. Centuries of such practices degraded the clergy and resulted in the accumulation of great wealth and property. The church became the largest landowner of Europe and the greatest of feudal lords and the greatest financial power in Christendom.[62] It was said that in the 11th century, "half the land of Germany had by this time been granted to the bishoprics and monasteries."[63] "So enmeshed in the feudal web, the church found herself a political, economic and military, as well as a religious institution, her material possessions, her feudal rights and obligations, a source of consuming controversy between emperors and popes."[64]

Two actions taken in quick succession by the papacy may also be considered as underlying causes of the religious reaction about to engulf the Church. The first action formalized the doctrine of transubstantiation. "About the year 1160 AD, the doctrine of transubstantiation, which sometime afterwards, Innocent III confirmed in a very solemn manner [Canon 1 of the Fourth Lateran Council of 1216], was required by the court of Rome to be acknowledged by all men. . . .Men fell down before the consecrated host, and worshiped it as god." [65] The second action, in 1229 AD, institutionalized the censure of scripture. ""We prohibit the permission of the books of the Old and New Testament to laymen, except perhaps they might desire to have the Psalter, or some Breviary for the divine service, or the Hours of the blessed Virgin Mary, for devotion; expressly forbidding their having the other parts of the Bible translated into the vulgar tongue."[66] In later years, Pius IV required the bishops to refuse lay persons leave to read even Catholic versions of the Scripture, unless their confessors or parish priests judged that such readings were likely to prove beneficial. [67]

The Distraction of the Crusades. The religiously volatile atmosphere of the first three centuries of the second millennium in Christian Europe cannot be described without reference to the crusades. For 200 years an odd assortment of warriors, Christian believers and adventurers conducted an inept and largely ineffective campaign to rescue the Holy Land from Islam.

Originally at the invitation of the Byzantine Emperor, Alexius I, Roman Catholic popes of the 11th century instigated and promoted a series of ill-conceived and poorly-executed paramilitary expeditions to conquer the Holy

Land. Ostensibly undertaken to protect Christian pilgrims, popes from Leo IX (1049 AD) to Nicholas IV (1288 AD) promoted the crusades principally as a means of unifying the princes and knights of Europe in common cause. A variety of expeditions was launched, with forces ranging in size from 20,000 to 40,000 participants consisting of knights, serfs and hangers-on and sometimes including a king or two. The expeditions were largely underwritten by extraordinary inducements from the church, promises of booty, and of forgiveness of past and future sins. Transportation was provided by Genoese and Venetian merchants, eager to establish new trading partners and routes.

The Crusaders proceeded across Europe and the Middle East en route to Jerusalem, suffering disease, famine and exposure, yet pillaging and plundering as they went. Encountering at first only weak resistance from Islamic forces, crusaders were able to conquer much of Palestine and establish the Latin Kingdom of Jerusalem. The fortunes and extent of control of the Latin Empire ebbed and flowed in subsequent years as the crusades came and went over 300 years. When at last the dust settled, little more than the coastal trade cities of Jaffa and Acre remained in Christian hands. Moslem control of Jerusalem and environs was confirmed in place, yet remained relatively benign, allowing Jewish and Christian pilgrims ready access to their holy sites.

The Crusades were like an awful B movie that wouldn't end; they had a life of their own. In truth, the expeditions as a whole never had a chance, for they were driven more by avarice and greed than by religious conviction, their supply lines were too long and their attention span too short; however they were instrumental in driving a permanent wedge between the western and eastern branches of Christianity rendering the schism of the 11th century a permanent arrangement.

Historians recount how the European Christian world was stunned by the failure of the crusades. "Men began to question how it was that the Almighty allowed His defenders to be so humiliated and the emboldened skeptical called into question the most basic tenets of the Christian faith while others agreed that failure of the Crusades refuted the claims of the pope to be God's vicar or representative on earth." [68]

In retrospect, given the spiritually bankrupt nature of the enterprise, as well as its ungodly progress and the decadence of the perpetrators, one can only wonder that the aftermath of the crusades didn't drive every thinking, conscientious Christian to flee from the church. Perhaps not without some connecting cause and effect, these events were coupled with or at least overlapped a significant period of upheaval and change in European life and institutions.

4. VITA APOSTOLICA.

Religious, Economic and Social Tumult. The first three centuries of the second millennium saw one of the most notable religious revivals ever to sweep over Europe both within and without the church. Its elements included the proliferation of monastic communities, the implementation of Gregorian reforms within the church, an economic revolution affecting all classes of people and, most significant of all, a massive exodus of determined dissidents from the church.

One monastic order after another was founded and numerous new or rebuilt convents appeared in the Christian landscape from the 11th to the 13th Centuries. "The orders of this period may be grouped into five main families: the family that followed the Benedictine rule; the family which followed the so-called Augustinian rule, the Carmelites, the hermit orders, of which the Carthusians were the chief; and the original mendicant orders, the Franciscans and the Dominicans."[69] Creatures of the papacy, the monastic orders tended to centralize church authority, drawing power away from the bishops and fostering the independence of the papacy.

The Gregorian reforms of the 11th century were concentrated on the two issues of papal absolutism and moral reform. Pope Gregory VII aggressively set out to solidify the pope's role as the sole Vicar of Christ, having absolute and final jurisdiction over all of Christendom, responsible only to God and to no earthly tribunal. The traction his efforts promoting papal authority were able to achieve, and it was significant, served society and the church well for a time – but inevitably, as the papacy subsequently degenerated into a more worldly institution, they led to intolerable tyranny over the hearts and minds of men, setting the stage for further rebellion and rejection. Gregory's moral reforms had mostly to do with clerical celibacy, secular investiture and the elimination of Simony. He attempted to enforce the long-standing but largely ignored prohibition against the marriage of clergy. He challenged the authority of monarchs and princes over control of appointments, or investitures, of church officials such as bishops, priests and abbots, and was able to reach a compromise favorable to the church. He sought to eliminate the sale and purchase of ecclesiastical office or spiritual authority.

Review of historical accounts of Gregory's papal administration leave the unmistakable impression that moral reform was a side issue, a secondary consideration. Throughout his twelve-year reign, the pope's time and energy were consumed with issues of church and state, struggles for prominence with emperors and kings. In fact for a few hundred of the medieval years, popes stumbled through a series of botched elections, invading armies, excommunicated emperors, deposed and vagabond popes, and enraged kings. These great contests of church and state played themselves out in the stratosphere, high above the hearths and homes of the simple people of the church, who attracted little interest from the Vatican. Perhaps the period can best be characterized by church leaders and members existing in separate worlds, matters of the world taking precedence over matters of the spirit.

Durant describes a three-century economic revolution in Europe coincident with upheaval within the church, beginning with the opening of the Mediterranean ports following the early Crusades. Elements of the revolution included the expansion of commerce and the emergence of a new class, the *bourgeoisie*, consisting of merchants and master craftsmen, inserting themselves between the nobles and the peasants. The elements of this new mercantile wealth and power rose in competition with and would eventually exceed that which came solely from the ownership of land. Intertwined with this was the emergence of nation states and a communal revolution in which cities began to assert their power and independence, drawing to their burgeoning slums large numbers of serfs by offering them employment and a measure of freedom. Lambert describes the formation of communities and the proliferation of new orders and guilds in the cities and towns. Religious excitement was awakened and heresy advanced by the emergence of charismatic interpreters of scripture coincident with increased literacy among the laity.[70] Under these circumstances, "Europe experienced in the 12th and 13th centuries such prosperity as it had not known since the fall of Rome . . . the dark Ages became a memory, and . . . the peasantry rose in the 12th century to a degree of freedom and prosperity that it had not known for 1000 years." [71]

Vita Apostolica. The coincidence of economic, social and religious circumstances of Christian Europe in the first two to three centuries of the second millennium formed a fertile seedbed for reform and dissent. Into this maelstrom strode a religious movement of significance anticipating that of the Protestant Reformation which was to follow several centuries later. From the perspective of religion, the period has been referred to as *vita apos-*

tolica, a great grass-roots movement where thoughtful Christians sought to imitate the apostolic life as manifest in the primitive church, with emphasis on preaching and poverty. The movement embraced three principles: return to the simple spirituality of the apostolic period, genuine concern and love for the souls of men, and poverty of the clergy. "It became, during the age of Gregorian reform [11th century] and after, a compelling program instinct, with the fervor, spontaneity, and humanity of the first [Christian] community at Jerusalem. . ... Such a momentous evolution of society, challenging the status quo in all its parts, demanded a reappraisal of the resources and ends of the church, the most powerful and tenacious defender of tradition."[72]

Peters refers to "the growth and variety of the forms of religious dissent suddenly [appearing] around the year 1000 as an important facet of the European experience during a period of profound change and social and cultural transformation. The religious sensibility of the 11th and 12th centuries was a manifestation of the deepest strata of European culture."[73]

Voices of prophetic dissent were heard and harkened to throughout Western Europe, with concentration in a regional belt of heresy extending from the south of France through northern Italy. "Of an independent ecclesiastical movement they had no thought, but they cried out for clerical reform, and the people after long waiting, seeing no signs of a reform, found hope and relief only in separatist societies and groups of believers."[74] "Writers and chroniclers describe the stirrings of a fully international movement, named differently in different countries, but having distinctive elements of belief and organization in common."[75]

Hundreds of dissident groups arose independently during this period, as if by spontaneous combustion, who, though differing in nuances of doctrine and practice, had much in common. What they offered was appealing to the common people and to the lesser nobility and they soon gained wide acceptance. "The greatest strength of the movement lay in its ethical appeal to populations who had been sufficiently affected by the religious sentiment of the age to value poverty and self-sacrifice – yet lacked orthodox instruction."[76] Characteristic among them was simplicity of ritual and service, piety and poverty of the clergy, and availability of the scriptures in the vernacular. As opposed to the main stream Christianity of this era, these elements better satisfied the spiritual aspirations of many.[77] "The fortress Christianity of the Dark Ages was giving way, in the more propitious circumstances of the age, to a religion which could touch the intellect of the layman."[78]

These dissidents came to view the evolution of doctrine and ritual in the Catholic Church as a steady deviation from its scriptural base. Rather than part from the church, they usually sought reform within the church. Their separation from the church most often resulted when their efforts toward reform were rejected, and as they in turn rejected the worldliness and dissolution of the clergy and the arrogance and ambition of the papacy.

Most of the dissident groups of this period invoked the New Testament as the basis of their religion and rejected anything introduced later by the church. They considered property and wealth to be inconsistent with the teachings of the Savior. They rejected the celibacy of priests, invocation of the saints, the veneration of relics, the use of images, auricular confession, mass for the dead, the primacy of the pope, and in some cases infant baptism. They drew their strength from the masses and were commonly portrayed by their adversaries as poor, illiterate and vulgar, and certainly, by comparison with their critics, they were unlearned.

These dissident movements are distinguished from those of the 15th century in that they found their basis in the people and not with the princes, the clerics or the sophisticated. Schaff writes:

> The vast majority of those who suffered punishment as heretics was of the common people. Their ignorance was a constant subject of gibe and derision as they stood trial before the ecclesiastical tribunals. Frequently they based the legitimacy of these teachings on scripture alone and the vision of the apostolic life they derived from it. Few of them were theologians and few of them were learned. Indeed the lack of systematic heretical 'doctrine' and the absence of learned men from these circles have led theologians to distinguish sharply between popular

and learned heresy throughout later medieval history. Learned or not, they too had their own answers to the question: "How should a Christian live in the world?"[79]

Some historians have characterized the dissident movement of this period as being primarily imported from the East, from groups such as the Paulicians, laden with Manichean baggage. Waddington counters:

> It required not a star from the East to indicate, even in these dark times, how distinct were the principles of the Church from the precepts of the Gospel; or to contrast the deformities of the Clergy with the purity of their heavenly master. Such incongruities intrude themselves perhaps most forcibly upon illiterate minds, and excite the deepest disgust in the simplest conscience. It is to this cause that the heresies of those early ages may most confidently be traced; They may indeed have been infected, in a greater or less degree, with some of the notions of the Paulician colonists – but that assuredly was not the cause from which they flowed.[80]

In 1140 AD the bishops of France informed the pope that, "Everywhere in our cities and villages, not only in our schools but on our street corners, learned and ignorant, great and small, are discussing the greatest mysteries. The reanimated [philosophical] fragments of the past. . . are intermingled with new interpretations of the gospel which were audaciously progressive, and with opinions, which. . .sought refuge in primitive Christian tradition against the innovations of Rome."[81]

Evervinus (1140 AD) of the diocese of Cologne writes of one such group claiming to be the church of God because they alone follow Christ, not seeking secular gains and possessing no property. Separation from the mother church did not interest them, but rather they sought a debate conference, and if they were proved wrong they would return to the fold. Instead, church authorities gave them three days to repent and, failing that, many of their number were burned, a fate they received with rejoicing. "They do not believe infant baptism to be a duty, but they put no confidence in the intercession of saints, and all things that have been observed in the church which have not been established by Christ himself or his apostles, they call superstitions. They do not admit of any purgatory after death, they make void all of the prayers and obligations of believers for the deceased. They maintain that the true faith and worship of Christ is nowhere to be found but in their meetings."[82]

Egbert of Schoenauge wrote that such groups increased to great multitudes thoughout all countries, and that in Germany these were called Cathari, signifying the pure, in Flanders, the Piphles, in France Tisseranus (meaning weaver – signifying humble laborers). [83] Milner further states that "their numbers were very considerable in [the 12th] century and that Cologne, Flanders, the south of France, Savoy,

Milan were their principal places of residence."[84] "Contemporary reports represent the number of heretics as very large. They were compared by William of Newburgh to the sand of the sea, and were said by Walter Map to be infinite in number in Aquitaine and Burgundy. By the end of the 12th century, they were reported to have followers in nearly 1000 cities. The Dominican Reinerius gave 4,000,000 as a safe estimate of their number and declared that this was according to a census taken by the Cathari themselves."[85]

Historical records do not support any firm number, but it is apparent that the 11th through 13th centuries witnessed hundreds of spontaneous dissident movements involving thousands of dissatisfied Christians seeking spiritual fulfillment outside the main stream. The reach of these dissidents was extensive even early in the 12th century when first historical records bring them to our attention, suggesting either extremely rapid growth and dissemination or that their origins lay in an earlier time. Though alarmed by their startling success, their foes seemed puzzled if not charmed by the dissidents' humility and righteous living.

Given the quantity and similarity of these dissident groups and the various appearances or branches thereof, it is not surprising that contemporary critics and historians alike confused and combined them at random. The Cathari, for example, achieved a sizable following and were spoken of throughout the 12th century. Kurtz portrays the Cathari as consisting of many sects or branches with varying doctrines and practices, but with the uniting principle of "basic enmity toward the Catholic clergy and hierarchy."[86] Several historians attribute to the Cathari Manichaen tendencies, that is, a sort of dualism drawn from Persian philosophies of the 3th century.[87] But then in the Middle Ages, opponents of Christian heretics often employed the name Manichaeism as a sort of pejorative, as a way of designating the heretic as beyond the pale. Historians are at pains to describe the dualistic doctrine of the Cathari in contrast to the teachings of the New Testament. However, it is not likely that the rank and file were adept at making the distinction between the good and evil in the spirit of the Mane as compared to the God and Satan of the New Testament.

The multitude of dissident groups, though united in doctrine and intent, had no central authority and produced hardly a single prominent leader whose reputation comes down to us through the centuries. This lack explains in part the plethora of names by which the dissidents were known. The council of Verona (1184) pronounced perpetual anathema against "first the Cathari and Paterenes, and those falsely called Humiliati, or Poor men of Lyon, also the Passigini, Josephini and Arnoldists, whom we put under perpetual anathema."[88] Names were generally derived from their founders or the locale of the originating group. Documents of the period speak of as many as 130 different sects.[89]

The German historian Kurtz wrote:

> The dissidents from the year 1030 in the neighborhood of Turin boasted a pope of their own

... In Goslar in 1052, a number of Manichean heretics were hanged at the emperor's command. In the 12th century, the number and extent [of heretical congregations] had grown to a startling extent. Most were located in Lombardy and the south of France, but large congregations were also found in Germany, Belgium, Spain and even England. It was said that in their prime they boasted an extensive hierarchy, including alone in Bulgaria a pope, 12 magistrates and 72 bishops. In the year 1167 [heretical movements] were sufficiently robust in France to convene a series of ecumenical councils in Toulouse.[90]

The writer designated Passau Anonymous, writing about 1315 AD, claimed there was "scarcely a land in which the Waldenses were not spread."[91] Pope Innocent III proclaimed "the number of heretics in southern France inumerable."[92] Hase states that "in the southern French region of Provençe, the Cathari and Vaudois were stronger than the church. The danger of their example could not be overestimated."[93]

5. THE EMERGENCE OF THE VAUDOIS.

Somewhere, somehow, into or out of this amalgam of dissatisfied Christians and organized dissidents, the Vaudois established themselves as a viable Christian denomination, in fact the most enduring of all the dissident groups. Their actual origin quite simply cannot be deduced from written historical accounts. However, perhaps the most likely scenario can be established.

Most evidence suggests that the Cathari were a dissident group distinct and separate from the Vaudois. Existing over the same time and space, they shared much in the way of practice and morals and perhaps for that reason they were not easily distinguished. One reads detailed discussions of their highly-esteemed morals, their exemplary citizenship, their successful missionary efforts, their endurance in the face of persecution, their dogmatic adherence to the New Testament as a basis for Christian behavior, and often one is unable to determine whether the account speaks of the Cathari or the Vaudois. Nonetheless, the two groups differed widely in doctrine. The Vaudois' long, perhaps even reluctant withdrawal from the Roman church was largely based on sacerdotal objections, that is, having to do with priesthood and its functions. The Cathari, on the other hand, took exception to the basic church doctrine regarding God and evil and the nature of Christ. Despite these differences, the Cathari and the Vaudois were kindred spirits throughout their existence, enjoying mutual toleration with little in the way of contention or rivalry.

The general consensus of modern historians concerning the origin of the Vaudois is that Pierre de Vaud, Peter Waldo (or Valdius) of Lyon was their founder and namesake. Yet, at the time that Waldo appeared on the scene (ca. 1170), Europe, and in particular the south of Gaul, was already home to a large number of dissident movements, sharing the tenets and practices attributed to the Vaudois. Mosheim, while asserting Waldo as the originator of the Vaudois, agrees that "there were in the valleys of Piedmont, long before this period [12th century], a set of men, who differed widely from the opinions adopted and inculcated by the church of Rome, and whose doctrine resembled, in many respects, that of the Waldenses."[94]

Robinson contends that the dissidents he characterize as *Old Waldenses* existed since the 8th century in the Pyrenees Mountains and that they were a liberty-loving, aggressive and doctrinally diverse grouping of dissident sects as opposed to the more conservative, homogenous dissidents, later known as Waldenses, of the Piedmont Alps. "The inhabitants [of the Pyrenees] seemed to have been the original Vallenses who undesignedly communicated their name with their doctrine in whole or in part to many other classes of people who were afterward called by the general name of Vellenses, Valdenses, or Ualdenses."[95] Their geographical base was the region surrounding Barcelona which in the 10th century bore the name Vallensis.

Milner attributes to the Cathari the Noble Lesson, normally thought to be of the Vaudois, calling them "Wallenses or Vaudois, from the valleys of Piedmont. They afterwards were called Waldenses from Peter Waldo, and by that name they are known to this day. But by the date 1000 AD they were evidently a distinct people before his time and most likely, had existed for generations. The seeds of the Cathari had in all probability been sown by Claudius of Turin in the 9th century." [96] The scant records of the period do not permit such a connection to be confirmed, only supposed, but to some the continuity of doctrine and practice was persuasive.

Biller asserts that the Vaudois were so diverse within their group that "Medieval *Waldensianism* is a mistaken name. It should be the plural: *Waldensianisms*."[97] The situation was further confounded in this period when various dissident groups, under pressure of persecution, to avoid detection or attack, adopted various names as a means of disguise.

Milner portrays the followers of Waldo as one of many sources flowing together in the 12th century and by no means the earliest. Passau Anonymous argues that the Italian Poor were not of Waldo but rather from the Humiliati of the 11th century.[98] At least one historian contends that Waldo's role was not as an originator, but rather to gather together the dispersed remnants of these dissident groups into one body of worship which took the name of Vaudois either because their principal place of refuge was in the Alpine valleys or because of their organizer's name.[99] Catholic detractors and persecuters found it convenient and useful to deny all claims of early existence of the Vaudois or other dissident groups and fixed their gaze upon Waldo of Lyon, as the founder.

> The later Vaudois' account of their ancient origin, dating preferably from the apostolic era, was partly true, to the extent that the same spirit never ceased to protest against the corruption of

the church, or its deviation from the Holy Scriptures. And perhaps there had been since the time of Claudius of Turin a direction maintained among peasant congregations in certain Alpine valleys, which corresponded to Vaudois beliefs, and which was to be further clarified through subsequent interaction with the Vaudois.[100]

Peter Waldo and his Immediate Forerunners. The generally-accepted thesis that Peter Waldo was the founder of the Vaudois in the same sense that Joseph Smith was the founder of Mormonism or Mary Baker Eddy the founder of Christian Science cannot be substantiated. We have not a single teaching of Peter Waldo, no wisp of his personal imprint on the Vaudois religion. That Waldo was a courageous and determined disciple of Christ and a persistent dissident is beyond dispute. His Bible translation was a key element in promoting the spread and duration of the dissident movement. But there is no basis to conclude that Waldo founded the Vaudois, or that he had anything but a peripheral role in the great missionary effort that spread the doctrines and practices of vita apostolica dissidence throughout most of Europe in the early medieval period.

Waldo had his contemporaries and immediate forerunners, those whose influence was prevalent in the South of France in his generation and who may have influenced him personally. Early in the 12th century there arose in Dauphine a priest by the name of Pierre de Bruys who protested against abuses in the church. Among his objections, he taught that the "ordinance of baptism was to be administered to adults only; that it was a piece of idle superstition to build and dedicate churches to the service of God, . . . who cannot be worshiped in temples made with hands; that the crucifixes are objects of superstition, and ought to be destroyed; that, in the Lord's supper, the real body and blood of Christ were not partaken of by the communicants, but only represented in the way of symbol or figure; and, lastly, that the oblations, prayers, and good works of the living, can in no way be beneficial to the dead."[101] De Bruys gained a substantial following in the south of France and added the name, Petrobusians, to the lexicon of *vita apostolica* dissidents. He was burned to death for his troubles by a mob urged on by the clergy at St. Giles in France, about the year 1130 AD.

In Peter's wake, and perhaps from among his entourage, came a Benedictine in 1125 AD named Henry of Lausanne, or Henry the Monk, to carry the dissidents' torch in France, raising his voice against the corruption of the church. A radical Gregorian reformer and an eloquent and compelling evangelist, Henry abandoned the convent but continued to preach and to practice poverty. His advocacy of simplicity in church rituals and his aggressive evangelism drew many to his side. Henry was one of the wandering preachers common to that era and may not have drawn the ire of ecclesiastical officials except that his recurring theme tended to marginalize the clergy and thus pose a real threat to the church. Known as Henricians, his followers were active in the Alps along the French-Italian border. In 1158 AD Henry was condemned, sent to a dungeon, and left there to die.

Meanwhile in the north of Italy there came another 12th century contemporary, a compelling preacher known as Arnold of Brescia who attracted many followers. Beginning as a priest and provost, Arnold instigated a reform movement based on criticism of the wealth among the clergy and the temporal power of the bishop. He proposed that "Clerics who own property, bishops who hold regalia [tenures by royal grant], and monks who have possessions cannot possibly be saved. All these things belong to the [temporal] prince, who cannot dispose of them except in favor of laymen."[102] Invited to Rome by pope Eugenius III for closer supervision, Arnold's rhetoric soared as did his ambition. He discovered "the pope himself was not what he professed to be – an apostolic man and shepherd of souls – but a man of blood who maintained his authority by fire and sword." [103]

Totally rejecting clerical rule, Arnold and his followers proceeded to establish a new Roman republic (1145 AD), take possession of the Vatican and expel the pope. Peyran[104] was almost surely mistaken when he claimed that Arnold of Brescia was a Vaudois pastor, though this misidentification suggests the difficulties of differentiating among the dissenters of the period. Arnold's ten-year rule came to a tumultuous end with the return of papal authority in the person of Adrian IV, whereupon Arnold was condemned by the church, excommunicated and executed by hanging or crucifixion in the year 1155.

Most of what we know of the life of Peter[9] Waldo comes from two accounts, the *Universal Chronical* of Laon Anony-

---

9 Some claim that the given name Peter was invented later to connect Waldo to Peter the apostle.

mous and the *Life of Alexander III* by Richard of Poitiers.[105] Born in 1140 AD, Waldo was said to have been a successful merchant of the city of Lyons, or he may have been a financial officer of the diocese. Certainly he was affluent by the standards of the day. Motivated by some spiritual experience, the sudden death of a friend or perhaps the tales of an itinerant entertainer, in 1173 AD Waldo decided to give away his property and enter into the life of a poor and humble follower of Christian teaching as found in the New Testament. Divesting himself of his abundant holdings, he deeded his immovable property to his wife, settled a large sum on his daughters and placed them in a convent. He then immersed himself in spiritual matters and the intense study of Christian doctrine and practice. Convinced that the scriptures should be made available to all in their native language, he engaged one Stephanus de Ansa to translate portions of the scriptures into the vernacular language.[10] He "saw it as his mission not just to be poor for his own soul's sake, but to encourage others to do likewise, and quite soon began to preach his mission of apostolic poverty in public."[106]

The Waldo-de Ansa translation of the Bible, occurring as it did in 1170 AD, centuries before the Protestant Reformation, can hardly be overestimated as a milestone in the history of Christian reform. The language was vernacular

---

10 Gilly argues that the language was Romaunt. Linguists believe that the Romaunt or Occitan language prevailed over the south of France and parts of northern Italy from the 8th Century into the medieval period, and that this was the language of the Vaudois.

in the purest sense in that it spoke to a huge swath of the European Christian world. "Lingua Romana or Romaunt was in one or another of its dialects, the vernacular language of the south of Europe from the time when pure Latin ceased to be spoken until the French, Spanish and Italian languages were completely formed, that is to say from the 8th to the 13th century. It derived its name from Romania by which the Gallic, Italian and Spanish provinces of the Roman Empire were designated by the northern nations."[107] Gilly claims that the copy of the Romaunt Bible kept at Trinity College, Dublin, was obtained by Archbishop Ussher[11] in the early 1600s from the Waldenses as a manuscript copy in the Provençal-Romaunt dialect faithful to the Waldo-de Ansa translation of 1170 AD.

Gilly believed that this translation, known as *La Bible des Paurves (Bible of the Poor)* was, "part of the earliest complete version of the New Testament which is now known to exist in any vernacular European language in the dark or middle ages. This and other translations of the Bible were rejected by Catholic authority, not because they were faulty or false, but "because they were vernacular, and it was the object of the hierarchy to check the spirit of scriptural inquiry, which was spreading among the people."[108] The Romaunt Bible was a hugely significant tool of scriptural inquiry, symptomatic of the age of *vita apostilica*.

Waldo, it seems, was an uncomplicated soul. Stumbling through the maze of Catholic hierarchy, welcomed here,

---

11 Archbishop of Armagh, distinguished scholar of the 17th Century, Primate of All Ireland to 1656.

rejected there, he was governed by two simple scriptures: The vow of poverty grew out of the Lord's admonition to the righteous rich man, who having kept all the commandments, came to Jesus to learn what else he must do. "Yet lackest thou one thing: sell all that thou hast, and distribute unto the poor, and thou shalt have treasure in heaven: and come, follow me" (Luke 18:22). Having achieved poverty, the second compelling commandment for Waldo was: "Go ye into all the world, and preach the gospel to every creature" (Mark 15:16). What church authorities expected from Waldo was obedience, subservience to the authority of the pope as the vicar of God. One could only excuse Waldo if he was unable to see in the popes of his day, men worthy of such a lofty mantle. To the prohibition they imposed upon him, he responded with a third scriptural reference, "Whether it be right in the sight of God to hearken unto you more than unto God, judge ye. For we cannot but speak the things which we have seen and heard." (Acts 4:19-2)

The archbishop of Lyon forbade Waldo to preach, not so much because his doctrines were incorrect or offensive, but because he was untrained and unauthorized. Proceeding to a council in Rome, (the Third Lateran Council of 1179 AD), Waldo and his followers presented their Bible to Pope Innocent III and appealed the archbishop's ruling, only to be adjudged schismatics. There is a fine line between the confession of poverty as practiced in the dissident groups and that later institutionalized by the likes of Domonic and Francis of Assissi. A timely nod of approval by the pope, an independent bent of local leadership, could make the difference between heresy and reform. Popes of the period embraced the movements initiated by Francis and Dominic as new monastic orders, appropriately growing out of the church itself. However, Waldo was rejected as an uppity lay person with good intentions but lacking in sophistication and learning. In time, Pope Innocent III attempted a reconciliation and recovery among the Vaudois by forming the Pauperes Catholici. In the end the Pauperes Catholici did not survive a generation and the bulk of Waldo's followers went their separate ways.

Canon 27 of the Third Lateran Council record condemns the Cathari, Publicani and Patarenes by name, but other sources indicate that Waldo and his group were considered at the council. They were embraced for their vows of poverty, humiliated because of their lack of theological sophistication, and advised to preach only as permitted by the local clergy. Failing to comply with this gag order, Waldo and his followers were declared contumacious and disobedient and were excommunicated. Their growing numbers drew the attention of Pope Alexander III, who urged stricter measures against them, causing their expulsion from Lyon and dispersion to other parts of Europe. In November 1184 AD at the Council of Verona, a new pope, Lucius III issued the decree *Ad Abolendam*, placing under anathema the Cathari, Patarenes and for the first time, the Humiliati[12] or Poor of Lyon. The council's specific reference to unauthorized preaching as a basis for anathema was thought to be

---

12 The Humiliati were a lay-monastic order under vows of poverty, sometimes, as in this instance, confused with the Vaudois.

specifically directed at the Vaudois.

Under the pressure of expulsion and anathema, Waldo removed first to Dauphiny and Piccardy. Persecution followed him there and eventually drove him to Germany and Bohemia where he died in 1218 AD leaving robust groups of his followers at each station along the way. Much as the expulsion of the primitive church from Jerusalem promoted its rapid growth in outlying areas, so also Waldo's exile from Lyon accelerated the expansion of the contagious doctrines and teachings of the dissidents. In the south of France, Waldo's missionaries found a fertile field, prepared by the likes of the previously mentioned Peter de Bruys and Henry of Lausanne. Evidently Waldo never set foot in Italy and certainly never led his followers into the Alpine Valleys.

The only surviving statement of Waldo's beliefs is the profession of faith[109] attributed to him as given at a diocesan hearing convened by the archbishop of Lyon in 1180 or 1181. It is an expression designed to demonstrate his conformance to Catholic orthodoxy and may have been dictated largely or wholly by the authorities of the church. As to the fundamental Vaudois tenets of poverty and preaching, it ends with a reaffirmation of his commitment to poverty but makes no mention of preaching. The statement bears scant relation to the beliefs and practices generally attributed to the Vaudois then or at any other time, supporting the conclusion that Waldo was not the founder of the Vaudois.

Bernhard of Fonteaulde, writing in 1190, reported the results of a debate between Catholic prelates and Vaudois representatives, whose name, he writes, surely derived from dense vale, "inasmuch as they were enveloped in a deep, dense darkness of error."[110] In this treatise he recounts the whole spectrum of Vaudois beliefs from denying the authority of the pope to rejecting purgatory, in sharp and total contrast to those attributed to Waldo just nine short years earlier.

Did the Vaudois begin with Peter Waldo? There is an abundance of convincing though fragmented evidence that dissident groups virtually identical with the Vaudois existed for decades, even centuries, before Waldo. Certainly, a group of Christians beyond the influence of and unfriendly to papal authority existed in the Cottian Alps as early as the 9th century. The region where the Vaudois flowered most abundantly, extending from southern France through Northern Italy, was the most productive area for the emergence and nurture of a variety of dissident groups growing out of the *vita apostolica* movement in the medieval period. The distinction between these various groups was seldom clearly defined, and there was little consistency to the names by which they were known, especially among their enemies. Waldenses, Poor Men of Lyon, Zabatati, Sandalati, and Leonists were names commonly used interchangeably with Vaudois. There is no lack of historians who wrote of the Cathari, Humiliati, Paterenes as if they were Vaudois. Historical accounts of the Inquisition describe the treatment of heretics called Vaudois throughout much of Europe by mid-13th century. "Innocent III describes the [Vaudois] heresy as established so widely in Bohemia by 1245 that it embraced not only the simple folk, but also the princes and magnates."[111] Such rapid expansion resulting in a substantial population of Vaudois from Bohemia to Britain, from Poland to the tip of Italy within 50 years of Waldo's death defies plausibility and is compelling evidence that much more was at play here than the humble followers of Peter Waldo.

The earliest mention of Waldo as founder of a dissident movement is by Stephen of Bourbon (1249) who wrote, "Now the Waldenses were so named for the founder of this heresy whose name was Waldes. They were also called the Poor of Lyon because it was in that city that they entered upon their life of poverty. They also refer to themselves as the Poor in Spirit. The sect began in this way, according to what I have heard."[112] "According to what I have heard" is weak affirmation. More interesting would be some real evidence of a connection between Waldo and the Vaudois. Other writers of the 13th century intimately familiar with the Vaudois, when writing of their origin, never mentioned Waldo, suggesting that his role as their founder was likely an invention of a later time. The absence of any reference to Peter Waldo in their writings suggests that (1) the Waldo origin theory emerged later than 1260 AD and (2) a scant 40 years after the death of Waldo the Vaudois were already considered as ancient. This, together with their widespread influence makes a compelling case that the Vaudois existed in some form well before the birth of Peter Waldo.

6. PERSECUTION, EXTERMINATION AND EXODUS.

The Church's Response. With the crusades winding down, Catholic authorities shifted their gaze from the infidel to the heretic, who they considered to be even worse than the Saracen [Muslim] or a person of depraved morals. The Abbot Werner of St. Blasius in Baden-Württemberg, preaching in 1125 AD stated that the "holy Catholic Church patiently tolerates those who live ill (*male viventes*) but casts out from itself those who believe erroneously (*male credites*)."[113] Had the wrath of the Catholic hierarchy ended there, with the casting out, we likely would not know of many of the dissident groups that followed, for often their notoriety resulted from the extreme action taken against them. "Casting out" did not suffice. The *vita apostolica* dissenters continued to grow in numbers and influence until economic isolation, social ostracism, confiscation of property, imprisonment and finally death-by-burning followed in rapid succession as the solutions of choice.

The wide-spread contagion of heresy centered in the south of France alarmed Pope Innocent III, who is said to have feared, not only for the survival of the church, but also the welfare of civilization. When friendly persuasion proved ineffectual, the pope resorted to more forceful methods. His next response was to authorize local bishops to "resist the ministers of diabolical error, who are ensnaring the souls of the simple, with all your might. We give you a strict command that by whatever means you can, you destroy all the heresies, and dispel from your diocese all who are polluted by them, and if necessary, you may cause the princes and people to suppress them with the sword."[114]

Local bishops and princes demurred, appalled at the prospect of persecuting law-abiding, exemplary subjects within their realms, and their implementation of the pope's decree was less than enthusiastic. Such a high-minded endeavor was beyond the comprehension of the local clergy and secular authorities who valued their heretical subjects. "How can we do it? We have been brought up with these people, we have kindred among them, and we see them living righteously." To assist the local bishops, Innocent appointed a papal legate to "make inquisition throughout France, and commanded him to offer a plenary indulgence to the king and nobles of France for aid in supporting the Catharist crusade."[115] On the basis of the Vatican's promise of material gain and the purchase of redemption, in 1207 AD papal authorities launched a crusade against the heretics of southern France.

Out of this turmoil emerged the quintessential Catholic institution that was to strike terror in the hearts of guilty and innocent alike in much of Europe for centuries to come: To extirpate religious dissent, the fierce tribunal of the medieval Inquisition[13] was established. Innocent III initiated the practice, but it was Gregory IX who institutionalized the process in 1231 AD. "Henceforth church and state [the Holy Roman Empire] agreed that impenitent heresy was treason, and should be punished by death. The Inquisition was now officially established under the control of the popes."[116] "The

---
13 See Chapter II for a more detailed description of the Inquisition.

creation of a permanent tribunal, staffed by Dominican friars who worked in conjunction with the local episcopate, endowed with papal authority first occurred in Languedoc in 1233-1234 AD."[117] The vital innovation of Gregory was to combine the inquisitorial and judgment processes by establishing a special tribunal, acting in secret and reporting to the pope. Those condemned by the Inquisition were generally remanded to secular authorities for punishment. Most dissident groups proved to be no match for the combined power of church and state.

Extermination and Exodus. Drawing most of the attention of the medieval Inquisition were the Cathari or Albigenses and the Vaudois. Innocent III gave unlimited authority to the annihilation of the heretics. [118] To this purpose he undertook a crusade against them. Comba reports, in the course of a few years in the first quarter of the 13th century, the destruction of 18 heretical cities, 124 villages and upwards of 60,000 inhabitants in the county of Toulouse (Languedoc). In Beziers alone, much of the population was destroyed, 7000 in the massacre at a single church. Heretics and loyal Catholics alike were caught up in the general conflagration. To Arnauld, the commanding legate of this genocide, was attributed the remark, "Kill them all. God will know his own."[119] Some powerful nobles in the area, such as Count Raymond VI of Toulouse, were sympathetic toward and may have joined the Cathari. At first they resisted the crusade but eventually the threat of the loss of all their realms compelled them to join in the effort. "By the first quarter of the 14th century the organized Cathari church had disappeared. After 1350 the heresies of the Cathari and the Vaudois were little more than memories in Languedoc."[120] In the wake of the crusade, "united in their death or destruction, Albigenses [or Cathari] and Waldenses crowded the highways, dazed with fright as they rushed pell-mell, mostly toward the east."[121] Pressing onward, the refugee stream soon overwhelmed the hospitality of their brethren in Dauphiny and spilled over into the mountain passes of the Alps.

The steep mountainous region forming a natural barrier between France and the Italian peninsula became the refuge for the fleeing dissidents and the traditional home of the Vaudois. The mountain ranges there known as the Cottian Alps are separated by the three major valleys of Lucerna, San Martino and Clusone; the latter further subdivided into the upper Clusone (Pragela) and the lower Clusone (Perosa).

From the vantage point of the mid-17th century, England's envoy to the Vaudois, Wm. Morland, has given us a vivid first-hand description of these valleys. A portion of the Valley of Pragela was ". . .in ancient times and yet is (1658) a part of Dauphine [a province of France] . . . as far as la Capella. . . as likewise it was the ordinary Passage of the French Armies into Italie."[122] The balance of the Vaudois Valleys lay in the Principality of Piedmont, since the 11th century part of the Duchy of Savoy. The valleys open onto the plains of Piedmont "watered like a pleasant Garden, and render[ed] . . . exceedingly fruitful in Cattel, Wine, Corn, Hay, Nuts and almost all other things in abundance.

These valleys are by nature strongly fortified, by reason of the many different Passages, as Bulwarks of Rocks and Mountains . . . designed as a Cabinet wherein to put some inestimable jewel."[123]

In his own bejeweled account, Lawrence describes the Valley of Lucena as ". . .the most fertile, the most beautiful [of the Vaudois valleys], possessing unrivaled charms. Its thick and almost perpetual foliage, its groves of mulberry trees,[14] its woods of chestnut, the waving fields of wheat, its vineyards climbing up the mountainside, its temperate air, its countless hamlets, its innocent and happy people, seem to rest in perfect peace beneath the shelter of the encircling Alps." [124]

Following a visit to the Valleys in 1860, Fredrika Bremer wrote:

> "Extending from the southern range of the Cottian Alps, these valley expand like a fan towards the plain of Piedmont, upon which they lie, between their mountain ridges, as upon a high terrace. The fertile heights and plain along the mountain ridges are covered with chestnut woods, which are just now laden with fruit, the manna of the valleys, as it is called, because it furnishes food to the inhabitants . . . the whole year through, from the one harvest to the other.

---

14 The Vaudois have long been accustomed to the rearing of silk worms, and by this means provide for their subsistence. The mulberry tree leaves are the only food of the silk worm.

> Lower down grows the mulberry tree in great luxuriance, the maize, the vine, &c., intermixed with beautiful pastureland; whilst through all three valleys, rivers dance and becks leap along clearer and fresher, it seems to me, than I have ever before seen elsewhere; such are the rivers Lucerne and Angrogna, and the wild Germanesco in the valley of San Martino. All proceed from sources in the Alps, and all contribute to swell with their pure waters the mighty Po, which leads them through Italy to the great ocean."[125]

Ms. Bremer's dated description from 1860 likely represents the condition of the people for centuries;

> "The people are poor . . . but their great frugality prevents the existence of any bitter sense of poverty. Polenta and chestnuts are the principal food, and both of them are palatable. Polenta is a kind of porridge made from maize, eaten with milk . . . Chestnuts are dried and smoked, and thus kept good the whole year round. Flesh meat is eaten very seldom. In the winter evenings several families will unite around one lamp, which in order to save wood they place in the cowhouse. Here the women sit and spin or knit, and the men, tired with the day's work, felling and cutting wood, lie to rest in the straw or talk. Occasionally someone reads aloud. Young men

at these times go from house to house, and sit for a little while in the sitting room, where they make acquaintance with young women."[126]

These Alpine valleys at the juncture of the Duchy of Savoy and the French province of Dauphine were in the 13th century a uniquely-suited region as a place of resort and refuge for fleeing heretics. First, there was hardly anyone there, and those who had made this region their home, were no friends of the Roman church, partly because the excesses of Rome were better known there than elsewhere. Second, the region, though nominally under the split jurisdiction of the Savoyard Duchy and the Kingdom of France and the diocese of Turin, was of little interest to the reigning secular or ecclesiastical authorities. Thirdly, the region was a natural fortress, easily defended against foes approaching from any direction. Some of the faithful saw the hand of God in their arrival and safe reception there, but as Hudry-Menos suggests "It is not necessary to explain their success by means of supernatural interference, it is sufficient to examine the configuration of the country carefully." [127] Fourth, the Romaunt or Occitan language, common to the south of France, was the predominant language of these valleys, so much so that they were known as the Occitan valleys, the western terminus of the cultural-historical region of Occitania. Lastly, the region of northern Italy had a long and well-deserved tradition of religious freedom. "There was a laudable passion for liberty, and the love of liberty was a fashionable virtue of the times, and there was no legal power in Italy in those times to put dissidents to death. The Italians always cherished a manly love of liberty and there under the eye of the people, in spite of ecclesiastical efforts, from the beginning until the Reformation, religious dissidents found shelter."[128]

The immense and relentless pressure of the Inquisition drove the refugees to this safe haven where they at last found a home base, nevermore to be dislodged. Comba writes that in these valleys the Vaudois "dwelt a long time before they were molested by persecution. The first colonists had sufficient time to establish themselves; they increased and prospered, and many of them died full of years, leaving to their children a safe asylum. With every returning spring came seed time, and with every autumn came the increase, and in the villages the sounds of the flail on the threshing floor were mingled with the voices of children at happy play."[129] "Thus in the absence of efficient repression, were established those Alpine communities whose tenacity of belief supplied through centuries an unfailing succession of humble martyrs, and who ennobled human nature by their marvelous example of constancy and endurance."[130]

7. CONCLUSIONS.

With the passage of years, there is no way to determine with any measure of certainty the precise origin of the Vaudois, but there is sufficient evidence to establish a most-likely scenario. Over the first 13 centuries of the Christian Era there were two significant stages or turning points in which Christianity changed course or was altered significantly. The first of these was the Constantine Intervention in the first half of the 4th century when the Roman Empire embraced Christianity and adopted it as the state religion. The second was the *vita apostolica* stretching over the first few centuries of the second millennium when material wealth, spiritual impoverishment and moral bankruptcy of organized Christianity coupled with a parallel cultural and economic upheaval in Europe prompted significant reform within the church as well as a massive exodus from the church. These two turning points lay the foundation and provided the opportunity for the appearance of a myriad of Christian dissident groups out of which eventually emerged the lone survivor: the Vaudous.

The replacement of pagan religion with Christianity was gradual, but by the time the Roman Empire was in serious decline in the 5th century, the transformation was pretty much complete. However, the state's adoption of Christianity was a two-edged sword. On the positive side it meant that the persecution of Christians would cease, that church leaders would have a seat at the table where great political decisions were made and that the financial prosperity of the church was assured. Perhaps more important, it meant that expansion by conversion would no longer be a matter of Christian emissaries searching out converts one individual or family at a time, rather, they would take the gospel to princes and kings, make them an offer they couldn't refuse and bring converts into the fold one kingdom at a time.

On the negative side, it meant that many of what had

previously been internal affairs of the church now became matters of state. It initiated a centuries-long contest between the power of the papacy and that of the secular kingdoms where Christianity prevailed, and it compromised the independence of the church. In addition, wealth and power did what wealth and power always do, in time they corrupted church officials and diverted their attention from the spiritual welfare of the members to the material welfare of the church.

In the period between turning points, the lost centuries of 400-1000 AD, some heretical leaders arose from time to time to be sure, but usually only as solitary voices with a ragtag following. None of them achieved lasting power or influence. These protested what the church was becoming and sought reform within the church, but there is no evidence that any of these movements survived, let alone prevailed. In some cases their protests led to minor reforms, but in most cases the originators suffered an untimely death.

The second great turning point occurred in the period from 1000-1300 AD with the wide-spread movement known as *vita apostolica* prompting the reforms of Popes Leo IX and Gregory. These reforms sought to reemphasize clerical celibacy, to condemn Simony, to reclaim papal authority to appoint church officials, and to establish the election of the pope by the College of Cardinals. The perceived dangers to the church during this period also spawned new mendicant orders such as those of Saint Francis and Saint Dominic. Dominicans and Franciscans went forth in poverty to stabilize the Christian flock and to reconvert and reclaim the lapsed.

In *vita apostolica*, an enabling combination of political, economic and cultural circumstances combined with the decadence within church leadership to produce or at least permit an unprecedented exodus from the church numbering in the millions. Each departing dissident group had its own concerns, yet most had some basic principles in common: rejection of the office of pope as the vicar of Christ and leader of the Christian world; embracing of the Holy Scriptures as the sole basis for Christian doctrine and practice; belief in poverty of the clergy; and rejection of relics, icons and rituals, and all but the most basic of sacraments. Hundreds of dissident groups emerged spontaneously from the main stream church, tolerant toward and even intermixing with one another, often confused and lumped together by their detractors. These medieval dissident groups may have found small remnants or congregations of the disaffected from earlier times and absorbed or embraced them, but a direct connection to any of these, if such existed, has never been established.

Along with reform and the effort to reclaim, the church implemented an escalating series of increasingly severe methods to staunch the flow of apostates and recover the willing. The approaches progressed from authorizing local episcopal tribunals through the Inquisition and included the medieval Crusades, launched first against the infidel and then against the heretic.

The exodus of the dissidents produced an array of Protestant groups with no centralized leadership, few sympathetic defenders among the kings and princes of the period, and little staying power. Though existing in large numbers, the dissidents soon fell prey to the organized and relentless pressures of the Inquisition, backed by the threatened and cowed princes of the world. The inquisitors discovered, denounced, tortured and condemned the heretics, while the political authorities disenfranchised, imprisoned and executed what few would not recant. Disheartened and decimated, a meager remnant of refugees who persisted in their heresy, escaped and were driven and fled to places of refuge. The most advantageous and convenient such place was the small triangular segment of mountainous terrain situated astride the Alpine passes connecting the Kingdom of France with the Duchy of Savoy. There, in the Cottian Alps, the fleeing dissidents gathered in anonymity and found refuge. There they hunkered down in silence and obscurity to await history. There they merged with and became the people of those valleys, the Vaudois, the Waldenses, the Valdesi.

According to this view, the Vaudois didn't begin, they simply emerged from the cauldron of earnest Christian dissenters of the first centuries of the second millennium, rising as a vaporous surviving remnant, terrorized and refined and purified by the hot coals of the Inquisition. Their spiritual ancestors include what few followers may have remained of the earliest heretics from the lost centuries. They include the dissident groups borne of the *vita apostolica*, reacting against the excesses of the church and seeking a more apostolic time and life. They include those who defied papal and secular authority to access the Holy Scriptures and to preach the gospel as they understood it. The Vaudois were the distillation of all the dissident groups and individuals who were spun off from the whirlpool of Catholic degeneracy, who felt there should have been, growing out of the legacy of Christ, a better way. Before all else, they were pure Christian survivors, sequestered in their strongholds, awaiting their tardy brethren of the Reformation yet lying far in the future.

CHAPTER II.
Bridge to the Reformation
(1250-1550 AD)

Only one heresy of the Twelfth Century survived in unbroken continuity into the 16th century to emerge from its hiding place and link hands with the Protestant Reformation. Waldensianism outlasted all the persecutions, only, in the end, in out-of-the-way places, generally in the lower ranks of society, and at the cost of loss of élan. But still it lasted to bequeath to Protestant histiography the memory that even in the depths of the Middle Ages there had been an evangelically based protest against Catholicism, and to leave to the historian the vivid stories of their resistance to persecution and a precious collection of vernacular scriptural commentary and religious literature.[131]

For the Vaudois, the three centuries from 1250 to 1550 formed a sort of bridge abutted on the front end by their beginnings as a small voice of dissent rising among a multitude of like movements, surviving and outspanning all of its contemporaries and connecting on the far end with the great upward thrust of the Protestant Reformation, when they found at last that they were not alone.

By the end of the 13th century, at the beginning of this bridge period, the original narrow gaze of the medieval Inquisition, focused as it was mostly on the heretics of southern France and northern Italy, had largely consumed its available fodder. The largest heretical protagonist of that period, the Cathari, had been virtually eliminated. Of the brutal armed crusade carried out against the Cathari with considerable collateral damage writes Cardew, "On him [Pope Innocent III] rests the responsibility for all the bloodshed and horrors which followed in Languedoc which ended in the destruction of the Provençal civilization."[132] The Inquisition was now preoccupied with broadening its scope and establishing its strategy as an enduring institutionalized tribunal of the Catholic Church.

The church hierarchy had lost its focus and drifted far from its original moorings, leading to much consternation and soul searching, dissent and upheavals within the church and even some effort at genuine reform. For a time, these together with the massive exodus of dissidents had shaken the church and undermined its domination, if not threatened its very existence. The most consequential reform involved the spawning of powerful mendicant monastic movements, among them the Dominicans and the Franciscans. Through the combined efforts of the early Inquisition and the example and the labors of the new mendicant orders, the mother church weathered the storm of dissent and was on its way to recovering its hegemony and dominion. *Unam Sanctam*, the papal bull of Boniface VIII issued in 1303 was thrown down as a gauntlet in the continuing contest with the kings of Europe, an extreme statement of papal supremacy over virtually every aspect of medieval life. The pesky little detail that Catholic supremacy had been reestablished mostly through brute force rather than serious reform was easily overlooked in the flush of victory and its unsettling consequences held at bay for another century or two.

During the bridge period, the great societal and religious forces of persecution and reform in much of the European theater largely played themselves out and like a retreating ice age, began to withdraw revealing how the world stage had been set for the great transformation about to unfold. The Inquisition wrought its peculiar havoc with the multitude of Christian dissenting groups, destroying most and driving the rest into places of resort and shelter and into each other's arms. With relief, the secular authorities in France and Italy, never really interested in suppressing heretics except as prodded by the church, turned their attention to their more natural pursuits, the accumulation of power and wealth and the building of nation states. Suppression of religious dissent became old news, and perhaps, one dared to think, no longer needed. One of the few remaining dissident groups, the Vaudois, were pretty much out of the way, their core group hunkered down in a tiny triangular enclave in the Cottian Alps, where they were able to find relative peace and safety for a time with the leisure to lick their wounds and regroup. Being the remnant of a conglomerate of many religious dissent groups, they employed this bridge time to consolidate and to discover who they were, to organize themselves and to develop and hone a strategy to ensure their long-term survival.

1. EUROPEAN LIFE IN THE LATE MIDDLE AGES.

The lives and times of the approximately 60 million inhabitants of Europe prior to the Renaissance had not changed significantly for centuries, and yet they were so far removed from those of the modern era as to be all but incomprehensible to the modern mind. Manchester describes them as follows:

> One significant dimension of the medieval man's mind was his lack of ego. To them their identity in this life was irrelevant. Nobleman had surnames, but less than 1% of the souls of Christendom were well born. Typically the rest were known as Hans, Sol, Carlos, Will or Will's wife, or Will's son, Will's daughter. If that was inadequate or confusing, a nickname would do. Because most peasants lived and died without leaving their birthplace, there was seldom any need for any tag beyond One-eye, or Roussic

(Redhead) or Biondi (Blondie) or the like.[133]

> Their villages were frequently innominate for the same reason. If war took a man even a short distance from a nameless hamlet, the chances of his returning to it were slight; he could not identify it and finding his way back was virtually impossible. Each hamlet was inbred, isolated and unaware of the world beyond its most familiar landmark: a creek, a mill, a tall tree scarred by lightening. There was no newspaper or magazine to inform common people of great events. . . their anonymity approached the absolute; so did their quiet acceptance of it[134]

Tuchman mentions yet another peculiar aspect of the period, the pervading violence of everyday life.

> The age had long been accustomed to physical violence. Violence was official as well as individual. Torture was authorized by the church and regularly used to uncover heresy. The tortures and punishments of civil justice customarily cut off hands and ears, racked, burned, flayed and pulled apart people's bodies. In everyday life, passersby saw some criminal flogged with a knotted rope or chained upright in an iron collar. They passed corpses hanging on the gibbet and decapitated heads and quartered bodies im-

paled on stakes on the city walls. Accustomed in their own lives to physical hardship and injury, medieval men and women were not necessarily repelled by the spectacle of pain, but rather enjoyed it.[135]

The nascent kingdoms of France and England were emerging in the west to challenge the loose confederacy of the Holy Roman Empire, which itself bumped up in the east against the established kingdoms of Poland, Hungary and Bohemia. These political entities were, for the most part, not nation states in the modern sense, but rather confederations governed by kings who exercised jurisdiction seriously limited by the autonomy of the nobles whose territorial units made up the kingdoms. The nobles, on the other hand, ruled their fiefdoms with near absolute authority and they themselves were "the constituent members of the 'nations,' a term referring to a relatively small class of blue-blooded persons who held titles and lands, not the population of 'the people' in terms of the modern democratic theory of popular sovereignty." [136]

The lore and power of knighthood in western Europe had peaked early in the Middle Ages. By the 14th century, their military potency had been largely neutralized and their functions replaced by mercenary troops equipped with fire arms and artillery. Knighthood was mostly reduced to legend and to the occasional foray to plunder travelers, merchants and peasants alike.

Overshadowing the peasants, small-holding landowners, chieftains and kings stood the Catholic Church as the predominant influence. Its view of the world over which it towered embraced a totality of influence and responsibility never before assumed or achieved by any other entity. In the words of one pope, "The church is independent of any earthly power, not merely in regard to her lawful end and purpose, but also in regard to whatever means she may deem suitable and necessary to attain them."[137]

The Church was engaged in a series of contests with the rising tide of aggressive monarchs, seeking absolute power themselves, which frays it entered from a position of considerable strength. It possessed enormous wealth, far more than any monarch, even to the extent that "the church became the wealthiest landowner on the continent, and the life of every European from baptism through matrimony to burial, was governed by popes, cardinals, prelates, monsignors, archbishop, bishop and village priest. The clergy, it was believed, would also cast a decisive vote in determining where each soul would spend the afterlife."[138]

The few aspiring monarchs who challenged papal authority had at first only limited success, but over the course of time, they began to prevail over the church, because ultimately the battering ram was more forceful than anathema, the sword more penetrating than excommunication. The repeated clashes between the church and the monarchs of Europe had the unintended effect of solidifying the power of the monarchs and nudging European society toward powerful nation states. Such clearly was the case in which Pope Boniface VIII applying unrelenting pressure on Phillip of France, forced that monarch to confirm his resistance and establish the nation of France. [139]

The intrigues of Vatican and king's court reached the peak of absurdity with the Avignon exile beginning in 1310 in which the seat of the papacy shifted from Rome onto French soil where it came under the power and influence of the kings of France for 70 years. It was during this period, known as the "Babylonian Captivity," that the church achieved

> the development of a financial system and the unscrupulous traffic which it plied in spiritual benefits and ecclesiastic offices. The theory was put into practice that every spiritual favor had its price in money. It was [Pope] John XXII's achievement to reduce the taxation of Christendom to a finely organized system [designed] to sustain the papal establishment in a state of luxury and ease. To contemporaries, commercial transactions at the central seat of Christianity seemed much more at home than services of religious devotion. Under John and his successors, the exploitation of Christendom was reduced by the curia to a fine art.[140]

The reconciliation of this Avignon exile was no simple matter, but involved another turbulent 40 years during which the office of pope was split in two and then three, each busily excommunicating the other. The resulting schism became as one historian described, "the greatest misfortune that could be thought of for the church. Western Christendom had never known such scandal, and nothing did so much as the schism to prepare the way for the defection from the papacy in the 16th century."[141]

Driven by the powerful Sigismund, Holy Roman Emperor, and the scholars of the University of Paris in their finest hour, a council was convened at Constance in 1414 to unseat the competing popes and resolve the schism. It was, some say, "the most important synod of the Middle Ages, and in fact one of the most important gatherings which has ever been convened in Western Europe, since it fairly represented the sentiments of Western Christendom more than any other council which has ever been held."[142]

This ecumenical council,[15] the Council of Constance, was attended by 37 cardinals, 47 archbishops, 140 bishops, 83 kings and their countless retainers. "It took four years to complete its work, but it was wildly successful. It united disparate forces, deposed the three popes and ended the schism which had been the source of untold havoc and scandal for 40 years. The council also exercised and proclaimed its status as the ultimate authority acting for the church in ascendancy above that of the pope. In a contradiction perhaps typical of an age seemingly devoid of logic, the council, fresh from trying and convicting a sitting pope (one of three, actually) for a multitude of mortal sins, including rape, sodomy, murder and incest; promptly tried the Bohemian reformer,

---

15 Prior to the Reformation, ecumenical signified 'plenary,' or whole, meaning a council potentially attended by all church officials.

Jon Hus, for heresy because, among other errors, he denied the infallibility of the pope.[143] The pope, John XXIII, for his sins, was defrocked. Jon Hus, for his dissent, was burned.

The council was the culmination of serious preparatory work by John Gershon and his colleagues at the University of Paris and had the potential to significantly alter the awful trajectory of the church in the early Middle Ages. Had the supremacy of council over pope prevailed, perhaps much of the abuse and debauchery of subsequent years might have been avoided. Unfortunately, in the event, the council and its reforms proved to be anomalous, an ingenious and necessary vehicle to momentarily pull the church back from the brink, but not capable of being sustained. The practices of Simony and wealth accumulation, though soundly condemned by the council, persisted thereafter pretty much unabated, as reported by Schaff:

> The healing of the schism was accomplished, but the abuses of the church went on, and under the last popes of the 15th century became more infamous than they had been at any time before. As for the theory of the supremacy of general council . . . it was proudly set aside by later popes in their practice and declared fallacious by the Fifth Lateran in 1516, and by the dogma of papal infallibility announced at the Council of the Vatican, 1870.[144]

How much of this actually affected the common man and how much did it detract from the power and influence of the church? Durant writes, that "throughout the 14th century, the church suffered political humiliation and moral decay, but the excesses and machinations occurred on a level quite beyond the awareness of the vast majority of the Christian populace."[145] The palace intrigues, playing out amid the splendor of riches and the squalor of depravity which characterized the papacy for several hundred years, were not enough to significantly lessen the power of the church. And yet, their relevance to the common man was manifest in his interaction with the parish priest, insofar as the priest reflected the depravity and corruption of his leaders. Historians of the period wrote of "the immorality and negligence widespread among the clergy, the decline of discipline among the friars and their rude manners as a permanent feature of the times."[146]

St. Bernadino of Siena, writing in 1420, decried the clergy's evil influence on the laity:

> Very many folk, considering the wicked life of monks and friars, nuns and secular clergy, are shaken by this; nay, oftentimes they fail in faith, and believe in nothing higher than the roofs of houses, not esteeming these things to be true that have been written concerning their faith, but believing them to have been written by the cozening invention of men, and not by the Lord's inspiration . . . they despise the

sacraments . . . and hold that the soul has no existence; neither do they . . . fear hell nor desire heaven, but cling with all their hearts to transitory things, and resolve that this world shall be their paradise.[147]

Meanwhile, nature showed her teeth early in the 14th century when the Baltic Sea froze over twice in 1303 and 1306-7 signaling the commencement of what came to be known as the "Little Ice Age." Unseasonable cold, incessant rain and shorter growing seasons spelled starvation and deprivation for much of the northern European population, which had only just established a delicate balance between nature and agriculture. The cold was to persist and worsen for 400 years.

In 1337 Edward of England and Phillip of France commenced hostilities that would grow into a war of unprecedented extent, devastating the population and property of the two countries for years to come. Fought principally over the prime property in the northwest corner of present-day France, the war would outlast the two kings and their posterity unto the fifth generation. The Hundred Years War, as it was known, featured the initial use of gunpowder, though to little effect, but also the emergence of the English longbow as the dominant military weapon. Lucrative plunder and ransom were the principal elements prolonging the war, but also armies and weapons of the period were simply insufficient to achieve decisive victory. "Medieval wars between Europeans were not aimed at strategic conquest but rather at seizure of dynastic rule at the top by inflicting enough damage to bring about the downfall of the opponent."[148] And so the war continued until the middle of the 15th century.

Into the relative chaos of the late Medieval period in Europe, like a thunderbolt from the blue "came the most lethal catastrophe in recorded history."[149] The black or bubonic plague is thought to have emerged from Asia, shipped in inadvertently along oceanic trade routes. Once having established its foothold in Europe in 1348, it wasted little time in infecting the entire continent, spreading a death toll from India to Iceland estimated at one third of the total population. By 1350 it had done its work and moved on, though return bouts continued to decimate the population periodically over the next 100 years.

To the suffering populace, the pestilence was particularly horrific because it seemed to materialize out of thin air and there was no escape for either peasant or king. Flight was the chief recourse, but "of the real carriers, rats and fleas, the 14th century had no suspicion."[150] The total impact of this catastrophe can hardly be imagined. Aside from the death toll, which was estimated at 20-25 million, an enormous psychological burden settled upon the survivors.[16] People said and believed, "This is the end of the world."

---

16 Some contemporary writers viewed the black death as fulfillment of the Book of Revelations prophecy where a pale horse symbolizing pestilence and is given power over ¼ part of the earth to kill (Rev. 6:7-8) and the number of 20 million may have been their guess of ¼ the population of the earth rather than a serious attempt at estimating the actual mortality.

Summarizing the age, Tuchman wrote...

> Mankind was not improved by the message of the times. Consciousness of wickedness made behavior worse. Violence threw off restraints. It was a time of default. Rules crumbled, institutions failed in their functions. Knighthood did not protect; the church, more worldly than spiritual, did not guide the way to God; the towns, once agents of progress and the commonweal, were absorbed in mutual hostilities and divided by class war; the population, depleted by the Black death, did not recover. The war with England and France (100 years war) and the brigandage it spawned revealed the emptiness of chivalry's military pretensions and the falsity of its moral ones. The schism shook the foundations of the central institution, spreading deep and pervasive uneasiness. People felt subject to events beyond their control, swept like flotsam at sea, hither and yon in a universe without reason or purpose. They lived through a period which suffered and struggled without visible advance. They longed for a remedy, for stability and order that never came.[151]

There has hardly ever been a time in recorded history more draining to the human spirit or less conducive to the advance of civilization than this awful interlude of two centuries just preceding the Renaissance and the Reformation. It was as if European society, like the addict, had to hit rock bottom before recovery could be initiated. It is with this backdrop of human despair that we consider how the Vaudois as a religious movement and a social community perpetuated itself.

2. CONSOLIDATION, EXPANSION AND REGROUPING OF THE VAUDOIS.

Consolidation. Recall that in the early 13th century the Vaudois were not much more than a loosely defined conglomerate of dissident refugee groups drawn together by common cause and thrust together in adversity. As an initial step in consolidation, a conference of representatives gathered at Bergamo, Italy to try to better define who they were and to resolve differences among them. This conference is the first indication of the existence of a consolidated, coherent religious group hereafter known as the Vaudois or the Waldenses. Two factions with somewhat differing viewpoints were represented at the conference. The record indicates that they reached agreement on a large number of issues, but did not achieve total unanimity. The disagreements that survived seem pretty minor, the most weighty having to do with their relationship with the mother church, and the validity of the Eucharist when performed by an unworthy priest. The Lyonists (French side of the Alps) still sought reconciliation with the Catholic Church and were willing to accept sacrament performed by unworthy priests.

The Lombardists (Italian side of the Alps) had irrevocably broken with the church. They rejected the sacraments and offices of a sinful priest. Conference results were communicated to what may have been a third party, a group of German-speaking coreligionists, brethren and friends residing beyond the Alps.[152] In this communication the Lyonists are generally referred to as the Waldenses or the Vaudois. Indications are that the Vaudois movement first took form at this time, as defined in their own minds, consisting of the bulk of the dissidents located in Piedmont (Northern Italy), Provence (southern France), with some extension into the district of Passau which formed part of the duchy of Austria (Bavaria).

The difference of opinion among the Vaudois factions persisted beyond the Bergamo Conference – but it did not lead to a schism in any sense. There was too much in doctrine and practice, principally in the rejected trappings of Catholicism that united them. The factions continued their loose confederation, exchanging ministers and ideas relating to practice and doctrine. The differences and their lack of consequence is further evidence of the ambiguity inherent in Vaudois theology – and "helps to explain some of the startling differences in emphasis between reports of the later Vaudois preaching originating from different parts of Europe."[153]

Remarkably, though all of the Vaudois rejected the Catholic Church as a failed religion since the time of Constantine, in a very fine distinction, none of the Vaudois factions were shy about accepting and participating in Catholic sacraments. "It was the authority of the persecuting church, not its moral standing or its sacramental services, which the heretics denied."[154] This ambivalence puzzles historians, but in fact it is a characteristic of a people who were simply trying their best to live Christ-like lives and did not take themselves too seriously. They knew they needed baptism and were willing to accept the ordinance at the hands of any "authorized" officer, provided he was worthy of his calling.

Expansion. For information of the whereabouts and extent of the Vaudois during this bridge period, we are almost wholly dependent on the records of the Inquisition, or from reports written by Inquisitors of their experiences.

Originally, the preaching of the word was essential to the Vaudois and proselytizing among their Christian neighbors was an early and persistent practice. The inquisitor Bernhard Gui wrote of them:

> Although they were ignorant and unlearned, these people, both men and women, went from village to village, going into people's homes and preaching in public squares and even in churches, the men in particular, leaving behind them a host of misunderstanding and mistakes. . . .God had ordered the apostles to preach the Holy Scriptures to all, they argued, taking upon themselves what had been said to the apostles, even having the audacity to declare themselves their imitators and successors on the grounds of their

poverty and disguised by a mask of saintliness. They did indeed despise prelates and the clergy, claiming that they possessed abundant wealth and lived a life of privilege.[155]

For the better part of a century, from 1150-1250 AD, the Vaudois performed extensive missionary labors, largely unhampered by opposition. Though most of the Vaudois were likely illiterate, they developed a culture of preaching and learning, and of drawing others into their faith. Of this Passau Anonymous wrote:[17]

> [Vaudois] men and women, great and lesser, day and night, do not cease to learn and teach; the workman who labors all day, teaches and learns at night. They teach and learn without books. They even teach in the houses of lepers. When someone has been a student for as little as seven days, he seeks someone else to teach, as one curtain draws another.[156]

These missionary efforts resulted in an initial expansion into the south of France and the north of Italy followed by a significant incursion into Austria and Germany. Monastier reports of Vaudois missionaries in Germany and Italy

---

17 Passau Anonymous was a Dominican Inquisitor of the 14th Century operating in German-speaking areas. His writings were published in Patschovski and Selge, *Quellen zur Geschichte der Waldenser*, Texten zur Kirchen- und Theologiegeschichte, Guetersloh, 1973.

as early as 1100 and in all parts of Europe by 1225,[157] and refers to the fruits of their labors as represented by a series of Vaudois communities established in a continuous line from Milan to Cologne. Blair describes numerous Vaudois communities along the Rhine, with Germany and especially Alsace being full of Vaudois.[158]

In the same period, Perrin has Vaudois fleeing French persecution over the Pyrenees and into Spain.[159] Cameron further describes substantial communities of the Vaudois in Languedoc early in the 13th century having emigrated there from Burgundy.[160]

Evidently lay members of the movement were engaged in preaching in the regions where they lived, whereas, those especially designated as their preachers traveled two-by-two to perform their missionary labors, expanding the movement into additional areas. Lambert reports. . .

> The mission into Germany set off from the borderlands . . . the first testimonies (of Inquisitors) date from 1231 -1233 as a result of severe persecution in the Rhineland and in Trier. There were also Waldenses tried in Bavaria towards the middle of the century. The worst persecutions were in Austria between 1259 and 1266 [which refer to] Waldenses being present in at least 40 parishes. Their settlement in Austria was to prove solid and lasting, at least until the end of the 14th century. From this stronghold, the expansion eastward was to continue after 1260.

Communities . . . were to reach and settle as far as Thuringa, Bohemia, Moravia, Silesia, Brandenburg, Pomerania and Poland. In the early 14th century, Waldensians were prosecuted in cities such as Prague, Vienna, Breslau, and Stettin. In 1315 an inquisitor declared, 'There may be more than 80,000 heretics in Austria, but in Bohemia and Moravia, their number is infinite.' The movement's prodigious spread eastwards clearly represented a major event in the history of the Poor of Lyons in the 13th century.[161]

Cameron states that:

The religious credibility of the Austrian Waldenses rested on their claim to a superior knowledge of the scriptures and superior moral conduct. Contemporary sources claimed that many knew the entire New Testament by heart, and that it was rare to find among them a person of either sex who cannot recite the text of the New Testament by heart in the vernacular. Even hostile sources showed no hesitation in reporting that the Austrian Waldenses were temperate, modest and well-behaved, commenting that it was the very appearance of piety on the part of the Leonists that made them so dangerous: apart from their anti-clericalism, they set a good example before the world – their behavior, restrained, virtuous and religious."[162]

Audisio characterizes a wide distribution of the Vaudois by the beginning of the 14th century "in little more than a century, the Poor of Lyons had reached as far as the limits of Europe and could henceforth be referred to as a diaspora."[163]

The incursion of the Vaudois into Bohemia was especially robust and productive. Wylie writes...

> Reynerius, speaking of the middle of the 13th century says, 'there is hardly a country in which this sect is not to be found.' The Waldensian refugees spread themselves in small colonies over all of the Slavonic countries, Poland included; they made their headquarters at Prague. They were zealous evangelizers, not daring to preach in public, but teaching in private houses, keeping alive the truth during the two centuries which were yet to run before Huss should appear. [164]

The Alpine valleys of Piedmont persisted as a stronghold and center of the Vaudois community throughout this period because they stood at a crossroads between nations and because it was an area which no one else wanted or was interested in. The piety, cohesion and unity of the Vaudois caused them to multiply rapidly, soon outstripping the limited abundance of their confined Piedmont valleys. The steep wooded valleys did not yield easily to the husbandman.

Eking out a living there was hard-scrabble work, not to everyone's taste, and with time the population outstripped the resources. Migration offered a solution, especially to destinations already populated by coreligionists or those who were already estranged from the Catholic Church.

The Vaudois of Lombardy and Piedmont pushed east through lower Austria into Bohemia and further north to the shores of the Baltic in Poland, Pomerania and Brandenburg. "From its base in Germany in the 13th century, Waldensianism achieved a remarkable expansion, traveling with the waves of German colonization into Bohemia[18] and lands further east. Waldensianism, transmitted from Germany and Austria, prospered in Bohemia and further east. [Adherents] were German speakers. The one frontier that was not crossed was the linguistic one; Czech speakers apparently remained orthodox. The burgeoning Bohemian Waldensianism was the fruit of colonization, mission and flight from persecution by German speakers flowing over the frontier from Austria into southern Bohemia."[165]

Vaudois were known to be in Bohemia as early as 1150. Cameron described the reach into German-speaking lands.

> By the middle of the 13th century, the German-speaking Waldensian heretics had gained enormous, even intimidating strength in the

---

18 The kingdom of Bohemia, centered in Prague, reached its zenith under the Luxemburg dynasty in the 14th century when it extended well beyond the modern day Czech Republic and Slovakia to include Silesia, Brandenburg, Pomerania and much of Austria.

Danube valley in the southeast corner of the Holy Roman Empire. Between the late 13th and the early 14th Centuries, they spread northwards into German communities, in the towns of Bohemia and Moravia, and even further north to the Baltic coast. Then in the middle of the 14th century, the movement began to decline. Several times within some thirty or forty years, it suffered catastrophic defections by some of the most educated and articulate leaders. It entered the 15th century irreversibly weakened and shrunken, yet did not disappear entirely. Rather its tattered remnants seemed to have merged with elements of the Bohemian heresy; ultimately the name of 'Waldensian Brethren', though little else besides the name, would be transferred to Czech dissenters who survived into the 16th century. [166]

The heart of the Vaudois system of belief and practice was strikingly similar to that adopted by Jon Hus in Prague 250 years later. Hus was a Catholic cleric influenced by the writings of Wycliffe, and historical research has found no direct connection with the Vaudois.[167] The Vaudois of Bohemia were eventually subsumed into the *Unitas Fratum* which has survived into modern times as the Moravian Brethren. Palacky offers the opinion that "the Hussite brothers were both students and teachers of their Waldensian brothers – but more the latter than the former."[168] It is interesting that when the *Unitas Fratum* was first organized in 1457, they turned to Vaudois officials to ordain their leaders.

The twin forces of persecution and poverty also elicited a resurgence of Vaudois back to the fertile lands of France along the river Durance in Provence, lands they had fled centuries before.

> The colony [in the Piedmont valleys] visibly prospered . . . the Waldenses were said to have multiplied furiously. Their increase beyond the power of the land to sustain them caused new swarms to leave the Alpine beehive. Some bands once more crossed to the [French] frontier to colonize on the banks of the Durance [where] their activity was soon crowned with unparalleled prosperity. [169]

A group numbering in the thousands of the Poor of Lyon settled in about 30 different locations in the valley of the Luberon, making this region, stretching 30 miles along a ridge of rugged hills east of Avignon, becoming one of the strongholds of Vaudois settlement in Western Europe.

There was a series of migrations of the Vaudois from Northern Italy to Calabria in the toe of Italy's boot. The first was in the period 1285-1309 when the king of Naples recruited textile workers from Piedmont into his kingdom.[170] Anxious to relieve the crowded conditions in the valleys, and hopeful of a better life, many of the Vaudois responded and resettled to Calabria. About a century later, another

Piedmont-to-Calabria migration occurred, this time driven principally by overcrowding in the valleys.[171] Yet another such migration was written of one century after that.[172]

As we have seen, the sheer power of the Inquisition had swept France clean of its intractable dissidents, crushing and compressing surviving remnants into the Alpine passes, but it was much like squeezing a balloon, for the irrepressible dissident movement spilled out the other side with resurgent energy into the reaches of central Europe. Within a mere two hundred years, Vaudois or Vaudois-like dissidents were found in very large numbers throughout Italy, Austria, Hungary, Germany and Bohemia and along the Baltic coast and some even sifting back into southern France.

How did the movement spread so widely, so rapidly? Considering that it was a lay movement without significant intellectual underpinnings, with no apparent central authority, no financial backing, no support from powerful monarchs, none but the most primitive means of communication, how were these simple, unlearned missionaries able to spread their doctrines and establish their church throughout most of Europe in one century? Perhaps the answer is: they weren't and they didn't. A more likely scenario is that the reported appearances of the Vaudois in such places as Bulgaria, Croatia, Dalmatia, Hungary, Germany, Bohemia, Alsace, Rhineland, etc. and their enormous numbers by 1530 (by one account, up to 800,000[173])[19] are largely a case of mistaken identity.

---

19 Down from the 14th century estimate of 4,000,000.

We only form some picture of the extent of the Vaudois through the records of their assailants, the inquisitors. The inquisitors, on the other hand, could only guess the identity of the Vaudois based on what they were able to learn of the beliefs and practices of those they interrogated. The Poor of Lyons, as Audisio characterizes them, never did use the term Vaudois or Waldenses to identify themselves until long after the Inquisition had pinned it on them. The Vaudois in the south of France simply "called themselves the 'Brethren.' Most interestingly, it was the outsiders, the gentiles, that is, the clergy, who called them the 'Poor of Lyon' and the 'Waldenses.' Cameron calls "*the Poor of Lyon* an ecclesiastical title: it would mean nothing either to those Waldenses [in France] or to others called by the same name."[174]

One can hardly acknowledge the inconsistency and sloppiness of the Inquisition in identifying heretics on the one hand while on the other hand trusting their records to determine the scope of the Vaudois movement. As a result, the actual extent of the Vaudois during the bridge period, 1250-1550, cannot be known. Yet ample evidence has been cited as to the whereabouts of those who were either Vaudois or indistinguishable from the Vaudois, and of the enormous hold these dissident beliefs had on the people.

Much of the business of the Medieval Inquisition was messy and imprecise. Inquisitors were often overwhelmed by the sheer number and the rich variety of heretical groups. Audisio writes, "it comes as quite a surprise to realize how many heretical movements there were, scattered throughout the whole of Europe, and to what extent non-conformist religious groups had multiplied. . . .the inquisitors' manuals providing lists of heresies and their leading characteristics intended to be exhaustive." One Dominican manual from 1376 and revised in 1578,

> listed 96 categories of heresy from the best known to the most obscure. Bernhard of Luxemburg, another Dominican friar, in his *Catologus haereticurum* issued in 1522, manages to distinguish between 432 categories of present or former heresy, to which he conscientiously adds 26 unclassified heresies . . . the courts of faith found themselves faced with a tangled web of heterodoxy. The inquisitors sought to disentangle the mesh by linking a particular error to a duly identified heresy, but in so doing, they only created further complications for themselves.[175]

A certain arrogance on the part of the inquisitors, or maybe it was just a matter of practicality, made it easy to lump the multitude of heretics under a few pejorative names. Oddly, Manichean was a favorite, after the 3rd century mystic, Mani, who synthesized the teachings of various religions into a dualistic theology having little similarity with any form of Christianity. Pursuers of heretics loved to dub their foes as Manichean, suggesting that they were a total loss, completely devoid of any Christian doctrine or principles. The name Cathari (the pure) or interchangeably Albigensian (from the French city of Albi) was commonly employed, probably because the actual Cathari were the largest single heretical group of the 13th century, and because they were partial toward the dualism of the Manichean.

But Vaudois or Waldenses was the most useful appellation, gaining early prominence and eventually prevailing over all others for several reasons. First, Vaudois practices and beliefs were representative of if not indistinguishable from those of most other dissident groups of the period. The three fundamental pillars of the Vaudois, namely: poverty, preaching and the scriptures were also the basic elements of virtually every other dissident movement growing out of the vita apostolica of the 11th through 13th centuries. Second, the Vaudois were not intellectually based, but rather emerged from the innate longing of the simple folk. As such they were easy to reject, to ridicule, to confound and to marginalize, or so it seemed to the learned whose writings of the period have come down to us.

A further reason the name of Vaudois became the heretical designation of choice was that the Inquisitors found solace in pinning their troubles on one child of the devil. The enormous ground swell of dissent resulting in the spontaneous emergence of hundreds of heretical groups was unthinkable to the devout Catholic inquisitor. He was much more comfortable if he could identify a single instigator, a poison apple, a skilled tempter, a charlatan who had led the masses astray. Such an one they found in Peter Waldo - hence the universality of the designation.

Gell argues that "instead of Waldo giving his name to the Vaudois or Waldenses, the reverse must have been the fact, the name of Waldo was given by the Inquisitors to Peter of Lyons, because of his connection with the Vaudois; and that subsequent inquisitors spoke of him as the head, intending to reduce the importance of their real and much earlier antiquity."[176]

So common was the use of the term Vaudois among the Inquisitorial community to represent all heretics that when the church's obsession with witchcraft reached its apogee in the 16th century, the name Vaudois morphed into vauderie (voodoo) to embrace both heretic and sorcerer.[177]

Regrouping. The expansion of the Vaudois and Vaudois-like dissidents through missionary work and other means, though hard to unequivocally identify, was impressive by any measure, but it proved to be relatively short-lived. Following the destruction of the Cathari in about 1250, the attention of the Inquisition turned with full force to the Vaudois[178] and other dissident movements of their ilk, and their attention was so intense as to eventually drive the Vaudois totally underground in the areas of France, Italy, Germany and Austria where they had flourished. Audisio writes of the great adjustment this imposed on the Vaudois, forcing them to abandon one of their basic pillars, to totally cease performing missionary work. Henceforward the movement was turned inward:

> The initial goal of converting others to evangelical poverty could henceforth be maintained only in an indirect, moderate way, since fear of being

> denounced compelled them to be silent. Public gatherings in churches and in public squares came to an end. A new era began, characterized by hasty meetings at dusk, limited circles of friends gathering by night around the hearth, veiled illusions, covert glances and signs known only to themselves.[179]

Over time this turning inward spawned significant consequences for the Vaudois, which from this turning point can no longer be labeled a movement, but rather a religious community. As will be seen, it would be wrong to assume that the Vaudois had thus lost their vitality, but it meant that future growth and expansion would be through propagation and inadvertent conversion. They had entered a 'hunkering down" period, one which, oddly, unified them and made them stronger:

> The fear of being hunted down, the feeling of belonging to the elect and the need to hide inevitably inspired a sense of tenacious solidarity and a satisfying conviction that they belonged to the same family whose members, in the face of adversity and general misunderstanding, had to rally together and provide one another with unfailing mutual support.[180]

The powerful forces hemming in the Vaudois thus contributed to the strength and cohesion of the community. The

Vaudois had entered another phase in which the typical adherent family was not a family of recent converts, but one of 2nd or 3rd generation members, those who grew up in the faith.

> All of the accused of Waldensian heresy interrogated in the second half of the 14th century and the 15th century and questioned as to the origins of their faith, came from families who were already members of the dissent. It was clear that the happy days of open preaching and converting were a thing of the past; henceforth the torch was passed within the family.[181]

Audisio also cites Inquisitorial accounts showing that in this period, 1250-1350, the Vaudois gradually shifted from the urban setting of their missionary era to a rural setting more suited to their underground nature. Proselytizing had flourished in the urban setting and many of the urban elite had joined the movement. Yet a rural setting proved more amenable to their clandestine community and "the poor of Lyon fled the towns."

> The reasons for their mission's success in the town were the same reasons for which they fled. The town had assured them crowds of eager listeners, but later multiplied the risks they ran. Urban areas were particularly efficient church networks. The first converts were townspeople, by necessity, their successors turned to the rural

world; later generations became country folk themselves. By turning away from the urban world, the Poor of Lyon lost contact with the most dynamic sector of society.[182]

However this may be, forcing the Vaudois movement underground, effectively shutting down their overt missionary efforts, did not succeed in eliminating their expansion. In spite of intense persecution, the period from the middle of the 13th century until the Reformation, saw the Vaudois, or those indistinguishable from the Vaudois, expand into southern Italy, northern Germany, Poland, and Bohemia. This expansion depended principally upon forces other than proselytizing and conversion.

The east-west interaction during this period largely involved the peaceful expansion of Germanic peoples into the eastern kingdoms. The drive to the east, *Drang nach Osten*, was "basically the result of population pressures in the German Empire combined with the presence of personal and economic opportunity outside the German-speaking world. During the 12th century, [as the medieval warming period wound down], an agricultural revolution had provided the basis for an unprecedented population boom. A combination of crop rotation, metal plowshares, use of horses instead of oxen, made agricultural productivity more intensive and extensive, and the consequential growth in population in Germany providing the human material for colonies or settlements in the less densely populated east."[183] From 1200-1350 there was a wave of German emigration to the kingdoms of Poland, Bohemia and Hungary.

3. THE ORGANIZATION OF THE VAUDOIS IN MEDIEVAL TIMES.

The egalitarian nature of the early Vaudois movement suggested and accommodated a loosely-structured, non-hierarchical church organization. Early on, the attraction of their message among the masses was especially powerful because the preachers were simple men and women like themselves, the more effective because they preached first from example. [184] This was in contrast to the Catholic clergy whose lives often didn't conform to the scriptures. "In the beginning, brothers, preachers, Poor of Christ, were all the same; synonymous terms all denoting members of the dissenting community."[185]

Robinson writes. . . "It is not clear that the ancient Waldenses had any clergy. It is certain that they practiced no coercion, and their opponents affirm that they thought none ought to be exercised. They held priesthood an abhorrence. They allowed women to teach, and laughed at the distinction between clergy and laity."[186] Such an organization, or better said the lack thereof, devoid of hierarchy, lent itself well to the early vigor and growth of the movement, but it was not well suited to provide for its longevity, its survival.

In the inquisitorial records there are occasional references to multiple officers among the Vaudois, including those of bishop, priest and deacon, though evidently not with the same functions as in the Catholic sense. There was even an occasional reference to a "sovereign pontiff or master." Whether such a structure was widespread among the Vaudois, whether they adopted it to mimic the Catholic Church or in simple compliance with their interpretation of scripture is not known. Certainly the three-tiered hierarchy of bishop, presbyter and deacon that prevailed in the primitive church was a compelling scripture-based model. On the other hand, during this bridge period, as the Vaudois strove to keep themselves from notice, they adopted practices and mores virtually indistinguishable from those of the Catholics. Many of the faithful, as a means of avoiding detection, even went so far as to attend mass and participate in confession even while maintaining their dissident religion.

Audisio observes that after 1450 the Inquisitorial records made no mention of bishops, priests or deacons among the Vaudois. "During the 15th century previous structures either fell from use or were simplified, and both in the eastern and western branches the Poor of Lyon returned to a binary organization. There were Masters or Brothers on the one side and the faithful or believers on the other."[187] There is so little evidence of the multiple church officials at all as to make one wonder if they were a myth manufactured by the Inquisitors.

As early as 1350 AD, the records speak of a dual hierarchical division among the membership, referring to lay members as believers and those who exercised leadership as lords, masters, confessors or *perfecti* (a term borrowed from the Cathari). The term *barbi* or uncles became a prominent designation of this preacher class in the western reaches of the community, but the functions of these *barbi* were the same as those of the Brothers elsewhere in the Vaudois diaspora. The term *barbi* emerged among the Vaudois sometime before the 15th century and

> is of Romance origin and is defined as a respectful title given to an elder in the community or to an uncle in the Piedmont Alps and in the county of Nice. In fact, even now (1989), uncle in the Piedmont dialect is *barba*. In 1530 Pierre Groit referred to the preacher with whom he traveled as "Uncle Georges." By night as the preachers arrived at a hamlet . . . a messenger went out to inform others that an uncle had arrived. The word was not unfamiliar to the culture and environment of the time; it was just transposed into the religious field. In this way the messenger could announce the uncle's arrival without unnecessarily arousing people's suspicions.[188]

This adjustment to a binary organization and breaking with the original notion of the strict overall equality of the faithful, occurred sometime in the 13th century and persisted throughout the bridge period until at least 1550. In those 300 years it became an identifying trait of the Vaudois. Under this regimen, "one part of the movement, indeed the greater one, became [ecclesiastically] sedentary, giving up itinerancy, poverty and preaching. This did not mean that the community as a whole turned its back on what had once been the keystone of its identity. A transfer occurred from the members as a whole to certain individuals within their ranks. This meant that a chosen few would maintain the original tenets, [i.e. the life of a mendicant preacher] while others by force renounced them. They [the chosen] would function as a nostalgic reminder of the movement's halcyon days. They would be the groups living memory, the outward proof that their faith had lived on. Symbolically they would represent the ideal life to which the followers aspired, however impossible it might be to attain."[189]

One wonders if anyone among the earliest Vaudois ever really thought that any kind of society, religious or otherwise, founded on poverty and dependent on alms, had any kind of sustainability. Might they not rather have known from the outset that in time, very quickly in fact, some accommodation to reality would have to be made? And given that, it seems very consistent with their basic principles and their commitment to simplicity, that they selected, or more likely settled into, an organizational scheme of the simplest nature, the very "hydrogen" of the organizational elements.

These *barbi* were not considered to be ordained priests in the Catholic sense, but individuals somehow separated from the general community of members and having authority to receive confessions and travel among the Vaudois in clandestine fashion preaching and encouraging the faithful. That they were acknowledged and highly respected by the faithful members is apparent, but what set them apart, if not ordination, is less clear. In some cases, they may have taken vows of poverty, chastity and obedience, and as reported by one of their number, Pierre Groit testifying to the Inquisition in 1532. . .

> None of us gets married. Our food and clothing are provided by alms of the people we preach to. We ministers hold all our worldly goods in common and receive them from the people's alms alone; they are more than enough for our needs.[190]

Alms were sometimes given in exchange for hearing a confession. "From the living and often from those on their death-beds we received abundant gifts of money. In this way the community supported a pastoral body so that it might serve it exclusively. It represented a concrete, financial expression of gratitude that reveals how useful the believers thought their preachers to be."[191] Celibacy seems to have been a late addition to the discipline of the *barbi*. There is ample evidence that married *barbi* were the norm prior to the 16th century.

The *barbi* were esteemed by the faithful as living apostolic lives, whose foremost duty was preaching, generally going about two-by-two. Such a task required the ability to read and write, which in 14-15th century Europe was had only by about 20% of the urban population, even less in rural areas where the Vaudois resided.

> [Their literacy] gives a clearer idea of the brothers' exceptional status. During their training

they learned to read and write. As a result of
their studies, they knew by heart whole chapters
of the New Testament, particularly the gospels
of Matthew and John and certain apostolic
epistles. The Brothers relied not only on their
memories but carried small books with them
from which they could read out passages to their
listeners. The reading was followed by a sermon,
both in the language spoken in the country, a
Romance tongue in the west and German in the
east. From the earliest days, preaching in the vernacular was a characteristic feature of the Poor
of Lyon.[192]

The *barbi* were sometimes referred to as "men of books," reflecting the scarcity of encounters the general populace had with literate people. Inquisitorial records speak of very small books, 6.7 x 9.8 cm. [roughly 2 ½ x 4 inches] containing portions of the New Testament or Vaudois texts such as the Liber Electorum. "The tiny size of such Vaudois books made it easier for the *barbi* to carry them and to hide them when in danger of discovery."[193] Surviving Vaudois books of the description from the 16th century exist in the libraries of Europe. The specific nature of the books employed by the *barbi*, their heretical content, their characteristic smallness, suggests the existence of scriptoria in the Vaudois communities where the texts were clandestinely copied.[194]

It seems also that the Vaudois texts were written both in Latin and in the vernacular – and some were especially designed to facilitate memorization. Writes Biller, "there are accounts of prodigious feats of memory, of a very long text: much of the New Testament. But in everyday life, with texts which were not scripture and in a mission which placed so much emphasis on memorization, there was a need to help more ordinary levels of memorization. One method was brevity. Another was the use of verse."[195] It should be noted that the two most prominent texts of the medieval Vaudois, the Noble Lesson and the Liber Electorum, both were written in abbreviated form and verse, evidently for the purpose of facilitating memorization.

We learn of the training associated with the selection and preparation of the *barbi* from a letter of two *barbi* from 1530.

> Candidates volunteered by addressing themselves to the college of *barbi* during a meeting. Those with good reputation were selected and enrolled for training which took place during the winter months only, over a three- or four-year period. They there learned to read, write and recite by heart books of the New Testament. When the winter training was over their practical apprenticeship began. An older *barba* took a younger one with him on his pastoral rounds to train him as a preacher. In this way formal training in winter alternated with practical training in summer. [196]

In contrast to the Roman Catholic clergy, the college of the *barbi* was highly traditional in its emphasis on learning by rote, an apprenticeship based wholly on the scriptures, not on commentaries, perfectly adapted to the aims and needs of the Vaudois community.

The *barbi* were governed by an annual synod where they came together to deliver tithes and alms, to report and to receive instruction. These synods were loosely organized and conducted by senior *barba*, as opposed to established and permanent leaders. Throughout the bridge period, the *barbi* were the enduring structure that somehow held together the disparate and scattered elements of the Vaudois community.

There may have been various types of church organization adopted at different times among the branches of the Vaudois over the centuries, perhaps including some with multiple offices. It is clear that there was no overall, official pontiff to whom the entire Vaudois community looked for leadership. In this, as in other matters, the Vaudois were not as particular as we might suppose. It didn't much matter to them who made the decisions. Theirs was a simple faith and correspondingly a simple organization. Remarkably over three centuries bridging from the origin of the Vaudois to their encounter with the Reformation, there have come down to us no names of indispensable leaders guiding the community, few founding fathers, no nurturing mothers – only the persistent survival of the community. The Vaudois organizational thread that runs all through the centuries from origin to Reformation is a membership bound closely to its *barbi*, its anonymous uncles, a two-tier structure with *barbi* or brothers drawn from the ranks of the faithful, not elevated to a plane above them, but standing on their level and supported by their alms – a priesthood, if we may call it that, on different, but not higher ground.

Lambert describes their impact as follows:

> [Their congregations] were held together by the simplest means, yet they had the resilience and outlasted heavy persecution. What held these Waldenses together was the mobile preacher, coming in secrecy and by night, known only by Christian name, to exhort, instruct, and above all to hear confessions. They came on average once a year, alone or with a pupil, to visit their believers who led them from place to place secretly and cared for them with food, money and necessities. Waldensianism lived in the family, and the wandering preachers were their essential lifeline. It was not the office, nor even the chapters, which counted in the last resort. It was the tenacity and mobility of preachers visiting their flocks, the *barbi* of the Alpine valleys, the Meister in Germany. They kept Waldensianism alive till the Reformation."[197]

4. PERSECUTION.

The Inquisition. Recall that Popes Innocent II and Gregory VI formed the medieval Inquisition in the 13th century in the south of France in response to the threat to the church posed by the heretical groups of the Cathari and the Vaudois. Having dispatched the bulk of the dissident movements growing out of the vita apostolica, the Inquisition morphed into a more permanent institution with the goal of eradicating all dissent everywhere within Catholic realms. As the Inquisition matured beyond its origin in the south of France, it expanded throughout Western Europe wherever heretics could be found. "By 1250 the Inquisition had penetrated throughout the greater part of Europe. The relentless energy of this dread organization, the secrecy of its proceedings, the ubiquitous character of its agents, the irresistible power they wielded spread terror throughout Christianity."[198] Thus, sadly, the relationship between the Roman Church and its heretical offshoots during the bridge period came largely to be defined by the Inquisition.

The workings of the Inquisition were relatively consistent over the years as techniques were first experimented with, then fine-tuned and finally institutionalized. Though the Inquisition was enormously powerful, it was not so much a well-oiled juggernaut as it was an insensitive and brutish beast, inexorably destroying whichever suspects fell within its lethal gaze. Kieckenhefer reminds us that in the Middle Ages, "extermination of heretics remained very much a haphazard endeavor, highly liable to distraction and marked by a strong degree of ineptitude." [199] Lea describes the Modus Operandi of the Inquisition:

> A few days in advance of his visit to a city, the Inquisitor would send notice to the ecclesiasti-

cal authorities requiring them to summon the
people to assemble at a specified time. To the
populace thus brought together, he preached
on the faith, urging them to its defense. . .summoning everyone within a certain radius to
come forward within 6-12 days and reveal to
him whatever they may have known or heard of
anyone leading to the belief or suspicion that he
might be a heretic. Neglect to comply with this
command incurred *ipso facto* excommunication
. . . compliance with it was rewarded with an
indulgence of three years. At the same time he
proclaimed a time of grace varying from 15-30
days, during which any heretic coming forward
spontaneously, confessing his guilt, abjuring,
and giving full information about his fellow
sectaries was promised mercy.[200]

The Council of Narbonne 1244 laid down the rules of evidence supporting a conviction of heresy. The accused could be found guilty if he was shown "to have manifested any word or sign that he had faith or belief in any heretics, or considered them to be good men."[201] Some officials added "visiting heretics, giving them alms, guiding them on their journeys, and the like" as sufficient evidence for condemnation.[202]

A crowning infamy of the Inquisitorial process "was the withholding from the accused all knowledge of the names of the witnesses against him. From the withholding of names, it was but a step to withhold the evidence altogether, and that step was sometimes taken. In truth the whole process was so completely at the arbitrary discretion of the inquisitor, and the accused was so wholly without rights, that whatever seemed good in the eyes of the former was allowable in the interest of the faith."[203] Since neither the witnesses nor the evidence was made available to the accused, there seemed no need for him to mount a defense. Inquisitional rules at first provided that the accused have access to counsel, but that practice was generally ignored, especially when the inquisitor was authorized to bring charges of heresy against anyone assisting the accused. Keeping the judicial process simple, without the "embarrassment of the vain jangling of lawyers in the conduct of the persecution,"[204] was an essential element of the proceedings.

Torture as a tool of interrogation was routinely employed by the Inquisition and was officially sanctioned by Innocent IV's papal bull *ad extirpanda* in 1252. Stallcup observes that "...church law forbade the clergy from shedding blood, which limited the type of torture they could implement, but the Inquisition still had a sufficient number of excruciatingly painful techniques at their disposal, such as water torture and the rack."[205] Use of torture techniques was justified by the medieval church's belief that the sufferings of the physical body mattered little compared to the salvation of the immortal soul.

The founding popes of the Inquisition, Innocent III and Gregory IX, cannot be burdened with the invention of the death penalty for heresy. There is Old Testament support for stoning to death those who have "gone and served other gods." (Exodus 22:18) Greek and Roman law considered blasphemy or heresy against the gods the same as treason and prescribed capital punishment. Augustine had taught that "certain wars that must be waged against the violence of those resisting are commanded by God, or by a legitimate ruler and undertaken by the good. We should be more afraid of the butchery of their minds by the sword of spiritual evil than their bodies by a sword of steel."[206] Similarly, Pope Innocent III reasoned that severe punishment should be administered against "traitors to the faith of Jesus Christ; for it is an infinitely greater sin to offend the divine majesty than to attack the majesty of the sovereign."[207]

Wakefield describes the medieval mindset:

> Heresy could not be a casual matter when religion was so vital an element in life. It had to be regarded as the most grievous sin and crime into which man could fall, for by denying the magistracy of the church which Christ had established, over which his vicar in Rome presided, the heretic became a traitor to God himself. Moreover, he imperiled others by his words and example; medieval writers were fond of likening heresy to a loathsome and contagious disease.[208]

To secure the support of the secular authorities, a *code of cooperation* was established in a series of agreements between the pope and the Holy Roman Empire between 1220 and 1239. Cardew reports...

> The principal provisions of this code were that any person suspected of heresy must purge himself at the command of the church. If he failed to satisfy the church he was deprived of all civil rights, and after such deprivation had lasted a year, he became liable to be treated as a heretic. All heretics were outlawed, their property forfeited, and their heirs disinherited. Their houses were to be destroyed and the site declared incapable of being again built upon. The heretic himself, after being condemned by the church, was to be handed over to the civil authority to be burnt. If through fear of death he recanted, he was to be imprisoned for life, and should he relapse, he was to be sent summarily to the stake. His children, to the second generation, were rendered incapable of holding any position of emolument or dignity, unless indeed they could obtain mercy by betraying their father or some other heretic. All fautors, favorers or defenders of heretics were liable themselves to be treated as heretics. All rulers and magistrates were to take an oath to exterminate all heretics within their dominions. If any temporal lord neglected to carry out this duty when called on by the church, he might be excommunicated,

and when excommunication had lasted a year, his subjects were released from their allegiance and any good Catholic might seize the country, always provided that the duty of exterminating heretics would rest on him.[209]

The medieval mind did not find it hard to justify the violent execution of a convicted heretic. Lea asserts that "The remorseless basis of St. Thomas of Aquinas rendered it self-evident that the secular power could not escape the duty of putting the heretic to death." [210] The burning of heretics was justified as necessary to eradicate all vestiges of the crime and the criminal so as to avoid any possible contamination of the faithful. Innocent III in *Vergentis in Senum* (1199) "charged those wandering away from the faith of the Lord with *lèse majesté* against the 'eternal majesty of God.' This innovative characterization of heresy as divine treason laid the foundation for more serious punishment through its allusion to the traditional penalties of secular treason"[211] Stallcup argues that "Burning at the stake was the preferred method of extermination because it allowed the church to avoid bloodshed, and because the dramatic and agonizing deaths served as a vivid deterrence to the general population."[212] Such a rationale even led to disinterment of heretic's remains to permit burning of the bones. Repugnant as these practices may seem to the modern mind, they are not altogether unlike those of ancient Israel as they entered the Promised Land. There the Lord commanded and Israel carried out the utter destruction of all peoples and their cities. (Joshua 6:21)

Cardew writes, "It would be a mistake to suppose that the ferocious [attack on] heresy outraged public opinion of the day. In the Middle Ages the mass of people were uneducated and readily accessible to the suggestions of their priests. Under his instruction, the word heretic had become a word of hateful connotation. A charge of heresy at once enlisted popular prejudice against the accused. The heretic was represented as a man in league with Satan to destroy good Catholic souls. No pity was felt at his punishment and no remorse for his fate."[213]

Catholic apologists assert that in the medieval period, unity of faith was essential to Western European civilization, and that therefore the heretic threatened the very foundation of society. Heresy was regarded as worse than any other crime, even that of high treason, and a crime which secular rulers were bound in duty to punish. They further claim that the methods employed were characteristic of the times and in fact less barbaric than their secular counterparts. As to the punishments inflicted by the church, these were restricted to those affecting spiritual life and involved various acts of penance, and in the extreme case excommunication. Confiscation of property, imprisonment and execution were all consequences inflicted by secular authority, but also in keeping with the times. In fact the argument has been made that the Inquisition was in part instituted to temper and attenuate overzealous secular authorities of the period who recklessly sought the indiscriminate destruction of all heretics. In short, Catholic apologists claim that historical evidence will "bear out the assertion that the Inquisition marks a substantial advance in the contemporary administration of justice, and therefore in the general civilization of mankind."[214]

Historians describe the systematic, inexorable destruction of heretics throughout most of western Europe through the instrumentality of the medieval Inquisition during the bridge period. Thousands were induced to return to the mother church or brought to judgment before these shadowy tribunals and their fates sealed. Communities were terrorized to the extent that those who escaped accusation were cowed into silence or the abandonment of their faith. Thus, almost all heretical groups were essentially stamped out during this period and among the casualties were many communities of the Vaudois.

Cardew reports that "The number of persons who actually suffered death at the stake is unknown."[215] Lea suggests that the number was considerably less than was originally supposed, (Some reports speak of millions of deaths.) but he quotes one boast ". . .that in a century and a half from 1400 AD the Holy Office burned 30,000 persons."[216]

One may be appalled at the methodology, but one can hardly deny the effectiveness of this organized assault on the heresies that threatened the church. Though early in the 13th century the numbers of heretics were huge, in some places approximating membership in the Catholic Church, by the end of the 15th century, the Inquisition's success was virtually complete. Lawrence reports that "The Inquisition provided an effectual remedy for the apostolic heresies. . ... The scriptural Christians of every land who refused to worship or adore the Virgin disappeared from sight, the supremacy of Rome was assured over all of Western Europe."[217] Lea testifies, "Thus heresy, deprived of its protection, was gradually stamped out, and the Inquisition established its power in every corner of the land."[218]

Vaudois Persecutions. Because of the difficulty of identifying specific heretics and differentiating between their various belief systems, the history of the persecution of the Vaudois during the bridge period, 1225-1525 AD, is difficult to characterize. Among those caught in its net were many Vaudois, but their numbers can never be known because they could often not be distinguished from members of other dissident groups. Though most religious dissenting groups succumbed to the power of the church and state arrayed against them, we shall see that the Vaudois were uniquely positioned and organized for survival.

The earliest evidence of persecution directed specifically against the Vaudois is a decree issued jointly from the offices of Alfonso, Marquis of Provence and the Bishop of Toulouse in the year 1192 AD. It set in place a pattern for years to come of secular and ecclesiastical effort to eliminate the Vaudois as a real danger to the established religious and secular leaders. It should be noted that this occurred before the establishment of the Inquisition and before the formation of the Dominican order, which order was to become the enabling implement of the Inquisition.

> We order that the Waldenses or Ensabates, who are also called the Poor of Lyon, and all the other numberless heretics, anathematized by Holy Mother Church, be expelled from all our states as enemies of the cross of Christ, violators of the Christian religion, and public enemies of our person and kingdom. Therefore, from this day forth, whosoever shall dare to receive in to his house, or listen to the preaching of said Waldenses or such other heretics, wherever it may be, or to feed or assist them in any way, is warned that he will thereby incur the wrath of Almighty God, and of ourselves; and that his possessions will be confiscated without appeal, according to the penalty provided against those who render themselves guilty of high treason. [219]

The decree was issued in 1192, early in Vaudois history as they flourished in the south of France, but it was characteristic of many to follow as secular authorities, prompted by the church, focused their wrath on the Vaudois. Nevertheless, the bulk of the Vaudois adherents proved to be relatively secure for upwards of 100 years while the suppression of more populous heretic groups raged around them "But now," reports Gell, "comes a new time with new dangers both of a secular and a spiritual nature. As yet the Vaudois had never been invaded in their interior retreats. But Pope John XXII, desirous of prosecuting the work commenced by Innocent III, began in 1332 AD to think of these heretics among the retired mountains, in the bosom of which a considerable part of them lay entrenched."[220] The last half of the 15th century saw the unfolding of the inquisition's persistent attacks on the Vaudois in areas surrounding their home valleys. "The Franciscan Borellius is said to have burned in 1393, 150 [Vaudois heretics] at Grenoble in the Dauphine in a single day."[221]

Somehow the Vaudois escaped the wholesale eradication of heretics that characterized the bridge period. What was their secret? There is no obvious single element, characteristic, doctrine or attribute that would serve as the basis for the Vaudois surviving this fiery furnace. It would seem to be more the location of their habitat, supplemented by the cohesiveness and self-reliance of the group. Also, it must be said, their survival was greatly enhanced by the relative independence of their secular rulers. Generally secular authorities in Vaudois territories were reluctant to join the battle to destroy the heretics. Successive dukes of Savoy gave the inquisitors but meager support. Wylie reports:

> The zeal of the pope was but indifferently seconded by that of the secular lords. The men they were enjoined to exterminate were the most industrious and peaceable of their subjects; and willing as they no doubt were, to oblige the pope, they were naturally averse to incur so great a loss as would be caused by the destruction of the flower of their population."[222]

The strategy of the Inquisition to intimidate and divide worked best in areas where the heretics were an easily-cowed minority and where the secular authorities were cooperative. These criteria held true for most of Western Europe during the medieval period. The Vaudois community inhabiting the valleys of the Cottian Alps did not fit the mold. Residing in a region famously independent of papal authority over previous centuries, inhabitants and leaders were not easily cowed. In their communities where they constituted the majority, they were unified and tightly knit, consisting of individuals not at all inclined to accuse their neighbors. Their secular authorities recognized them as long-standing model subjects and were not inclined to comply with the wrecking ball of the Inquisition, especially after having witnessed the destruction of Provence wrought in the previous century by the Inquisition-inspired crusade against the Cathari. An illuminating scenario is reported from the 14th century, when after repeated efforts to obtain confessions,

> the Inquisition issued a summons to all the inhabitants of Val Perosa reciting that their land was full of heretics and that they must appear before him in Pignerolo and purge themselves and their communities of this infamy. They did not obey but through the intervention of the Piedmontese chancellor, they agreed to pay Count Amadeo 500 florins a year, for which he was to prevent the inquisitors from visiting Val Perosa, and they were to be exempted

from obeying his citations. This was too much to endure and the inquisitor shook the dust of Pignerol off his feet, denouncing the officials of Val Perosa as having incurred excommunication and the penalties of contumacy, the only result of which was to call down upon his head the wrath of Count Amadeo.[223]

In addition, secular authorities were emboldened by their history of independence. On the Italian side, the Duchy of Savoy for hundreds of years, stood independent of the greater kings and kingdoms, and on the French side, the province of Dauphine was far removed from the seat of French power and often neglected. Repeated efforts by the Inquisition to penetrate the Vaudois society and set to rout the people were not successful, as they "wasted their energies on the Piedmontese Waldenses without reducing them to subjection."[224] In contrast to almost all other areas where the Inquisition flourished, the Vaudois of the Alpine valleys, on occasion, responded to the constant pressure of the Inquisition with armed force. The Vaudois began to engage during this period in a pronounced pushback as they developed a significant military capability for their protection, which interestingly enough, was to become one of their characteristic traits and prove to be a valuable bargaining chip in later years.

The conventional Inquisitional procedures described above, having failed among the Vaudois, the commencement of the 15th century signaled a new approach. Casting aside all pretense to investigation and identification of individual heretics, church authorities undertook a sustained program of assault on whole communities with overwhelming force of arms, a war of extermination. This new approach was in part undertaken in retaliation for the pushback of the Vaudois.

At the demand of the pope's legate, a century-long war of extermination against the Vaudois began with an attack by Savoyard armed forces against the valley of di Susa or Pregalas on Christmas Day 1400 AD. Wylie reports that the entire community was either killed or driven from their homes in mid-winter with a reported loss of 50 (some say 80) children frozen to death in the cold.[225] Having this taste of success, this new brute-force approach was soon institutionalized by papal bull (Innocent VIII) in 1487 denouncing the heretics of the Piedmontese valleys for their false worship and their "simulated sanctity," which had the effect of seducing the sheep of the true fold, therefore he orders that that "malicious and abominable sect of malignants, if they refuse to abjure, to be crushed like venomous snakes and to be exterminated."[226] The papal bull "called upon the king of France and the duke of Savoy and other princes to proceed with armed expeditions against them ... and promised to all princes, lords and others, who would arm themselves with the buckler of the orthodox faith, plenary indulgence, remission of their sins once in their lifetime, and what was not less tempting, it granted permission to each person to appropriate to himself any possessions of the heretics, whether lands or goods."[227]

In response, the Vaudois rose in arms, slew the parish priest in the square at Angrogna and "besieged the inquisitor in a castle where he had taken refuge, so that he was glad to escape with his life."[228] Other Inquisitors were slain by the Vaudois in Bricarax and in Susa. Attempts were made over years to dislodge the Vaudois from their mountain retreats but none were met with success. Each time the Vaudois pushed back with powerful effect, and when necessary, retreated for refuge to higher, more secure positions.

Subsequent battles are reported throughout the 15th century having the effect of reducing the Vaudois population, proscribing their boundaries and driving them further into the mountains where they could defend themselves. "The heretics scattered throughout the towns of Piedmont were mercilessly dealt with by the Inquisition, but those who inhabited the mountain valleys were safe, except from assault by overwhelming forces."[229]

Their effective acts of resistance eventually earned the Vaudois a seat at the conference table with Charles I, the duke of Savoy in 1489, in which they were granted peace and had their ancient religious privileges restored. It didn't mean the end of persecution, only a brief respite, for again in 1513 all the provisions of the Inquisition were reinstated, renewing a cycle that had come to seem endless.

However, the peace of 1489 provides a convenient landmark to pause and assess the condition and extent of the Vaudois people and communities. The ravages of 300 years of persecution had taken a mighty toll and essentially decimated the Vaudois population. From tens, perhaps hundreds of thousands in many lands they had been reduced to a precious few scattered across and hidden within the kingdoms and fiefdoms of Europe with a few thousand concentrated and sequestered in the valleys of Piedmont, northern Italy. The central, remaining community of the Vaudois was located in the triangular enclave of Alpine valleys situated astride the Alpine boundary between the Dauphine region of France and the Duchy of Savoy. Vestiges of Vaudois communities remained in the Durance and Luberon valleys of Provence, on the plains of Piedmont and huddled together with and finally indistinguishable from the like-minded Hussites of Bohemia. It was, however, for the most part, only the few thousand faithful of the Alpine valleys and a few outlying groups who figured in further Vaudois history.

5. THE ENCOUNTER OF THE VAUDOIS WITH THE REFORMATION.

The encounter of the Vaudois with the Reformation did not occur in a sterile environment, and the reaction of the Vaudois must have been informed and profoundly influenced by surrounding events. Tourn writes of the atmosphere surrounding the first contact:

> By 1530 the Reformation was no longer a question to be discussed primarily among theologians. Suddenly it burst out as a popular force, sweeping aside venerable institutions like a flood. Just five years previously Prussia had be-

come Lutheran; Sweden followed two years later, Basel in 1529. By 1531 military lines were drawn right across Switzerland; the leader of the reformation in Switzerland, Ulrich Zwingli, met his death in a pitched battle. This was a time when political and military turmoil spared no one. In 1527 Rome itself was sacked by Imperial troops; in 1529 the Turks threatened Vienna. Confronted with immense problems in his realm, the young emperor Charles V (of the Holy Roman Empire) signed a treaty with the protestant princes which recognized the Reformation. The Confession of faith written by Melanchthon, outlining the theological standards of the new movement, thus received sovereign sanction.[230]

The Duchy of Savoy and portions of France, the small corner of Europe that was home to most of the Vaudois, was situated between the great powers of France and the Holy Roman Empire. The Duke of Savoy, Charles III, himself marvelously theologically ambivalent, tried to carefully balance between papal warnings and the wave of the Reformation from the north. His failure to safely navigate these troubled waters led to armed conflict with Bern and eventually the severing of the Vaud, the Swiss portion of the duchy. Hence the international atmosphere surrounding the Savoyard neighborhood at the time was one of political and military stress with Bernese troops poised on the frontier to push the Reformation further south.[231]

It was early in the 16th century when word first crept into Vaudois enclaves of this new and amazing development in the history of Christian dissent. For the first time since the great east-west schism of Christianity in the 11th century, whole peoples were declaring their independence and throwing off the yoke of Catholicism. One can only imagine the sense of marvel and amazement the Vaudois representatives must have felt as the great reform movement unfolded on their doorstep, how they must have longed to be a part of it.

The differences between the two parties engaged in this encounter, the Reformers and the Vaudois, were remarkable and relevant. " Luther, Bucer, Œcolampadius, Zwingli, Lambert, Melanchthon, Haller, and later Calvin and the majority of Reformers were former clerics and also urban dwellers, grounded in Latin and scholastic methods of university training. They had nothing in common with the Waldenses and their deliberate, organized simplicity."[232]

Milner's description offers a good perspective. "As they [the Vaudois] were, for the most part, a plain and illiterate people, they furnished no learned divines, no profound reasoners, no able historians. The vindication of their claims to the character of a true church, must therefore be drawn principally from the holiness of their lives and the patience of their sufferings."[233]

First contact evidently occurred when *barbi* from the valleys journeyed to Switzerland in 1526 and returned with news of the progress of the Reformation and with books expounding its principles. Four years later an official Vaudois delegation consisting of Georges Morel and Pierre Masson entered into consultations with Swiss Protestants, Œcolampadius, Bucer and others. Morel was a good theologian and already known for his openness to Reformation ideas.[234] Wylie writes "The visit of these two pastors of this ancient church gave unspeakable joy to the reformer of Basel [Œcolampadius]. He heard in them the voice of the church primitive and apostolic speaking to the Christians of the 16th century and bidding them welcome within the gates of the city of God. What a miracle was before him. For ages had this church been in the fires, yet she had not been consumed. Was this not encouragement to those who were just entering into persecutions not less terrific?"[235]

The Vaudois emissaries arrived with a precious document in hand, written in Latin, "and giving a complete account of their ecclesiastical discipline, worship, manners and doctrine – requesting advice on several parts."[236] Of this document, Audisio writes:

> The tone is clearly sincere and candid. [Morel, the presumed author] was speaking of his community, presenting it to his listeners who were not even aware that the [Vaudois] existed. For this reason the *barbi's* list of questions present the following pattern: these are our beliefs, these are our practices, what do you think of them? The delegates sought details, explanations and comparisons related to their Bible readings. Morel and Masson wrote to Œcolampadius: "It is

our hope and our confident belief that the Holy Spirit will speak to us through you and enlighten us over numerous things which, because of our ignorance and our laziness, we doubt, and also we do not know at all which is, [we] strongly fear, much to the detriment of us and our people, whom we teach in a manner which is hardly competent."[237]

Of peripheral interest is Morel's reference in his memoirs to his estimate of the population of the Vaudois at this time at 800,000 souls located in the valleys, on the plains of Piedmont, in Naples and Calabria and in the countries of Germany.[238]

Most striking in this petition is the humility and sincerity of the Vaudois representatives. In all their years, they had never been properly grounded intellectually, their faith never based on great theological arguments, their doctrines never justified by learned theologians. From the 12th century the Vaudois had been characterized "as poor wandering preachers, unlearned, who saw it as their objective to preach repentance to all Christian peoples."[239] Over the centuries they had retained the simplicity of their roots, a simplicity based on reading and applying the teachings of the New Testament, which they took literally, without the need of interpretation. Reports Audisio, "it meant refusing all interpretations,, all adaptations, even those which were the fruit of centuries of reflection, discussion and debate."[240] Matthew, Mark, Luke and John they knew. With Paul they were not so much acquainted, and as to Augustine, in him they had no interest.

As always their articles of faith began with the Holy Scriptures and the infallibility thereof. They wrote of stark differences from the Catholic faith in practices, including their refusal to take human life, to swear oaths; their rejection of purgatory, worship of relics, vigils, sufferings for the dead, and adoration of the Virgin or the other saints. Surprisingly they also included, as their own, a large measure of Catholic doctrine and practice, such as transubstantiation, auricular confession, celibacy of the *barbi*, and the seven sacraments, though Morel admitted that they had erred in thinking that there were more than two sacraments.[241]

Their practice also included attendance at Catholic mass, permitting their babies to be baptized by priests, and confessing to priests. Blending in with the Catholic background had become part of their spiritual lives and their religious practice and had rendered them in many ways indistinguishable from their Catholic neighbors, which had after all been the point of their dissimulation in the first place. Meeting clandestinely in their homes for instruction by the *barbi* had been an essential element in the maintenance of their separate existence. The Poor of Lyons lived a double life. On the one hand they behaved to all appearances like Catholics to safeguard their relative tranquility; on the other, they observed a certain number of rites and habits among themselves which ensured that their community continued to exist.[242]

The delegates posed a number of questions for their

Protestant advisors, which are phrased in such a way as to display an endearing humility as well as apparent feelings of guilt and inadequacy. What is striking about their questions is their lack of theological relevance. For the most part they demonstrate a concern about concrete aspects of their practical lives, with some minor issues in understanding the Bible. "In these questions, [Morel] evinced the intense preoccupation with practical ethics. He sought specific answers to practical questions relating to things like marriage, rent, property, usury, and self-defense. He also mentioned the classic 'issues'of Vaudois protest and 'heresy': judicial execution, oaths, prayers for the dead, the ministry of corrupt priests."[243]

With little supporting evidence, historians write of the struggle the Vaudois had with the reformers' theology, principally the role of free will and good works versus the grace of God. Such issues lay at the heart of the great controversies raging at the time between Luther, Zwingli, Farel and the like. The historian would have the Vaudois absorbed into this maelstrom, but the evidence suggests otherwise. Doctrinal issues were not important to the Vaudois, never had been, for they allowed *barbi* and even lay members to read the Bible and decide for themselves. They had no central authority, they had no theological elite, and they did not interpret.

True, encounters with the Reformer theologians raised the issues uppermost in the Reformers' minds and those issues thus became part of the dialogue. The Vaudois representatives, who were not unacquainted with the writings of Erasmus and Luther, wondered how their history of emphasis on good works could be fitted into all these new interpretations, but it did not seem to overly concern them. Living in harmony with those around them, doing good to their neighbors, worshiping the Savior and walking in obedience to the Lord's commands, these things they taught and did, without much thought as to why, or whether they were essential to salvation. They did them for the love of God and their fellow men. The arguments about nuances in doctrine mostly passed right over their heads. They didn't care.

Audisio writes of the:

> ideal cherished by the Waldenses since the origin of the movement, the desire to live in accordance with the evangelical model and to meditate on the Sermon on the Mount (Matthew 5), a central text of the Waldensian reflections, rather than debating doctrinal speculations. Their line of thought was moral rather than dogmatic, practical rather than speculative. Their approach was characterized above all by its pastoralism.[244]

The awful success of the Inquisition had driven them to a clandestine status, the status of an underground organization, so intense that many stooped to closely emulate their Catholic neighbors as a disguise, attending mass and partaking of the Eucharist. For centuries they had been subjects, victims of the ruthless power of the papacy. Relief in any permanent form was surely not expected. Nor had they in the 400 years of their existence ever experienced the presence of any other dissident group with staying power, let alone one seriously competing with the church. For centuries their life had been one of hanging on by their fingernails. Little wonder that on hearing the incredible news of the Reformation sweeping western Europe, they were anxious to confer, to connect and, if possible, to join hands.

One is also struck by their humble and teachable attitude. They had been at this reform business for 400 years, and yet they welcomed new ideas and were eager to be taught by the newcomers. To understand this attitude and the reception the new ideas received, it is helpful to recall that the Vaudois' ecclesiastical history was one of ingrained theological ambivalence. In contrast, the Reformers they encountered were part of a great, historic movement with world-wide consequences. "Facing this reticent troubled community, towered the world of the Reformation, learned, self-assured and triumphant, irrespective of the hostility it inspired."[245]

En route back home, as a stark reminder that the advent of the Reformation did not signal the end of the Vaudois' ordeal, one of the emissaries, Masson, was apprehended and executed, and Morel was left alone to deliver the Protestant response.

The introductory greeting of Œcolampadius, dated October 13, 1530, which Morel brought back to his people, was one of tender and respectful acceptance:

> We render thanks to our most gracious Father

that he has called you into such marvelous light, during ages in which such thick darkness has covered almost the whole world under the empire of the Antichrist. We love you as brethren.[246]

But, Œcolampadius and his colleagues, fresh from the jousting involved in establishing the Swiss Reformation, "wished the Waldenses to rework their theology and to declare themselves openly a part of the mainstream of the Reformation."[247] To this end they had some advice for the Vaudois. They counseled them to abandon the popish notion of transubstantiation and to recognize only the sacraments of baptism and the Eucharist. They chastised them for their lives of deception and their disinclination to stand forth and preach their gospel. They took issue with their propensity to act like Catholics if they really weren't. They should openly declare their faith, come out of their homes, build places of worship and face the world as true believers with no more dissimulation. Œcolampadius felt that the Waldenses "should be ready to face martyrdom rather than deny Christ. Those who know they are redeemed by the blood of Christ should be stronger."[248]

One has to wonder, would the Vaudois have justifiably experienced some measure of annoyance at these newcomers' admonitions to openness, these people who had no idea of what sustained persecution is like, of the pressures it brought to bear and the extremities to which one might be driven. Perhaps they identified with the catacombs and ancient Christians who hid there from their persecutors. What must the theologically unsophisticated *barbi* have thought on being subjected to metaphysical discussions involving whether the bread and wine of the Eucharist were actually the body and blood of Christ or just alongside the actual body and blood of Christ, when all they wanted to do was partake of the bread and wine in remembrance of him?

To assist the Vaudois in assimilating true reformist doctrine and practice, William Farel, one of the more radical Swiss reformers, but a native of Dauphine and acquainted with the Romaunt language, was dispatched to accompany Morel and counsel further with the Vaudois at home. We say "dispatched" as if there were some central organization or Protestant church calling the shots. In truth, there was none, but rather an assortment of articulate and combative theological warriors, acting on their own recognizance, pursuing their own agendas, pressing forward the reform movement in their own ways. It was to be another 34 years before Swiss Protestantism first reached a consensus as to doctrine and practice with the publication of the Helvetic Confessions. Farel, in addition to forcefully and persuasively delivering his own slant on the reformist message, urged the Vaudois to establish schools and afterwards collected money for them and sent four teachers.[249]

The new doctrines and wrenching advice were received by the Vaudois in council the following year, evidently attended by *barbi* and lay members alike. Muston writes "a great synod was held in the hamlet of Chanforan, in the valley of Angrogna. It began on the 12th of September 1532, lasted six days and was attended by representatives from all the Vaudois communities of Savoy, Italy, France and Dauphiny and by the entire Vaudois population all around."[250]

Out of this synod came a declaration of conclusions. Cameron reviews the Chanforan propositions of 12 September 1532 as reported by Vinay[251] in twenty-three articles. Among the most controversial were:

> 1. A Christian may lawfully take an oath in the name of God.
> 2. External good works may or may not be done, but are not commanded.
> 5. Auricular confession is not commanded of God. Confession is to God alone.
> 6. Work on the Sabbath is not forbidden by God.
> 10. It is not lawful for a Christian to take revenge on his enemy.
> 13. Marriage is not forbidden to anyone.
> 19. All those who are already and will be saved were pre-elected before the foundation of the world.
> 20. Whosoever would establish free will denies entirely the grace of God.
> 22, 23. Ministers ought not to move from place to place and may possess personal property.
> Additional. Christ left us with only two sacraments: baptism and the Eucharist.

Baird lists 17 articles adopted by the Vaudois in conference from the year 1535, a list which includes all of the above, but reverses article 6 to conform to the Ten Commandments. His account of the conference reaffirms the harsh doctrine of predestination, but side-steps the faith-works controversy with the bland statement: "No work is called good but that which is commanded of God; and none evil but that which he forbiddeth."[252]

Monastier characterizes the propositions emerging from the conference as "a confession of faith which may be considered a supplement to the ancient confession of faith of the year 1120[20] which it does not contradict in any point."[253] He further states that:

> they adopted a decisive resolution for the
> well-being of the Vaudois Church, which had
> been compromised for a number of years by the
> fear of persecutions. It was decreed by common
> consent, that they should cease entirely from
> all acts of dissimulation by which they had
> hoped to escape the notice of enemies of the
> faith; that henceforth they would take no part
> in any of the popish superstitions; they would
> not acknowledge as a pastor any priest of the
> Romish Church and never have recourse to his
> ministrations in any case, or under any circumstances. They likewise resolved to cease from all
> concealment in their religious assemblies; that
> the worship should be carried on openly and

---

20 He likely refers to the Noble Lesson, originally thought to have been written in 1120 but subsequently found to have been written in 1420.

publicly, in order to give glory to God.²⁵⁴

Audisio, on the other hand, has a different view. He claims a host of principles and practices contrary to their traditions were adopted by the Vaudois, transforming their entire religion. The principle of predestination was accepted totally. "All those who have been or will be saved were pre-selected before the creation of the world. Those chosen to be saved cannot fail to be saved." Similarly, as to sacraments: Christ's teaching only authorizes two: baptism and the Eucharist. Regarding free will and grace, a compromise was agreed to, recognizing that external works were optional. They abandoned evangelical poverty, they accepted oath taking, they authorized private property for ministers, and they rejected confession. Instead of Luther's concept of consubstantiation, they instead adopted the Zwingli belief concerning the Eucharist, which was quite opposed to their traditional stand (the presence of Christ in the gathering of believers). "On a doctrinal level the changes proved radical. The Poor of Lyon were giving up what had been their particular spiritual essence, their common practices and their understanding of religious intelligence."²⁵⁵

Audisio concludes:

> With Chanforan, in principle and in practice around 1560, Waldensianism died out. Practically everything that made up the religious characteristics of this dissident movement – and that defined its specificity in Europe – disap-

peared. I repeat, religiously speaking, being a Waldensian and being a Reformer is contradictory. One could only be one or the other. Waldensiasm was drowned in the Reformation. It is appropriate to speak of death. No continuity is possible between Waldensianism before and after Chanforan. As a consequence, the Valdese church, which claims to be its legitimate descendent is anything but its heir. [256]

Melia, on the other hand declares "The new Reformers had good reason to regard the old Waldenses as their ancestors, because nearly all the points, in which the Waldenses during three centuries disagreed with the Roman Church, were likewise assumed and kept by the new Reformers, although with a good many additions of their own."[257] Schaff maintains that it was the flexibility of the Vaudois at this critical juncture that ensured their survival and that they became "the only medieval sect which survived to this day [1910] because they progressed with the Reformation and adhered to the Bible as their rule of faith."[258] Of the Chanforan conference outcomes, Wylie writes, "The lamp which had been on the point of expiring began, after the synod, to burn with its former brightness. The ancient spirit of the Waldenses revived."[259]

Surely the truth lies somewhere between these extreme claims: Audisio proclaiming death and others claiming new life. Melia lists fourteen well-documented[21] doctrines which the Waldenses held in common with the Reformers before their encounter with them and finds only five that were contrary. Of these five only two are substantive: acceptance of seven sacraments and the celibacy of ministers, and these latter were revised after consultation with the Reformers. These discrepancies hardly seem substantive enough to warrant the conclusion of Audisio that "The Poor of Lyon were giving up what had been their particular spiritual essence."[260]

Cameron asserts "The building up of the 'Synod of Chanforan' as a symbol and decisive turning point for the movement is, however, a deeply misleading piece of historical construction, and as such to be avoided."[261]

What the reformers decried and where they differed from the Vaudois of 1530 was not the foundation which had under-girded and animated the Vaudois for 400 years. Instead, these differences were mostly the practices and doctrines which the Vaudois had gradually and reluctantly adopted to save themselves from total destruction – and in some cases had made them look and act like their Catholic neighbors. These they were only too glad to abandon with, one imagines, some sense of relief. In their haste to do so, they may have failed to anticipate the consequences of discarding the mechanisms that had kept them alive. Or, if they did anticipate the consequences, then their willingness to accept these

---

21 A detailed, organized list of beliefs is lacking for this period because almost all we know about Waldensian beliefs comes from documents of Inquisitorial interrogations.

constitutes an act of remarkable faith and courage.

At the Chanforan conference the Vaudois reached an additional significant decision, evidently with considerable prompting from their Reformer advisors, that is, to commission a new translation of the Bible. The version then in use by the *barbi* was in the Romaunt language and was based on the Church of Rome's Latin vulgate and judged to be inaccurate. The new translation was to be prepared by the Swiss reformer, Robert Olivetan, a cousin of Calvin, and to be drawn from Hebrew and Greek texts and, oddly, it was to be in the French language. Furthermore, the new bible would be published in a large in-folio version making it very difficult to carry or hide. It seems odd that the Vaudois would commit their resources and energy to produce a bible of so little use to them. And in fact, the new Bible did not sell well and apparently was used sparingly by the Vaudois. It appears that the Reformers pressed vigorously for the project, largely in their own interest rather than that of the Vaudois, and some say is a stark indicator of "the ascendancy of the 'Swiss' then had over the *barbi*, persuading them to agree to the new edition and to pay for it."[262]

Perhaps the Vaudois were, as some historians suppose, the naive dupes of the Reformers, having no will of their own, simply doing whatever they were pressured to do. But, more likely, they recognized in this new Bible, an opportunity to perform a selfless act, to make a significant contribution to the general Reform effort, to which, incidentally, they had dedicated their lives for the previous 400 years. This would explain their willingness to support a translation which would benefit them very little, but instead would prove serviceable to their French-speaking neighbors. Audisio states that:

> Olivetan's Bible is a real landmark. On a linguistic level, at the time when French was still very variable, it fixed a language that could be understood by all Franco-phones; it was also the first Bible in French based on Hebrew and Greek. Furthermore, on a religious level, the translation, which in the following centur[ies] was to be [repeatedly] updated, was the edition in which generations of French Protestants read the word of God, often in secret, particularly during the arduous Wilderness period from 1685-1787, when the *Religion Pretendue Reformeè* was forbidden.[263]

These controversies aside, what is relevant about this great encounter with the Reformation is what the Vaudois did about it afterward. What changed in their practice of religion and in their teachings and what impact did these changes bring for the Vaudois people?

CHAPTER III.
Survival (1520-1686 AD)

"Avenge, O Lord, Thy slaughtered saints, whose bones
Lie scattered on the Alpine meadows cold!
For them who kept the truth so pure of old,
When all our Fathers worshipped stocks and stones.
Forget not, in Thy book record their groans
Who were Thy sheep, and in their ancient fold,
Slain by the bloody Piedmontese, they rolled
Mother with infant down the rocks. Their moans
The vales redoubled to the hills, and they
To heaven."[264]   *-John Milton*

Oh, that my head were waters and mine eyes a fountain of tears, that I might weep day and night for the slain of the daughter of my people." (Jeremiah 9:1)

1. GENERAL IMPACT OF THE PROTESTANT REFORMATION.

Europe, in the 16th and 17th centuries, was buffeted and transformed by the confluence of elemental forces: the emergence of nationalism, the rise of monarchies, the exploration of the New World, the expansion of knowledge and scientific thought, the invention of the printing press and the Protestant Reformation. Throughout Western Europe nations began to take form as we know them today. Monarchs arose to challenge and in time diminish the power of the pope. Just when Christian expansion to the south and east was blocked by the wall of Islam, intrepid explorers circled the globe and opened new pathways by the introduction of Christianity into the Americas and the Far East. The likes of Galileo, Bacon, Kepler, Copernicus, Hobbes and Newton launched an unprecedented expansion of scientific and social knowledge. Within fifty short years the Protestant heresy had blossomed into established religions, engulfing England, Scotland, Switzerland, all of Scandinavia and half of Germany and significantly penetrated many other Europeans lands. It was a frightening and exciting age for all and especially for Christians.

Luther has been described as a catalyst, igniting an explosive generation. What began by Pope Leo X's characterization as some little trouble with a "drunken German who would soon be sober," blossomed into a movement that changed the western world. The Protestant Reformation awakened Christianity, opened whole new vistas to freedom of thought and worship and ended the hegemony of the Roman Church, splintering Christianity into a multitude of pieces. Leo altered his initial view of Luther to that characterized by his bull of 1520, *Exsurge Domine*, in which he penned a confidential warning to his God: "Arise O Lord and judge thine own cause. A wild boar has invaded the vineyard." This wild boar split off whole kingdoms of independent, reformed religious denominations, together with their cathedrals and their clergy, leaving the mother church splintered, bereft and staggering.

Beyond its purely religious implications, Luther's revolution led to the popularization of public schooling, including the education of women, increased literacy of the common man, an unprecedented advance of personal liberty, and contributed significantly to the political instability of Europe and its attendant wars of the 16th and 17th centuries. Perhaps as significant as the religious protests themselves was the timely introduction of the printing press, thus giving the voices of dissent an unprecedented audience and range of influence.[22] By 1620 Francis Bacon listed the printing press together with firearms and the nautical compass as the three inventions that changed the world.

Though its force and extent could not have been anticipated, the Protestant Reformation surely did not come as a surprise to the Roman church. The abuses within the church

---

22 Though preceded by the Chinese centuries before, it was Gutenberg's moveable type and printing press invention that heralded a world-wide printing revolution from 1439. By Luther's time printing presses in Western Europe had produced over 20 million volumes.

and its vulnerable condition were perhaps the worst-kept secret of all time. The enormous wealth of the church and the excesses of the hierarchy and clergy were widely known and acknowledged from the humblest of parishioners to the loftiest members of the Holy See. At the dawn of the Reformation, a papal commission had bravely "paint[ed] in the darkest manner the corruption which had made its way into the church," and predicted that if "Leo X refuses to heal the wounds, it is to be feared that God himself will no longer apply a slow remedy, but will cut off and destroy the diseased members with fire and sword."[265]

Another papal commission "put into writing the abuses of the church, stating that the popes themselves, by their sins, crimes and financial greed had been the prime source of ecclesiastical deterioration."[266] The renowned jurist, Caccia wrote, "I see that our Holy Mother the Church has been so changed that she seems to have no tokens of her evangelical character, and no trace can be found in her of humility, temperance, continence and Apostolic strength."[267]

Such advance warnings went largely unheeded until the Reformation compelled closer introspection and initiated what became known as the Counter-Reformation, which has been characterized as, "the spiritual battle for souls, the psychological battle for hearts, the intellectual battle for minds, the physical battle for bodies."[268] Under a succession of popes, from 1521 to 1559, some determined on reform and others oblivious to the problems, a stop-and-go effort at Counter-Reformation was undertaken, attempting to implement reforms within the Catholic Church and staunch the expansion of Protestantism.

An early stage of the Counter-Reformation sought reconciliation with the dissidents. Protestant representatives were invited to debate in church councils in an attempt to engage them in cordial intercourse. However, by then the Protestant Reformation had a life of its own and was not to be so easily subsumed. Cordial conversation soon deteriorated into rancorous debate and the effort was soon abandoned.

Another stage of the Counter-Reformation was reform from within. Luke-warm attempts at reform ebbed and flowed over the period until the threads of reform were drawn together in an Herculean effort at the seventeenth ecumenical council of the church convened at Trent in 1545. The council met for a period of eight years under the direction of four different popes and the watchful eye of Charles V, the Holy Roman Emperor. A wide range of genuine reforms was considered and many implemented, including measures dealing with absentee bishops, granting of indulgences, morals and discipline of the clergy. In the end much was resolved by armed force far from the councils of the church. Durant claims:

> The counter reformation [within the church] succeeded in its principal purposes. Men continued, in Catholic as much as in Protestant countries, to lie and steal, seduce maidens and sell offices, kill and make war. But the morals of the clergy improved and the wild freedom of

Renaissance Italy was tamed to a decent conformity to the pretentions of mankind. All in all it was an astonishing recovery, one of the most brilliant products of the Protestant Reformation.[269]

Concurrent with these efforts, the Inquisition, mostly dormant now for 200 years except for its robust and notorious survival in Spain, was called back to life (in 1536) and launched with renewed vigor. The Society of Jesus was founded (1540) in time to provide a cadre of highly-educated, militant monks eager to replace the Dominicans as able administrators of the institution. Baigent and Leigh report:

> In 1542, the Holy Office was created as a permanent tribunal patterned after the Inquisition of Spain, with four procedural rules:
> 1. punish on suspicion,
> 2. have no regard for the great,
> 3. be severe with any who seek shelter behind the powerful, and
> 4. show no mildness, least of all towards Calvinists.[270]

The machinations of the resuscitated Inquisition became legendary in their cruelty and injustice, exceeding even those of its antecedent of 200 years before. Baigent and Leigh further write: "There ensued then a purge of the kind that anticipated those perpetrated in our century by Hitler, Stalin and other more petty tyrants of their ilk."[271] One Catholic historian wrote...

> The hasty and credulous pope lent a willing ear to every denunciation, even the most absurd. The inquisitors, constantly urged on by the pope, scented heresy in numerous cases where a calm and circumspect observer would not have discovered a trace of it. An actual reign of terror began."[272]

Cardinal Caraffa, a zealous anti-heretic, was appointed to the Holy Office as the first president of the revived tribunal. Upon his elevation to the papacy in 1555 as Paul IV, the Inquisition expanded its activities and promulgated the Roman Index of Prohibited Books, a list of forbidden publications considered detrimental to the faith. Though an abject failure in its efforts to extirpate the heresy, the Counter-Reformation was hugely successful in halting the progress of the Protestant expansion principally through the application of intimidation, bloodshed and destruction. Within 100 years, through a combination of Jesuit proselyting and Inquisitional intimidation, it succeeded in eliminating virtually all vestiges of Protestantism from many European nations where it seemed to have taken root.

Though only a peripheral part of the enormous Reformation movement and the Catholic response, the Vaudois, as we shall see, suffered mightily during this period, which became, for them, an almost fatal age of renewed and intensified persecution.

2. IMPACT OF THE PROTESTANT REFORMATION ON THE VAUDOIS.

Luther's foundational premise that sacred writ, as interpreted by the individual, was authoritative, and that every Christian should have access to the Bible in his own tongue, though an earthquake to Christianity, was old news to the Vaudois. This had been their consistent position for over four hundred years. However, the post-Reformation survival period witnessed several significant changes among the Vaudois, precipitated by their encounter with the Protestant Reformation. Audisio chronicles a gradual transformation in culture and practice throughout the early 16th century reflecting alterations in church organization, construction of chapels, swearing of legal oaths, all of which suggest that by the mid 17th century, "The Poor of Lyon became full-fledged Protestants, not just in word but also in deed."[273]

Encouraged by their new-found Protestant friends, the Vaudois undertook the publication of confessions of faith, a new experience for them. The earliest of these, "signed by the community of Cabrieres d'Avignon, was sent to the inquisitor, Jean of Roma, in 1533. The Poor of Christ from that region wrote telling him that they were good Christians and sent as confirmation of this 'the faith and belief that we hold and believe in.' The ensuing text is quite simply the Apostle's Creed, in French, transcribed in full."[274]

Within the next twenty years the Vaudois drew up several additional confessions, all of which conformed almost fully to the Calvinist reform model, such as: justification by faith, recognition of two sacraments, baptism and the Lord's Supper, with additional articles vindicating their orthodoxy and denouncing the errors of Roman doctrine. These documents were prepared and submitted to various governmental and legal entities as a defense against accusations of heresy. Rather than genuine adherence to the Calvinist model, these confessions demonstrate that "The Poor of Lyon were capable of great versatility, according to their situation."[275] Or one might assert that these confessions illustrate how indifferent the Vaudois were to the details of Christian theology.

Interaction with representatives of the Reformation also had an impact on the intellectual leadership and the organizational structure of the Vaudois. They had encountered theological sophisticates before on many occasions, but generally in a contentious environment with their adversaries. Their history is replete with the ridicule by learned Dominican Inquisitors who were amazed to discover that this persistent, indestructible group of heretics employed no great thinkers, no bona fide theologians. There were no profound spokesmen to expound, no persuasive disputants to engage, just simple people trying to be good Christians. Their intercourse with the Swiss Protestant representatives now convinced the Vaudois that this time-honored approach of "aw shucks" was insufficient to the times. They decided that more sophisticated ministers would be needed, along with a more effective church hierarchy to provide direction. Quite naturally they turned to their new-found friends from Switzerland for a model.

Vaudois representatives joined Protestant delegates from all over France in a synod in Paris in 1559, where it appears they differed very little from their co-religionists. The synod drew up confessions of faith in conformance to the model of the Swiss Reformed churches and provided a corresponding document which the Vaudois representatives presented to the Savoyard Duke Emmanual Phillibert as an apologia and confession. From this period, the organization of the Vaudois church, which had hitherto featured a simple *barba*-minister model, now began to conform to the more common Protestant standard with parishes and ministers, presbyters and deacons.

For some years, a Swiss Protestant academy, a school of the prophets, had been functioning, initially in Geneva, but later also in Zürich and Strasbourg, in a movement initiated by Zwingli in 1525 and perpetuated by Calvin. The school provided regular instruction to an organization called The Congregations of the Company of Pastors. The school received participants from a variety of groups, but for pastors serving within the Republic of Geneva and surrounding areas, participation was mandatory. The purpose of the school was to provide a ready pool of pastors such as to "preserve purity and concord in doctrine among ministers of the word. The common cause of the Reformation led to a plan of a broad platform of regular meetings and discussions in which unity of doctrine was a primary aim."[276]

Under the heavy hand of John Calvin, the Company of Pastors functioned as a governing body, selecting, training, and dispatching pastors throughout the French-speaking Protestant community.

Sometime about a third of the way through the 16th century, the Vaudois began to request and to receive pastors trained in the Geneva academy. By mid-century, there was a steady flow of such trained ministers into the ranks of the Vaudois clergy. The Registry of Pastors reports ten such trainees sent into the field in support of the Piedmont communities in the years 1555-1557.[277]

Under the influence of the Protestant Reformation the Vaudois abandoned their ancient leadership structure of *barbi* and adopted a church government more akin to the Swiss Presbyterian model. Each commune consisting of a cluster of hamlets employed its full-time pastor who was generally educated abroad, principally in the Calvinist Academies at Geneva and Lausanne. Synods of pastors and laymen met periodically as needed to decide pressing issues. These issues were usually more social or sacerdotal than they were doctrinal. Three pastors together with two lay members formed a "Table," which acted as the Vaudois governing body between synods. One of the two pastors was designated Moderator to preside over the Table.

Fast forward three-quarters of a century to the time when the plague devastated the valleys of the Vaudois in the 1630s. Among the estimated 10,000 casualties were the pastors, for it was reported that twelve of fifteen of them fell victims to the plague. All were replaced by relief forces prepared in the Geneva Academy, schooled in the Calvinist doctrines and speaking French.[278] Over the century stretching roughly from 1530 to 1630 the surviving Vaudois gradually adopted the Calvinist doctrines, the structure of the reformed religious organizations and even their language. Monastier reports:

> From this period may be dated the use of the French language in the worship of the Vaudois valleys of Piedmont. Hitherto it had been carried on in the common language of the country, that is, in the Romance language, in which all their ancient writings were composed. Henceforth French was generally employed, for the various editions of the Bible printed at the expense of the Vaudois and circulated in their houses were in this language, and the body of the pastors likewise spoke it, owing either to their origin, or the course of their studies.[279]

By 1650 the Vaudois people had totally abandoned the old Romaunt language of their heritage. They began giving their children French names and reading their scriptures and documenting their transactions in the French language.

Also during this survival period, a peculiar circumstance directed the gaze of theologians and religious historians of both the Protestant and Catholic persuasion toward the study of the origin, beliefs and practices of the Vaudois. This heightened interest arose from their interpretation of the final instruction of the Christ to his disciples in Matthew: "Go ye therefore, and teach all nations, baptizing them in the name of the Father, and of the Son, and of the Holy Ghost: Teaching them to observe all things whatsoever I have commanded you: and, lo, I am with you alway, *even unto the end of the world. Amen.*"(Matt. 28:19-20) This instruction was thought to mean that the church Christ established would never lose its identity, but provide a continuous and visible succession until he came again.

Eusebius, Christianity's earliest historian, had claimed that the whole intellectual, spiritual and institutional life established by the Christ was preserved in the Roman church from apostolic times. Though subsequent Catholic theologians abandoned their strict requirement of the unchanging succession of doctrine and practice, they nevertheless held strongly to the principle of the succession of church administration. The reigning pope in Rome was alleged to be the successor in an unbroken line of authority beginning with Peter, the chief apostle of the Savior's time. Their principal attack on the upstart Protestants was that their religion had only been around for fifty years and therefore could not be the church that Christ established.

The Protestant apologists, on the other hand, sought to demonstrate that the true church had always existed independent of Catholicism, though driven underground. Cameron writes:

> At this point the Protestant theologians discovered the Waldenses, as just one of the whole

mass of anti-papal, anti-sacerdotal heretics whose condemnation and exclusion from the church coincided very neatly with the apogee of papal power and medieval scholasticism. Articles on the medieval Waldenses were written into theological histories and treatises, which sought to demonstrate the continuity of the True Church within the dissenting tradition. All of these historical traditions began at roughly the same time, in the latter half of the 1550s, as Protestant historical writing was taking off.[280]

This must have been a welcome and unexpected confirmation for those among the embattled Vaudois who had long claimed the antiquity of their origins. As previously observed, there was no lack of Vaudois theologians or historians who supported the case for their ancient beginning in publications, including Leger (1690), Peyran (1823), Perrin (1847), Allix (1821), Worsfold (1835), Wylie (1860), Bresse (1827) and Faber (1838) as well as the British benefactors, Morland (1658) and Gilly (1848).

Jesuit scholars of the period responded that, yes, the Waldenses had existed over many centuries but their doctrines and practices could not be considered proto-protestant in any sense.

Citing mainly documents provided by the Inquisition, Jesuit scholars, led by Jacob Gretser of Ingolstadt (1561-1625) laid out an array of documents providing compelling evidence of the variety and changing nature of the Vaudois practice and teaching which could hardly be considered a foundation for the Lutheran or reformed religions of the Reformation.[281] Ironically, the great minds of 16th century Christianity seeking to illuminate the origin and history of the Vaudois, gave more credence to the Vaudois' claim of antiquity than they themselves had done.

3. SURVIVAL.

When the Vaudois engaged the Reformation, their central and ancestral home was in the Piedmont Valleys lying along the south-eastern border of France, one portion in the Duchy of Savoy and the balance in the French province of Dauphine. Centuries of persecution and harassment had landed them in the relatively safe embrace of the mountains. Loosely-connected outlying communities of the Vaudois were situated in the Luberon region in France's Provence and in Calabria forming the toe of Italy's boot, with some small remnants in Bohemia, the modern-day Czech Republic. Not particularly interested in theological disputes, the Vaudois had wasted little time in identifying with the nearest protestant neighbors, the Calvinist version of Protestantism, centered in the Swiss Confederacy. It didn't take much of an adjustment in the minds of these rustic, faithful Christians, to adopt many of the doctrines espoused by the Helvetic Confessions I and II of the 16th century. The great heated debates of the Protestant theologians about such weighty matters as faith and grace, and the literal presence of the Eucharist, were largely lost on the simple Vaudois. These were insignificant details of little interest to them.

However their long-standing policy of seclusion and dissimilation, for them an essential element of survival, was anathema to the Reformation. Their new Swiss friends, enjoying as they did the backing of the state and the safety of numbers, could not understand true Christians who eschewed openness and hid their candle under a bushel. Shamed into compliance, the Vaudois began to emerge from their shell and with unaccustomed audacity, to openly espouse their religion, even beginning for the first time to build places of public worship.

This openness led to no immediate consequences in the small duchy of Savoy, for the Vaudois there enjoyed some measure of grudging acceptance. They had long been recognized as good citizens and loyal subjects. Though uncomfortable with the existence of reformed religionists in their duchy, the ducal authorities had come to rely upon them for their loyalty and their military expertise. The duchy had often been rescued by the timely arrival of crack Waldensian battalions, disciplined, trained and ready for combat. Thus over the years, the Vaudois had been alternately tolerated and persecuted, but always winked at and allowed to exist.

Elsewhere in France and Italy, however, these protections did not exist. The coming-out of the Luberon and Calabria branches of the Vaudois proved to be wildly imprudent, drawing as it did the immediate and vigorous attention of powerful Catholic and secular authorities.

Provence. The fate of the Provence branch of the Vaudois in the early 16th century came partly from drawing attention to themselves, but it was also dictated by events playing out in neighboring countries. Europe had recently suffered through the Peasants' Revolt in Germany, arguably an outgrowth of the religious upheavals initiated by Luther's ninety-five theses on the chapel door in Wittenberg. Beginning in 1525 in the Alsace, there was a spontaneous rising of the peasant class directed toward the aristocratic landowners and against all things Catholic. The revolt was ill-conceived and poorly led, largely economically motivated, but partly also a desperate expression of the innate desire for freedom sparked by the hope of the religious awakening. The revolt soon spread to all German-speaking lands where it became the largest and most destructive uprising ever seen in Europe.

The battles between the peasant and aristocratic forces were seriously one-sided and the revolt was quickly suppressed, but not before an estimated 100,000– 300,000 of the peasant insurgents were killed, with the attendant destruction of property, livestock and crops. The contagion of revolt spilled over into the very heart of Catholic orthodoxy when insurgent peasants sacked Rome in 1527, driving the pope from his throne and committing atrocities against nuns and monks. Fear that such anarchy and chaos might cross the borders became a compelling motivation for Francis I of France to eliminate, so far as possible, all traces of religious reform from within his realm. The pursuit of that goal embroiled much of the kingdom of France in a series of wars of religion stretching over thirty-six years.

By the middle of the 16th century as this blood-bath began, the reformed churches of France, mostly Huguenots, counted upwards of two million adherents including roughly half of the nobility. For half of the 16th century, the attention of the French was occupied by a series of military campaigns principally between Catholic forces backed by Spain and Protestant forces with the support of England. Battles erupted throughout the land, pitting powerful families against each other, punctuated by new edicts, periods of peace and palace intrigues followed by renewed warfare. This bloody era reached a peak in 1572 with the slaughter of an estimated 30,000 adherents of the reformed religion. Hostilities left the French countryside in ruins and the economy in a shambles. Peace was finally achieved with the publication of the Edict of Nantes in 1598 permitting a tentative coexistence of Catholic and reformed religionists within the realm of the first Bourbon king, France's Henry IV.

In the Provence region of France, the Vaudois became a minor footnote in these religious wars, but this footnote constituted a level of destruction seldom matched in cruelty and injustice. An army sent by the Parliament of Aix gathered near the village of Mèrindol in the Luberon on 13 April 1545 just before Easter where, as Audisio reports:

> A truly bloody week ensued, for the army advanced in formation, banners raised as if in battle, the troops convinced it was a crusade, when in reality they were pitted against bewil-

dered groups of fugitive peasants. Eleven villages were burnt or razed, the inhabitants shot, hunted down or imprisoned. Unmentionable atrocities were then committed by the unruly soldiery, followed by bands of pillagers who finished what the soldiers had begun. The final toll is sobering: an estimated 2700 dead and 600 men sentenced to work in the galleys[23] . . . to which must be added the prisoners, orphans and widows and ruined families, exiles, ruined crops, the countryside wrecked, the surviving population hit by famine, trials and debts."[282]

According to other accounts, by the year 1560, twen-

---

[23] Over the years, several thousand of the Vaudois men were captured, condemned and consigned to the galleys. A life sentence to the galleys was a punishment favored by French courts for those convicted of belonging to the reformed religion, giving comfort and aide to those of the reformed religion, and even those caught fleeing the country in search of religious freedom. Galleys were the principal naval vessels used by European powers for the conduct of warfare for almost a millennium through the 17th century, particularly in the Mediterranean sphere of operations. A typical galley was a formidable fighting machine featuring up to five cannon and a crew of 500, roughly 1/10 of compliment found on board a modern nuclear aircraft carrier. Of the 500, roughly half the galley's contingent was made up of galley slaves chained to their benches, usually for life. Successful propulsion and maneuvering of the vessel relied upon a well-disciplined and practiced crew, which, since there was no relief, could be required to row for as much as 24 hours without interruption. Any rower faltering in his duties would be beaten in place until he either returned to function or collapsed and was thrown overboard. 25 trained alternates stood ready to replace those slaves who died in the harness.

ty-two Luberon villages of the Vaudois had been burned, 10,000 inhabitants affected, 5000 lives lost and 700 men sent to the galleys.[283] The families of the Vaudois of the Luberon were eradicated and the final traces of the Vaudois in their original homeland of Provence disappeared forever.[284] It is not supposed that all of the Luberon Vaudois were killed, but those who were not destroyed both recanted and became Catholic or quietly merged into the beleaguered community of the Huguenots.[285]

Calabria. The southern Italian branch of the Vaudois fared no better. After a discreet existence of two hundred years, the Vaudois communities of Calabria, caught up in the Protestant euphoria of the times, also began to assert themselves with open public meetings and proselyting efforts in neighboring communities. This out-of-character posture of drawing attention to themselves and their message, commendable as it may have been, proved for them to be a fatal strategy, for the response they drew from the Catholic and secular authorities was swift and powerful. Tourn writes:

> Late in 1560 Cardinal Allessandrino, who was to become Pope Pius V, sent two inquisitors to Calabria. Aided by the efficient arm of the governor of the region, they spread terror with their torture, secret accusations and arbitrary fines. The Waldensians had no alternative but to abandon their villages and flee to the woods and mountains where a most unexpected turn of

events occurred: well hidden, and in a moment of desperation, the Waldensians fell upon their pursuers and killed a number of them, including the governor of the province himself. Authorities from Naples reacted with a vengeance. Punitive action was carried out by the Spanish military. What followed belongs to the chronicle of unspeakable violence. There were sporadic attempts at resistance, but their [traditional] respect for authority led the Waldensians to give themselves up. On June 5, 1561, the town of San Sisto, with its 6000 inhabitants, was burned to the ground, as also the neighboring village of Guardia Piemontese. Prisoners were burned like torches, sold to the Arabs as slaves or condemned to die of starvation in the dungeons of Cosenza. The military operations, enhanced by Jesuit indoctrination, aimed to obliterate every trace of Waldensian presence in Calabria.[286]

Bohemia. What of the Vaudois remnant in Bohemia? The early 17th century saw an extension of Catholic Counter-Reformation zeal and success marked by the commencement of the Thirty-Years War in 1618. To further facilitate and oversee the anti-heretical endeavors, the Council for the Propagation of the Faith and the Extirpation of Heretics was established in 1622. Originally founded as sacred congregation *de propaganda fide*[24], by Gregory XV, it soon

---
24 It is from this organization that the English word 'propaganda' has its origin.

expanded to take on the nasty business of extirpation. In a great convulsive, battle-scarred period, Hungary, Poland, Bohemia and Austria, after seriously imbibing the Protestant cocktail, were largely reclaimed for Catholicism.

It was during this war that the remnants of Protestantism in Bohemia suffered their own extinction. The Vaudois had assisted in establishing the Bohemian Protestants, the Bohemian Brethren, in the 15th century, though the subsequent relationship between the two religious groups is unclear. Conflict between officials of the Hapsburg Empire and the Brethren reached a crisis when Protestant insurgents penetrated Prague Castle in 1618 and evicted the imperial authorities there by throwing them out the window in the "Prague Defenestration."[25] The Hapsburg empire struck back, defeating the insurgents in the Battle of White Mountain and additional military actions culminated in the decapitation of the Bohemian nobility and the re-establishment of Catholicism as the state religion of Bohemia. Over time whatever Vaudois were present in Bohemia either recanted or merged with the Bohemian Brethren, who were then forced to find refuge elsewhere.

Piedmont Valleys. Throughout much of the 16th century, persecutions in the Alpine valleys were muted and subdued in comparison to those experienced by their brethren in France and Italy, largely because of the intermittent support, or at least the acquiescence, of Savoyard authorities. Dukes of Savoy, subject as they often were to the whims of more pow-

---
[25] Derived from the German word for window, *Fenster*

erful neighbors, ran hot and cold in their treatment of the heretics, but in general in these years they acquiesced in the coming-out of the Vaudois in their new role as proselyters and temple builders.

France, the Duchy of Savoy and much of Europe at this time fell under the compelling influence of Spain, which under Philipp II came to dominate the continent. In this period, Philipp became, among European monarchs, the chief defender of the Catholic faith and a determined, powerful foe of Protestantism. In February 1560, Duke Emmanuel Phillbert of Savoy, under pressure from the French and Spanish monarchs, issued from his residence in Nice an uncommonly harsh edict which initiated a new round of persecution of the Vaudois in his duchy. "It forbade on pain of fine and being sent to the galleys, listening to Lutheran[26] preaching in the Val Pellice or elsewhere."[287] The decree was promptly further enhanced by an edict commanding attendance at mass under penalty of death.[288] In the wake of these decrees, came a series of confiscations, arrests, tortures and deaths in the Piedmont plains, sending the surviving faithful fleeing to the refuge of their mountains. These actions were soon followed by a more conciliatory policy as the duke had second thoughts. This scenario had played itself out to good effect on numerous occasions over the centuries of the Vaudois survival.

In dealing with entrenched, powerful opposition, the Vaudois had established a pattern and employed a survival strategy and feigned compliance perfected with long prac-

---

26 The term 'Lutheran' here employed may be read as 'reformed.'

tice, namely this:
- The duke, usually under outside pressure, issues an edict limiting or even forbidding their religious practice.
- The Vaudois react with shock and amazement, engage powerful friends, enter a series of pleas for reconsideration, reminding the duke of their constant fealty and past services rendered.
- The duke dispatches an armed force, usually allied with the French and sometimes under their command, to enforce of the edict.
- The Vaudois declare their fealty to their rightful ruler, the duke, but respectfully refuse to comply and actively resist the forces deployed against them.
- A few engagements are fought - some won, some lost.
- The duke experiences a change of heart, decides he cares for his Protestants and can't live without them and resolves to resist outside pressures.
- A new edict is issued or an agreement is signed and peace returns.

Consistent with this time-honored strategy, in the face of the renewed threat the Vaudois issued a plea of innocence to the charge of heresy:

> First we do protest before the Almighty and

All-just God, before whose tribunal we must all one day appear, that we intend to live and die in the holy faith, piety and religion of our Lord Jesus Christ, and that we do abhor all heresies that have been and are condemned by the word of God. We do embrace the most holy doctrine of the prophets and apostles, as likewise of the Nicene and Athanasian Creeds; we do subscribe to the four councils[27], and to all the ancient fathers in all such things as are not repugnant to the analogy of faith."[289]

Such might be the plea of any accused heretical group, but that of the Vaudois was powered by the unique claim that they had been true to their vision of Christianity, passing from father to son, for 1500 years, and

> if they were heretics, so too were the first four councils and so too were the apostles themselves. They were willing any moment to appeal their cause to the general council, provided that council were to decide the question by the only infallible standard they knew, the word of God. If on this evidence they should be convicted of even one heresy, most willingly would they sur-

---

[27] Protestants commonly accepted the first four ecumenical councils of the Roman Church as authoritative in clarifying the nature of Christ and God, namely: Nicaea (315 AD), Constantinople (381 AD), Ephesus (427 AD) and Chalcedon (451 AD).

render it. "Show us," they said, "what the errors are you ask us to renounce under penalty of death, and you should not need to ask a second time."[290]

There is a certain combination of beauty and naiveté in this position, which could come only from the mouths of a simple, unassuming, humble people, oblivious to and bewildered by the world of nuanced doctrinal disputes and political power struggles. For some reason at this time in the middle of the 16th century, the process of edict and appeal resulted in unprecedented agreements defined in two watershed documents that came to be identified by the locations of Puy and Cavour.

Heretofore, the two major regions of the Vaudois Valley, the Pellice (Piedmont-Savoyard) and the Pragela (Dauphine-French), though united religiously and in many ways confederate, had not always acted in concert militarily or diplomatically. Confronted with a renewed and persistent invasion of their territories by overwhelming French and Savoyard forces under the command of Count la Trinité, representatives of the two valleys came together in the village of Puy near Bobbio in the Pellice Valley to formally unite their defensive efforts. In the dead of winter, while most military activities were in repose, on 21 January 1561, they achieved a landmark agreement that came to be known as the *Covenant of Puy*. Wylie quotes it in full:

> In the name of the Vaudois churches of the Alps, of Dauphine and Piedmont, which have ever been united, and of which we are the representatives, we here promise, our hands upon our Bibles, and in the presence of God, that all our valleys will courageously sustain each other in matters of religion, without prejudice due to their legitimate superiors.
>
> We promise to maintain the Bible, whole and without admixture, according to the usage of the true apostolic church persevering in this holy religion, though it be at the peril of our life, in order that we may transmit it to our children, intact and pure, as we received it from our fathers.
>
> We promise aid and succor to our persecuted brothers, not regarding our individual interests, but in the common cause; and not relying upon man, but upon God.[291]

The 1561 Covenant of Puy was an affirmation of faith and a mutual commitment that unified the Vaudois and became a rallying point for the faithful.

> The covenant was to be a living inspiration across years, since for the Waldensians faith had meant and would mean holding fast to the gospel which is discovered and lived in the context

of solidarity and in the concreteness of history. Their church would not be rigorously organized as in Geneva, nor still would it be a political confessional movement as with the Huguenots. The Waldensian church would be a free union of congregations, bound together by a common commitment to solidarity. No wonder that from 1561 on, the covenant was to be reaffirmed over and over again.[292]

This agreement marked a turning point in the conflict, for from that moment the Vaudois forces began to prevail, until by mid-year the enemy forces had been driven from the valleys. The ducal and French representatives who then came to the armistice table at Cavour, did so with a renewed respect and diminished expectations. The resulting document, drawn up at Cavour on June 5, 1561, tendered the duke's pardon, absolved the defenders from all acts committed during the war, and forgave damages to ducal property. More importantly, the Cavour document acknowledged Vaudois rights and authorized Vaudois worship.[293] The Edict of Cavour defined the whole Alpine Reformed area as an autonomous and responsible unit in which the practice of religion was to be tolerated without government interference. For the first time a community of country people effectively resisted the absolute power of their sovereign and succeeded in establishing the people's right to reform their church. Tourn writes:

This strange parchment spelled out for the first time in European religious history the fact that subjects who practiced a religion different from that of the ruling power possessed officially recognized rights. Up to this time the rule had always been that the religion of the prince determined the religion of his subjects. Even more important was the fact that a Catholic prince tolerated 'heresy' and renounced the destruction of it.[294]

This document was more than just another agreement hammered out between the leadership and the aggrieved, but rather it constituted a landmark event with enormous portent for the Vaudois and for all future religionists. It was a significant milestone in the onward march of human freedom, orchestrated by an unsophisticated minor religious group and dearly purchased through centuries of tragic suffering.

Whereas this agreement provided unprecedented freedom of religion, it also formed a peculiar, restricted enclave, a kind of religious ghetto. Religious freedom prevailed within the specified zone, but anyone departing, not just emigrating but simply traveling outside the boundaries, was subject to arrest and punishment as a heretic. Flawed though it was, this arrangement was to serve the Vaudois reasonably well for the next 100 years.

This hundred-year period of relative peace (roughly 1560-1660) was the calm before an approaching storm, during which a strange new climate evolved preparatory to a new level of repression and massacre that awaited the Vaudois at the midpoint of the 17th century. Intolerance of the reformed religion was on the rise in the France of Louis XIII and Louis XIV as France superseded Spain as the dominant power of Europe. A widowed sister of the French King controlled the ducal throne of Savoy as regent. A number of militant Catholics, driven out of Ireland by a Protestant wave of resurgence under Oliver Cromwell, had joined ranks with the French as mercenaries. Years of bloodshed and destruction had driven back the Protestant wave in much of the continent, yet somehow the religious wars of Europe had left unscathed a small, annoying Protestant Alpine group, right under the noses of their Catholic majesties. The Vaudois enclave at the time was the only surviving outpost of Protestantism imbedded within a predominantly Catholic neighborhood - only about 18,000 of them. How hard could it be to wipe them out altogether? Eventually the powers of western Europe, both secular and religious, turned to the task with a will.

Of all the atrocities perpetrated against the Vaudois over the centuries, perhaps none exceeded in intensity and outrage the massacre known as the Piedmont Easter or the Bloody Pascha of 1655. The pretext leading to the hostilities was economic, and may be traced back to the restrictive religious zone established a hundred years earlier. Over the ensuing years, the Vaudois had found it increasingly difficult to maintain themselves in their small, relatively infertile domain, and so had expanded beyond the agreed-upon borders. Their breaking out was perceived as an attempt to expand the faith and to threaten the surrounding Catholics. Tensions among neighbors mounted and incidents occurred. Questions of who destroyed the Vaudois temple and who burned down the Catholic monastery soon led to armed conflict. The tried and true Vaudois strategy of confrontation, conciliation, pleading and resistance was invoked as of old, but the new forces now in play precluded its success. The overwhelming, unchecked power of the state was brought to bear with fearful consequences.

In 1655, under the command of the Marquis of Pianezza, a ducal force of 4000 (some say 15,000[295]) soldiers and assorted militias including French troops and Irish mercenaries:

> were rallied for a renewed crusade against the Waldensians. The latter sent delegations and representatives to affirm their submission. In April Pianezza ordered that the Waldensians house his troops, which amounted to forcing them to offer hospitality to those who came to pillage them. The Waldensians eventually had to accept. The military occupation of the villages rapidly degenerated into a massacre which would appear to have been far from spontaneous. It became known as the Piedmontese Easter: brutality, sadism, torture, slaughter and pillaging were widespread. Those who got away took to the hills; the soldiers, weighed down with booty, returned to the plains.[296]

Leger writes that the troops were lodged by subterfuge, claiming that a truce had been established and their intent peaceful. Then after a few days of peaceful coexistence, at 4:00 AM on Easter morning, by pre-arrangement, the occupying troops rose against their hosts and perpetrated a general massacre.

In prior centuries the ultimate refuge of the valleys had been repeatedly established at Pra del Tor, a natural fortress and a place of safe resort. On Bloody Pascha, April 24, 1655, even this citadel "was taken by assault, reduced to rubble and plundered. Within a few days the same fate befell Villar and Bobbio. Similar ghastly scenes were multiplied throughout the Valleys – unarmed people were tortured sadistically and massacred; the terror-stricken fled for their lives."[297] Some say that 1700 Vaudois, men, women and children, were massacred on that fateful day.

Accounts of the massacre of the Vaudois perpetrated in the crucial year of 1655 are mainly based on the eyewitness accounts of the historian Leger and the report of Oliver Cromwell's personal emissary, Samuel Morland. They provide a lengthy and detailed record of unmentionable atrocities perpetrated by the assaulting forces. Morland's descriptions and sketches describing the Bloody Pasha massacre and subsequent encounters are explicit and detailed, with many specific references and eyewitness attributions. They are excruciatingly painful to consider, and if devoid of exaggeration, constitute an uncommon level of cruelty and depravity in human history. Nowhere does one see quantitative information of this attempt at genocide, leaving the extent and magnitude of the destruction an open question.

The reports of this massacre are filled with horror unspeakable, the superlatives piled upon one another, until one can hardly fathom the depravity of the perpetrators. In their despair the Vaudois penned a poignant message to the world.

> Our tears are no longer water, they are blood; they do not merely obscure our sight, they choke our hearts. Our hands tremble and our hearts ache by the many blows we have received. We cannot frame an epistle answerable to the intent of our hearts and the strangeness of our desolations. We pray you excuse us, and to discern amid our groans, the meaning of what we fain would utter.[298]

In all of their centuries of endurance and survival, this was perhaps the most perilous, for the pogroms instituted among them in this era left the Vaudois teetering on the edge of absolute extermination. After the failure of their tried-and-true strategy of appeasement and mitigation, and the futility of pitched battles against overwhelming forces, the Vaudois found themselves in extremity. As their organized society was gutted and armed resistance destroyed, the Vaudois turned to the time-honored alternative of guerilla warfare. Into this opportune atmosphere stepped an unlikely guerilla leader, one Joshua Janavel of Rora, his second in command, Barthelemi Jahier of Pramollo, and the minister-historian, Jean Leger.

Within a month of the Bloody Pascha of 1655, the ducal troops had conquered all of the valleys except the small community of Rora, situated high in the mountains just south of Torre Pellice. The effective resistance of a small guerilla band under Janavel and Jahier preserved the village of Rora for several days until the masses of Pianezza's troops (on the order of 10,000 men) could be assembled to finally overcome the defenders and lay waste the village. Having captured the wife and children of Janavel

> Pianezza wrote to the hero of Rora, offering him his own life and that of his wife and daughters if he renounced his heresy, but threatening him, on the contrary if he persisted in it, with the loss of his head and that his family would be burned to death. Janavel replied, "that there were no torments so cruel, nor death so barbarous, which he could not prefer to abjuration. That if the marquis made his wife and daughters pass through the fire, the flames could only consume their poor bodies; that as for their souls, he commended them to God, trusting them in His hands equally with his own, in case it were His pleasure that he should fall into the hands of the executioners."[299]

The fate of Janavel's family in this gruesome standoff has not been recorded, but this small band, beginning with as few as six warriors, but growing in time to near 500, maintained a constant running battle with the invading forces in the months ahead and became an essential element in preventing the total annihilation of the Vaudois as a religious group.

The guerilla leaders Janavel and Jahier grew a formidable force to carry on the conflict. Wylie reports:

> The massacre had reduced the Vaudois race to all but utter extermination, and 500 men were all the two leaders could collect around their standards. The army opposed to them, and at this time in their valleys, was from 15,000 to 20,000 strong, consisted of trained and picked soldiers. Nothing but an impulse from the God of battles could have moved these two men with such a handful, to take the field against such odds. To the eye of a common hero all would have seemed lost; but the courage of these two Christian warriors was based on faith. They believed that God would not permit his cause to perish, or the lamp of the valleys to be extinguished; and few though they were, they knew that God was able by their humble instrumentality to save their country and church. In this faith they unsheathed the sword; and so valiantly did they wield it that soon that sword became the terror of the Piedmontese armies.

Nothing could withstand the fury of their attack. Post after post and village after village were wrested from the Piedmontese troops. Soon the enemy was driven from the upper valleys. The war now passed down into the plain of Piedmont, and there it was waged with the same heroism and the same success. They besieged and took several towns, they fought not a few pitched battles; and in those actions they were nearly always victorious, though opposed by more than ten times their number. Their success could hardly be credited had it not been recorded by historians whose veracity is above suspicion, and the accuracy of whose statements as attested by eye-witnesses. Not infrequently did it happen at the close of a day's fighting that 1400 Piedmontese dead covered the field of battle, while not more than six or seven of the Waldenses had fallen. Such success might well be termed miraculous; and not only did it appear so to the Vaudois themselves, but even to their foes, who could not refrain from expressing their conviction "that surely God was on the side of the Barbets."[300]

The efforts of the military leaders were supplemented by the no less effective services of Leger, the pastor-propagandist. Leger's vivid accounts of atrocities committed against the Vaudois, amplified and promulgated by William Morland, Oliver Cromwell's ambassador to the Vaudois, soon generated outrage throughout the Protestant countries of Europe. Encouragement, supporting funds and weapons began to arrive, empowering the guerilla forces and prolonging the resistance. Envoys, plenipotentiaries and messages of protest accumulated at the doors of the ducal throne in Turin and the palaces of Versailles. The influence of Oliver Cromwell, Lord Protector of England, as enhanced by the sovereigns of Sweden, The Dutch States General and the Evangelical cantons of the Swiss, was instrumental in averting the total annihilation threatened by the tidal wave that was engulfing the Vaudois.

The result was yet another treaty, which put a temporary end to military hostilities and ostensibly "confirmed the ancient franchise, the prerogatives and privileges granted and settled in times past."[301] The uncertainty and chaos of guerilla warfare had left the people and the countryside exhausted. Janavel's lieutenant, Jahier, was killed and with a price on their heads, Janavel and Leger accepted banishment for life to ensure the peace. Taking refuge in the friendly Swiss Republic, Janavel wrote a manual of military tactics[302] to be of valuable future use to the Vaudois, and Leger wrote the first definitive history of his people.[303]

Of this latest treaty, Wylie writes:

> When the treaty of 1655 was published, it was found to contain two clauses that astonished the Protestant world. In the preamble the Vaudois

were styled rebels, whom it had pleased their prince graciously to receive back into favour; and in the body of the deed was an article, which no one recollected to have heard mentioned during the negotiations, empowering the French to construct a fort above La Torre. This looked like a preparation for renewing the war. By this treaty the Protestant States were outwitted; their ambassadors were duped; and the poor Vaudois were left as much as ever in the power of the Duke of Savoy and of the Council for the Propagation of the Faith and the Extirpation of Heretics.[304]

Morland wrote of this treaty and its aftermath:

In the meantime, this treaty being published to the world and more thoroughly examined by wise and sober men was found to be no other than a leper arrayed in rich clothing and gay attire. A treaty was full of grievances as poor Lazarus of sores. The greatest part of the articles directly clashing with the peoples' interest and ancient privileges, and the remainder made up of expressions that look as many ways as the points of the mariner's compass. In sum it cannot be more fittly compared to anything than to Ezekiel's roll, which though it were sweet as honey in the poor people's mouths, yet there was written within nothing but lamentation and mourning and woe: indeed, the Swiss ambassadors had no sooner turned their backs and departed towards their own country, but a numberless number of grievances and difficulties, almost inexpressible, like so many hornets out of a rotten or hollow tree, and from that very day to this have never ceased stinging the people to death. [305]

4. IN CONCLUSION.

As we have seen, the two hundred survival years following the time of Luther were for the Vaudois a period of euphoria with the discovery that they were not alone, followed by a period of relative peace but finally punctuated by unprecedented persecution, cutting off their outliers, decimating their ranks and rendering them an endangered species. Embracing their tardy Protestant brethren, heeding their urgings and emerging from their self-imposed concealment was a near-fatal mistake, for as the 17th century drew to its close, the Vaudois stood at the brink of extinction.

Morland, on his departure from the valleys in 1658 gave this mournful assessment of the conditions and prophetic view of the prospects of the Vaudois as the dust settled on the infamous massacre of 1655.

> It is my unhappiness that I am forced to leave them where I found them. To this very day they labor under most heavy burdens . . . the enemies

of truth plough and make long furrows upon
their backs . . . by forbidding them all manner
of traffique and commerce for their sustenance
. . . by robbing them of their goods and estates
. . . by driving them in a most savage manner
from their ancient houses and habitations . . . by
forcing them to sell their birthright for a mess of
pottage . . . by banishing their ministers . . . by
ravishing their women and maidens . . . by murthering many innocent souls as they pass along
the highways about their private occasions . . .
by cruel mockings and revilings . . . by continual
menacings and threats. Their miseries are more
sad and grievous than words can express; and
they are in a manner of dying while they yet live.
No grapes in their vineyards, no cattle in their
fields, no herds in their stalls, no corn in their
garners, no meal in their barrel, no oyl in their
cruse. The stock which was gathered for them
by the good people of this and other nations
wasting apace, and when it is once spent, they
must inevitably perish, except God who turns
the hearts of the princes as the rivers of water,
be graciously pleased to incline the hearts of
their sovereign prince to take pity on his poor,
harmless and faithful subjects.[306]

One wonders how during this survival period the Vaudois viewed themselves with respect to the world in which they lived. Precarious and uncertain don't begin to describe their situation, subject as they were to capricious and unpredictable forces and movements far beyond their ken, let alone their control. Perhaps with this perspective in mind, sometime in the early 17th century, the Vaudois adopted, as the symbol of their faith, the candlestick surrounded by seven stars, with the Latin phrase – *lux lucet in tenebris* (Into the Darkness, Light). The seven stars are thought to be symbolic of the seven churches addressed by St. John's Book of Revelation. Perhaps this symbol was a crying out against the darkness, a plea for help, a distress signal to friendly neighbors or to a greater power. Or, more likely it was a declaration of faith and determination, a message that, no matter the intensity of the persecution, the power of the opposition, or the magnitude of the darkness, "We are still here, still maintaining the sacred flame."

CHAPTER IV.
Expulsion and Return (1686-1690 AD)

"The little flock of the Waldenses of Piedmont, from the first moment it came into notoriety, has been indestructible and inseparable; like the flaming bush, it has burned, but it has not been consumed; and there it remains to this day in the very valleys where it first made its appearance."[307]

'The hammers are broken, the anvil remains."

Above the small Italian town of Torre Pellice not far from the border with France, stands a modest monument at a place called Sibaud. There on special occasions, for centuries, remnants of a small Protestant group have assembled to renew the covenant of their ancestors to keep their faith pristine and secure. Sibaud bears witness of countless persecutions together with acts of transcendent bravery. Today the monument stands in silent testimony of the remarkable Protestant heritage of the Waldenses or the Vaudois.[308]

As with Luther, the Vaudois survived the overwhelming power of the Roman church during those turbulent centuries "in consequence of the favour of their princes and feudal lords,"[309] one of whom, the Duke of Savoy, confessed in 1602, "We are obliged to tolerate heresy in the valleys of our realm."[310] Their extent in earlier times is not verifiable, but it is clear that prior to the 17th century, there were several hundred thousand of the Vaudois faithful ranging from the Baltic Sea to the tip of Italy's boot, and from Poland to Brittany.[28] Whatever their earlier numbers, the Vaudois were eventually worn down by the persecutions of kings and priests to fewer than 50,000[311] in the latter half of the 17th century, roughly 17,000 of whom were confined largely to their ancient homeland. These Vaudois valleys formed a triangular section in the Cottian Alps on the border of modern-day Italy and France, covering approximately 150 square miles, roughly the size of the District of Columbia.

As the 17th century faded into history, fate tipped up this seemingly insignificant dustpan of people and swept every one of them into oblivion. Then suddenly the world of the Vaudois righted itself yet again. Following a three-year hiatus, a ragged remnant of this beleaguered people returned in the face of overwhelming opposition and in another inexpli-

---

28 Numbers are hard to verify. Moreland (215) estimates the population of the valleys in 1675 at 50,000, but cites Morel as identifying 800,000 professing the Waldensian faith in 1530.

cable turning of the great wheel of fate, were permitted to reestablish themselves in their ancient homeland.

1. RELIGIOUS-POLITICAL DEVELOPMENTS.

In the hundred years after Luther's revolution, approximately 25% of the estimated 80,000,000 people living in Western Europe had become Protestant, of which 65%, or 13,000,000 espoused the Confession of Augsburg, that is, the Lutheran persuasion. The balance of 7,000,000 Protestants included the Anabaptists, Calvinists, Separatists, Methodists, Huguenots, Anglicans and the Vaudois. By mid-17th century the religious wars of Europe were almost over. A measure of religious freedom had been established by three landmark documents: the Peace of Augsburg (1555), the Edict of Nantes (1598) and the Peace of Westfalia (1648). Protestants and Catholics were permitted a limited exercise of religious freedom though rulers most often resorted to the principle of *curius region eius religio*, that is, the religion of the ruler is made obligatory upon his subjects.[312]

Peace of Augsburg. In the aftermath of the Peasants War and other central European religious conflicts, in 1555, the princes and electors of Germany extracted from the emperor the "Peace of Augsburg." This treaty encompassed the commitment that throughout the Holy Roman Empire "those espousing the Augsburg Confession [i.e. Lutherans] shall be left to the free and untrammeled enjoyment of their religion, ceremonies, appointment of ministers. Likewise

[they] shall let all who cling to the old religion live in absolute peace and in the enjoyment of all their estates, rights, and privileges. However, all such as do not belong to the two above named religions shall not be included in the present peace but be totally excluded from it."[313] This agreement set the stage for the prolonged peaceful coexistence of the Austrian (Catholic) and Prussian (Protestant) kingdoms within the loose confederation of the Holy Roman Empire.

Edict of Nantes. What then of the other Protestant movements? Their relief began when Henry IV ascended the throne of France in 1589, the first of the Bourbon dynasty. Henry was a Protestant, a Huguenot, a religious conviction he was required to abjure to ascend and retain the throne. The Huguenots were Calvinist in origin and had become quite fashionable, attaining considerable popularity among the skilled artisans and nobility of France. Once having consolidated his power, Henry didn't forget his old friends. He issued the Edict of Nantes, defining a measure of restricted religious tolerance within the French kingdom for the so-called reformed religion (i.e. the Huguenots):

> [We do] herewith permit, those of the said religion called Reformed to live and abide in all the cities and places of this our kingdom and countries of our sway, without being annoyed, molested, or compelled to do anything in the matter of religion contrary to their consciences.

He then broached a particularly outrageous practice that had long been part of the doctrine of persecution: the abduction of children.

> We also forbid all our subjects, of whatever quality and condition, from carrying off by force or persuasion, against the will of their parents, the children of the said religion, in order to cause them to be baptized or confirmed in the Catholic Church.[314]

Peace of Westfalia. The Thirty-Years War in the first half of the 17th century delivered similar concessions to other Protestant groups in Bohemia, the Netherlands and parts of the German nations. At the war's conclusion, representatives of Ferdinand III (Holy Roman Emperor) and Louis XIV (King of France), meeting in Muenster, Germany on October 24, 1648 signed the Peace of Westfalia. "His Most Serene and most Puissant Prince and Lord, Emperor of the Holy Roman Empire joined his seal and signature together with that of his Most Serene and Most Puissant Prince and most Christian King of France" and thus concluded a war fought principally by their fathers of the same names (minus I) and left for them to resolve.

The Peace of Westfalia extended religious toleration throughout all of western Europe excepting the Iberian and Italian peninsulas, establishing "Liberty of the Exercise of Religion in the same manner as the abovesaid Agreement [Peace of Augsburg] has been made also with those call'd the Reformed, in the same manner, as in the words of the abovesaid."[315] The 17th century legal terminology seems to have been rendered particularly awkward in this document because having betrayed their traditional Roman Catholic heritage by once writing the words of religious toleration, the negotiators could not bear to repeat them.

The result of four years of hard negotiations, the Peace of Westfalia was a harbinger of the European Union "the first time that a European community of sovereign states was established. And it was only possible because all of its members recognized each other as having equal legal standing, and guaranteed each other their independence [bound by an] international community of law." [316] There was a naiveté and yet a certain beauty in the final wording:

> That there shall be a Christian and Universal
> Peace, and a perpetual, true, and sincere Amity,
> between his Sacred Imperial Majesty, and his
> most Christian Majesty; as also, between all and
> each of the Allies, that this Peace and Amity be
> observ'd and cultivated with such a Sincerity
> and Zeal, that each Party shall endeavour to
> procure the Benefit, Honour and Advantage of
> the other; that thus on all sides they may see this
> Peace and Friendship flourish, by entertaining a
> good and faithful Neighbourhood . . . that no
> body, under any pretext whatsoever, shall practice any Acts of Hostility, entertain any Enmity,
> or cause any Trouble to each other . . . that they

shall not act, or permit to be acted, any wrong or injury to any whatsoever . . . and [previous] Words, Writings, and Outrageous Actions, in Violences, Hostilitys, Damages and Expences shall be entirely abolish'd [and] . . . bury'd in eternal Oblivion.[317]

These three landmark documents of religious toleration, though reluctantly granted and resentfully and oftimes indifferently enforced, nonetheless established a measure of religious freedom heretofore unknown in European lands since the time of the Caesars, and they provided the framework to overturn centuries of blind bigotry and irrational hatred. Courageous and visionary documents, these three seemed to burst upon these dark centuries as a shaft of light, bringing a measure of relief and the hope of more to come.

The French Reversal. Politically and culturally, the 17th century of Europe belonged to Louis XIV, the Sun King of France, who ruled from the age of five (1643) until his death twelve years into the next century. During this period, "France exercised almost hypnotic dominance over western Europe, in politics, in language, literature, art and much else. France was a geographically compact nation of 20,000,000 people, united under a strong central government, the strongest state in Christendom."[318]

Near the end of the 17th century, Louis XIV began to be troubled that the hegemony of his glorious Catholic reign was disturbed by the presence of 1.5 million annoying

Protestant heretics, most of them Huguenots. Among the Protestants were some Vaudois scattered over the south of France, with upwards of 4000 located in the upper portion of the Valley of Clusone, the balance of approximately 13,000 Vaudois occupying the portions of the Valleys under the Duke of Savoy. Louis was a firm Catholic believer but not an uncompromising one. He exercised an enlightened intolerance that waxed and waned throughout his reign. His official posture regarding Protestants, if it can be pinned down at all, is best expressed in his memoir and advice to his son:

> As for the great number of my subjects of the RPR (*religion pretendue reforme*) which was an evil which caused me then and still causes me today (1671) great pain, I decided right then how to behave with them. It seemed to me that those who chose to use violent remedies did not understand the nature of the problem, which must be allowed gradually to pass and die away rather than exciting it anew by strong contradictions, which are in any event useless when the disease is spread throughout the state. I thought that the best way to reduce the number of Huguenots was no longer to press them with any new rigor, and to see that the guarantees that they obtained from my predecessors were observed, but I granted them no new ones and saw to it that they be kept within the narrowest limits that justice and fairness would allow. But as for those

favors that depended on me alone, I decided to allow them none, and that through kindness rather than anger, so that they would be forced to consider of themselves, from time to time and without violence whether they had good reason to deprive themselves of the advantages which otherwise they would have shared with my other subjects."[319]

If his benign policy was designed to secure converts, by the 1680s it was a failure. The enclaves of French Protestant evangelism remained largely intact. Additionally, Huguenots had achieved a disproportionate level of involvement in the commerce and defense forces of the French nation. Such was the context in which Louis XIV did an abrupt about face.

It is puzzling to consider why the French king, after years of leniency, decided to revoke the Edict of Nantes and revert to a policy of extermination or conversion by force. Some have argued that Louis caved in to pressure from the Catholic hierarchy in general and from his Jesuit confessors in particular. It is clear that there was a persistent urging on their part as well as from the French clergy, for action to suppress the heretics. But Louis was his own man, and he had explicitly divorced the French church from Rome, declaring in articles drawn up 1663 and repeated in 1682:

> that the kings and sovereigns are independent, by God's order, from all ecclesiastical powers

in temporal matters, that they cannot be deposed, directly or indirectly, by the authority of the head of the church, and that their subjects cannot be dispensed from the submission or obedience they owe them.[320]

Louis was the most absolute of the monarchs of his time and it is not likely that pressure from Rome forced him to action. Rather, evidence suggests that Louis' lifting of the sword against the so-called reformed religionists in his realm grew out of misinformation. Louis' counselors, notably his Secretary of State for War, Louvois, advised him that the Huguenots were flocking to the Catholic standard, such that the king wrote his son, "I must have done the right things since God has granted that it result in a very real number of conversions."[321] In their Catholic zeal, his counselors had grossly inflated the conversion numbers. Louis believed them, and in a letter to Cardinal d'Estees in January 1686, "flattered himself that out of 800,000 to 900,000 Protestants, only 1200-1400 remained."[322] It wasn't the first time that a head of state was misled into an unfortunate decision through persistent misinformation from his advisors. On October 18, 1685, in the loneliness of his own chambers, King Louis XIV revoked the Edict of Nantes, since it now appeared to be obsolete, offering this justification:

> And now we perceive, with thankful acknowledgment of God's aid, that our endeavors have

attained their proposed end, inasmuch as the better and the greater part of our subjects of the said R.P.R. [so-called reformed religion] have embraced the Catholic faith. And since by this fact the execution of the Edict of Nantes and of all that has ever been ordained in favor of the said R.P.R. has been rendered nugatory, we have determined that we can do nothing better, in order wholly to obliterate the memory of the troubles, the confusion, and the evils which the progress of this false religion has caused in this kingdom, than entirely to revoke the said Edict of Nantes . . . as well as all that has since been done in favor of the said religion.[323]

The Revocation of the Edict of Nantes reversed the benign French policy of 100 years toward Protestants, declaring:

> Be it known that . . . the edict given at Nantes in April, 1598, in its whole extent, together with all [later appended] articles . . . we declare null and void, together with all concessions . . . in favor of the said persons of the RPR[29] . . . and in consequence . . . it is our pleasure, that all the[ir] temples . . . shall be demolished with-

---

29 Pretended reformed religion

> out delay. We forbid our subjects of the RPR
> to meet any more for the exercise of the said
> religion in any place or private house, under
> any pretext whatever. As for children who may
> be born of persons of the said RPR, henceforth
> they [shall] be baptized by the parish priests.
> We enjoin parents to send them to the churches
> for that purpose, under penalty of five hundred
> livres fine . . . and thereafter the children shall be
> brought up in the Catholic religion. [324]

Nor was it enough for those of the reformed religion to simply flee the regime, for the decree forbade it:

> We repeat our most express prohibition to all
> our subjects of the said RPR., together with
> their wives and children, against leaving our
> kingdom . . . or transporting their goods and
> effects therefrom under penalty, as respects the
> men, of being sent to the galleys, and as respects
> the women, of imprisonment and confisca-
> tion.[325]

2. THE EXPULSION OF THE VAUDOIS.

Provisions of the revocation were swiftly implemented throughout the kingdom, in actions that reflected the most ill-conceived decision of the Sun King's reign. They proved disastrous for France. In the revocation's aftermath, hundreds of thousands of the Huguenots fled the country, finding generous refuge in surrounding Protestant lands. The French economy and defense forces suffered the loss of thousands of skilled citizens,[326] and western Europe, including Great Britain, the United Republic of the Netherlands, the Holy Roman Empire including the German states unitedly took up arms against the French.[327] Meanwhile, the religious atmosphere was about to change in the neighboring Duchy of Savoy.

The ancient ruling House of Savoy had begun with Humbert I, White Hands,[30] who became the Count of Savoy in 1032 AD. The Savoyard State, home to most of the Vaudois, was neighbor to France extending west as far as Chambery and south to include the Mediterranean port of Nice. On the southern border lay the republic of Genoa as far as Monaco. On the north and east, Savoy bordered the Spanish principality of Milan and the canton of Berne, Switzerland. Over the years the Savoyard domains alternately stretched and shrank with the fortunes of its rulers, as they progressed from counts to dukes to kings, culminating in the elevation of Victor Emmanuel I as king of Italy when that nation was formed in 1861. The only constant in its history was its strategic importance, lying as it did on both sides of the French and Italian Alps guarding the intersection of power in 17th century Europe. It lay at the crossroads where the Kingdom of France, the Holy Roman

---

30 "White Hands may have had reference to his generosity or a textual mistranslation of an early Latin record which actually refers to the walls of his castle, not his hands, as white." (Regalis, Dynastic and Royal History)

Empire and the Roman Catholic Church came together. Additionally, the Savoyards traditionally were able to put a sizable and well-equipped professional army in the field, giving the Duke of Savoy a measure of power and influence well beyond that warranted by the size of his domains.

With the revocation of the Edict of Nantes, Louis XIV urged his neighbor to the east, with whom he shared dominion over the Vaudois valleys, to adopt a policy similar to his own, namely extermination of the Protestants within their realms. To that end, during the latter half of the year 1685, Louis applied considerable pressure to Victor Amadeus II, the Duke of Savoy, sending through his ambassador, Marquis D'Arcy, numerous official, detailed requests. The surprised duke, who considered the Vaudois his loyal subjects and an integral part of his armed forces, was not easily persuaded. He repeatedly delayed his responses and declined to act. The King offered a division or two of French soldiers to join the Savoyard armies in effecting the extermination. Victor Amadeus again demurred. Through his ambassadors, the king forcefully declared

> You must strongly represent to him that all gentle treatment of such a set of people will only serve to render them more obstinate. The only course for him is, by one stroke, to take from them all favours and privileges which have been granted to them by his predecessors, to ordain the demolition of their places of worship, to prohibit them from the exercise of their reli-

gion, and at the same time to lodge his troops with the most obstinate of them. And by this firmness of conduct he will succeed so much the more easily, that the wretches will hope for no assistance, and that even if they should be able to resist the forces of the duke, they will reflect that he will always be supported by mine in the execution of his design.[328]

Failing in all else, the king ultimately made the duke an offer he couldn't refuse: if the Duchy of Savoy wasn't equal to the task, the French forces would come to help and afterward stay on as an occupying force. This threat got the duke's attention, and brought him in line with the objectives of Louis XIV. In response he signed the ducal edict of January 31, 1686.

Monastier informs us that when unexpectedly the duke caved in, "all at once the alarming words of the edict resounded, ordaining the complete cessation of every religious service in the duke's domains except the Romish, under pain of death and the confiscation of property; the demolition of temples; the banishment of ministers and schoolmasters, and in the future the baptism of all the children by the popish priests, who were to educate them in the Romish religion."[329] In addition, the edict contained an attempt to buy off the Vaudois ministers by offering them and their widows after them an increased salary if they would abjure.

The Vaudois, though no strangers to the whims and caprice of their princes, yet were surprised to find themselves suddenly subject to an edict more severe and immediate than ever before imposed upon their forefathers. They appealed to the duke to reconsider, to no avail. Word of their plight spread to their Protestant neighbors. The Dutch, the English, the Germans, but most prominently the Swiss, in the early months of 1686 sought to intercede on behalf of the Vaudois. They appealed to the duke's humanity, reminded him of the ancient privileges granted the Vaudois by his predecessors, made reference to the Vaudois' history as model subjects and consistent military supporters. "But neither the reasoning of the ambassadors, nor their own pressing solicitations, nor the letters of intercession from many other Protestant princes, could avail anything with the court of Turin."[330] It soon became clear that the duke and his agents had already exhausted these issues in their intercourse with the French king.[331]

As the French and Savoyard armies gathered to enforce the edict, those Vaudois who would not deny their ancient faith nor abandon their homeland, prepared for battle. Some estimate that a combined force of 25,000 troops gathered against the Vaudois, though these numbers may have been inflated. However, Muston reports that 2586 Savoyard soldiers took the field, joined by a "number of regiments of cavalry and dragoons [and] seven or eight battalions of infantry [from the French]," which could easily have totaled 20,000- 25,000 men at arms, mostly French.[332]

There were an estimated 17,000 Vaudois in the valleys of Piedmont as the Duke and his French allies began the religious purge of 1686, of which an estimated 2500-3000 were men under arms. First it was decreed that all Vaudois who had resided in the valleys less than forty years were to be immediately expelled. Thus all who had entered the valleys since the previous purge and massacre in 1655, about 3000, departed.[333] These first refugees were routed through Switzerland and found new homes in Germanic lands, principally in the kingdom of Württemberg.

As the armed conflict commenced, the duke sought to avoid bloodshed by issuing another edict, that of April 9, 1686, declaring amnesty for the belligerents provided they would immediately lay down their arms, return to their homes, abide by the previous edict, demolish their places of worship with their own hands, and pay for the expenses thus far incurred by those seeking their extermination. In addition, those who wished to depart the realm were permitted to do so, carrying their goods with them and engaging agents to sell their remaining possessions within three months after their departure. "By this act, which put an end to all ulterior negotiations, since it settled beforehand all the points under discussion, nothing was left to the Vaudois, but to choose between entire submission to the absolute and arbitrary will of their sovereign, and an exile encompassed with dangers, snares and perplexities."[334]

The Vaudois vacillated in uncertainty; some wanting to fight, others to submit. After much consultation, and contrary to the united counsel of their ecclesiastical leaders and the Swiss intermediaries, the delegates assembled from each of the Vaudois communes meeting in solemn assembly at Rocheplate on the 19th of April, bound themselves and their people, to " defend their country and their religion unto death, as their fathers had done."[335]

Meanwhile, the French and Savoyard allied forces marched into the Vaudois valleys and engaged the Vaudois in battle. Outnumbered ten to one, the 2500 Vaudois patriot soldiers

> had made in each of their valleys some entrenchments of turf and rough stones. If they had concentrated their forces instead of scattering them; if they had abandoned their advance posts, to retire into the retreats of the mountains; above all, if they had been of one mind as to the course to be pursued; if they had had at their head experienced men, of courage and influence; if at least, they had not numbered among their ranks the irresolute, the cowardly and probably the treacherous, the issue would have been different; but in the actual state of things it could not be otherwise than disastrous."[336]

Though, by modern standards, the weapons were relatively primitive, warfare in the 17th century was as always, brutal and highly destructive business. Both France and the Duchy of Savoy had only recently established standing uniformed armies. These consisted of roughly one third cavalry and dragoons (soldiers who traveled on horseback but fought on foot) and two-thirds infantry. Native soldiers were usually supplemented with a substantial contingent of mercenaries (troops for hire), often to as much as one half the complement. The typical infantryman was equipped with sword and musket and perhaps bayonet and very likely no personal armor. The soldiers of the best equipped armies would have flint-lock muskets with socket bayonets. Those less fortunate carried the cumbersome and unreliable match-lock muskets with (if they were lucky) a plug bayonet, which, once fixed to the musket barrel, rendered it unable to be fired again, bayonets having recently replaced the pike as the preferred weapon for infantry combating cavalry.

Financing an army was a huge problem for most nation-states of the period. Hence most didn't pay their soldiers, but rather employed the concept of "'war paying for war,' implying depredation, contribution and despoliation of agriculture."[337] Boeri comments on

> the brutality of the armies (especially French and Imperials) who wasted the country and showed no mercy for the ordinary people and peasants. Small villages and towns were often burnt to ashes, after being pillaged, the fields and farms wasted, Any act of resistance or a slow obedience to impositions of military authorities were brutally punished. All this exasperated the country folk and contributed to make them ready and eager to attack the enemies as the chance arose. Often the French executed to the last man the small garrisons of

villages or small forts; in many instances they were repaid with the same reward when they had to surrender in their turn.[338]

Bernier also affirms that "Armies in the 17th century were almost as devastating as the worst natural catastrophe; looting, arson, rape, murder - these usual accompaniments of all military operations left the countryside ravaged and deserted."[339] Even so, "a soldier's life was not unattractive. Battles were infrequent; there was the prospect of loot and plunder, whilst living conditions were no worse than those endured by civilians. The greatest danger was disease, particularly prevalent in crowded and unsanitary camps."[340]

Because of the inaccuracy of weapons, soldiers fought at hideously close quarters and battles devolved into hand-to-hand struggles. Unlike modern armies where independence and skill are highly valued, "a good soldier of the 17th century was a solid and reliable member of a close-knit team who held his place in the formation without flinching. Here was no requirement or scope for individual heroism or initiative."[341]

Armies of the period seldom engaged in face-to-face, open field battles. Most engagements involved one army laying siege and assaulting the fortifications of the opposing force. Hence, armies were accompanied by a siege train consisting of cannon of various sizes and a company of grenadiers, trained in attacking fortifications with hand-held grenades and light, mobile cannon.

Once a breach of fortifications was established permitting the passage of infantry, Childs reports:

> According to the unwritten but widely accepted customs of war, at that point the [garrison commander] could sue for honorable terms, and be assured of receiving fair and favorable treatment. However, should the besieged forces continue the fight and lose, the invading army enjoyed the historic right to put the garrison to the sword and plunder the town for three days, but such a conclusion was rare. Normally, once [the fortification was breached] it was accepted that the game was over and the garrison troops were allowed to surrender on honourable terms in recognition of the fact that they had not caused the attackers unnecessary bloodshed and expense by resisting the inevitable. Prisoners of war were expensive embarrassments, so garrisons were usually paroled and allowed to march to a specified destination.[342]

In this instance, as the invading forces moved against them, various Vaudois groups engaged the enemy in battle from fortified positions, initially with considerable success. However as the overwhelming force of invasion became apparent, a common theme repeated itself in hamlet after hamlet, in valley after valley, through the summer and fall of 1686. French or Savoyard troops advanced and engaged the Vaudois defenders in battle, always with a significant numerical advantage. At length, as the situation grew hopeless, the defending Vaudois garrison raised the flag of truce.

At this point the French and Savoyard forces then enjoined the Vaudois to "lay down your arms immediately, and trust yourself to the clemency of his royal highness. On these conditions be assured that he will show you favor, and that you shall not be injured, either in your own person or in that of your wives and children."[343] On this promise, each group of Vaudois insurgents, recognizing their hopeless situation, surrendered their arms and the opposing armies took them prisoner and occupied their entrenchments.

For the Vaudois, this regrettable but seemingly harmless outcome proved to be an unprecedented catastrophe. Instead of being conducted safely to the duke for the act of submission, families were separated and escorted to prison. In this manner, "Twelve to fourteen thousand persons, men, women and children, were, in the course of a few days, dragged from their native soil, distributed in 13 or 14 fortresses, where they endured a thousand evils. About 2000 children, abducted from their parents, were at the same time dispersed throughout Piedmont among the papists."[344] The exact numbers are impossible to verify. Muston reports 13,596 imprisoned and 396 children abducted.[345]

Except for a small guerilla force remaining in the mountains (fewer than a hundred men), the duke and the king had at last succeeded in wholly eradicating the Vaudois from their valleys.

> From the gardens of the palace of Lucerna,
> whither he had come to enjoy the victory, Victor
> Amadeus II could behold the ravages made by
> his triumphant army. The fields that lay before
> his eyes were deserted, the hamlets on the sides
> of the mountains, the smiling villages, with their
> green bowers and rich orchards, no longer con-
> tains one of their ancient inhabitants; the valleys
> no longer resounded to the bleatings of flocks,
> and the voices of the shepherds; the fields the
> meadows, the vineyards, the alpine pasturelands,
> scenes once so beautiful, all these districts, so
> happy in the previous spring, were reduced to
> one vast solitude, dreary as the wildest rocks.[346]

Their property was confiscated by the regal officers and later offered for sale. "The Vaudois who had become Catholics were permitted to remain for a few months longer on their lands, in order to dispose of them as they best could, after which they were transferred to the Piedmont province of Verceil."[347] By November even those making up the guerilla force, acknowledging the hopelessness of their situation, were given passports and persuaded to withdraw to Switzerland.

Burnett describes the expulsion of the Vaudois from Savoy as a scandalous affair for the court of Turin:

> All the court were ashamed of the matter; and took pains with strangers to convince them that the duke was, with great difficulty, forced into it - that he was long pressed by repeated entreaties, from the court of France – that he excused himself from complying therewith, representing to the court of France the constant fidelity of the Waldenses . . . and their great industry, so that they were the most profitable subjects the duke had, and that the body of men which they had given his father in the last war with Genoa, had done great service for it and saved the whole army. But the duke was not only pressed to extirpate the heretics from these valleys, but was also threatened that if he did not do it the king would send his own troops to extirpate the heresy.[348]

What was the fate of the approximately 14,000 imprisoned men, women and children? Of those captured by the French, the able-bodied men to the number of 500 were consigned for life to the galleys at Marseille. For eight months the remainder languished in prisons where conditions were overcrowded and barely sufficient for survival. Swiss emissaries were busy throughout the period, seeking their liberation. Some claim that as many as 11,000 perished in prison.[349] Evidence suggests that though hundreds died, others abjured and were released. Based on Turin State Archives, Muston reports that of 1973 Vaudois families residing in the valleys in 1686, 424 (2226 individuals) became Catholic, that is 21%.[350] Those who thought to advance their fate by changing religion were instead exiled from the valleys to an undesirable clime where they were further ostracized and generally less-favorably treated by their enemies than those who remained true.[351]

In the 17th century, European prisons were not used for punishment, but rather as holding pens to retain and monitor undesirables. They often consisted of rooms or holes in the foundations of local fortifications, cellars under halls, or subterranean chambers, and were usually regulated by unpaid, local authorities who were expected to earn their livelihood by charging prisoners and visitors for services and supplies. Rather than prolonged incarceration, convicted criminals were punished by fines, enslavement, whipping, the pillory or the gallows, often followed by dismemberment. Prison populations consisted of those awaiting trial or sentencing, debtors, political prisoners and those confined for safekeeping at the behest of their families.

> On entering the [typical prison] one was confronted with the noise and smell of the place. It was seldom easy to distinguish those who belonged in the prison from those who did not. Only the presence of irons differentiated the felons from the visitors or from the debtors and their families. The jail appeared to be a peculiar kind of lodging house with mixed clientele. Some of its inhabitants lived in ease [if they had

the means] and others suffered in squalor. There was little evidence of authority. Some prisoners gambled while others stood drinking at the prison tap.[352]

How is it that 14,000 prisoners could be reduced to 3-5000 in eight months? One can only imagine fourteen prisons unexpectedly receiving 1000 new prisoners - each. Food supplies and living conditions depended on the means to pay, and destitute prisoners were lucky to receive daily rations of bread and water. Disease, starvation and neglect in the heat of the summer would soon take its toll. If the numbers are accurate, the mortality rate of those unfortunate Vaudois prisoners exceeded that of any they had experienced in the preceding 400 years of persistent persecution, leaving the unavoidable conclusion that they may have fared better had they fought their oppressors to the death.

When at last on Christmas Day 1686, their freedom was proclaimed, the first contingent of the 3-5000 surviving, prison-wasted souls emerged, on condition that they depart that very day and make their way unassisted across the Alps to refuge in Switzerland. Not unaware of the dangers of such a crossing in winter, nonetheless, they made the attempt. Lawrence reports:

> In the fearful winter of 1686-7, when the Rhone was frozen to its bed and the Alps were incrusted with ice, the papists drove the surviving remnant of the prisoners over the precipitous

passes of Mont Cenis. The aged, the sick, women, children, and the wounded, and the faint, climbed with unsteady steps the chill waste of snows, and toiled onward toward Protestant Geneva. Many had scarcely clothes to cover them; all were feeble with starvation. The road was marked by the bodies of those that died by the way. The survivors staggered down the Swiss side of the mountains, pallid with hunger and cold; some perished as they approached the borders of the friendly territory; others lingered a while, and expired in the homes of the Swiss.[353]

Hundreds died en route. The balance, after unspeakable suffering, were met, rescued shall we say, by generous Swiss intermediaries stationed along the way to offer succor. Following the suffering and death of many in the first few contingents released from Piedmont prisons, and in response to the outrage of Swiss intermediaries, the duke took measures to mitigate the sufferings of those subsequently released. In the following months, the stream of released prisoners fared better. One refugee reported:

> After having made promises to us to get us to embrace Catholicism, they allowed us to depart on February 27, 1687. We set out in good order. The children and persons who could not walk were put in carts. When the road was too bad for vehicles, they gave us mules, asses and horses.

> We passed through nearly the whole of Savoy on horseback, and when the Savoyards did not do their duty, the sergeant gave them blows with his stick. Our sergeants were very good. They were careful that no harm should be done to us. [354]

Over a period of several months, the surviving "two-thousand six hundred Vaudois, men, women and children, were received within the walls of hospitable Geneva."[355]

In order to secure the release of the Vaudois from the Savoyard prisons, the representatives of the Swiss cantons had made a deal with the duke. The refugees were to be given a new home and were never to return to their homelands. Already burdened with thousands of Huguenots refugees, the Swiss handed off the Vaudois to generous Protestant princes further north in the German states of Württemberg and Brandenburg. There most of the estimated 6,000 Vaudois survivors made their homes.[31]

3. THE EXILE AND THE RETURN.

Among the refugees remained a substantial contingent who longed to return to their valleys, though they must have realized the success of such an endeavor was highly unlikely and could only be accomplished by stealth and by force.

---

31 The generosity of the German princes was partly due to the fact that their lands had been largely depopulated through the Thirty-Years War. Württemberg alone, from a population of 450,000 in 1620 had been reduced through the devastations of war and disease to 100,000 in 1640. (Childs 76-77)

The Vaudois patriots made two abortive attempts to return in 1687 and 1688. Neither was well-planned and each was intercepted and frustrated by the watchful Canton of Berne gendarmerie. A successful return awaited the convergence of favorable international circumstances, the appearance of leaders equal to the task, and sufficient encouragement, funding, weapons and ammunition.

On the international scene, Louis XIV was anxious to engage his large army (the largest ever assembled in Europe up to that time, with half a million under arms)[356] against some pliable neighbor – preferably Protestant and weak. His glance fell upon either the Dutch Republic to the north or the Lower Palatinate to the east. His choice of the Palatinate set in motion events favorable to the Vaudois' returning to the valleys.

When France began its invasion of the Lower Palatinate in 1686 precipitating the Nine-Years War, William of Orange, Stadtholder of the Dutch Republic, felt free to seek his fortune across the channel, where by virtue of his favorable marriage to Mary, heir to the English throne, he might expect a welcome. James II, Mary's father and king of England, was particularly vulnerable because of his crude attempts to re-impose the religion of Rome upon his subjects against their will. In quick time, James II fled and in effect abdicated, and William and Mary assumed the English throne, precipitating the Glorious Revolution and setting England on the path of limited, constitutional government. Their ascension returned the island kingdom to the Protestant fold and rendered it the most liberal kingdom of Europe. Thus

William of Orange, long-time champion of the Vaudois, now became King William III of England, Scotland and Ireland, their powerful and better-funded benefactor.[32]

In another unintended consequence, the sudden and unexpected presence of French armies in the Lower Palatinate (modern Rheinland-Pfalz section of Germany), sent many of the newly-settled Vaudois fleeing back in the Swiss direction. Though the electors of Brandenburg and the Lower Palatinate had welcomed hundreds of refugee Vaudois into their realms, the local inhabitants and sometimes the local Protestant clergy, were less welcoming. In some cases their opposition was based on fear of Calvinist dogma and practices, in others the drain on local resources, and in still others, harboring religious refugees of French origin was viewed as an unneeded provocation to the ruthless French invaders.[357] In addition, the Duke of Savoy, allied as he was with the French, transferred much of his occupying army (at least three divisions) from the Vaudois valleys to support French military adventures further north.[358]

The aggressive belligerence of France brought into the field an opposing allied military force called the Grand Alliance, the first effective organized European response to French aggression, consisting of Great Britain, the Dutch Republic, Spain, Denmark, Sweden, and the Holy Roman Empire.[359] These nations, if not the planets, were favorably aligned. All that remained was leadership to set the restive Vaudois patriots in motion.

---

32 William of Orange as stadtholder of Holland had championed Protestant causes throughout Europe prior to ascending the British throne.

Henri Arnaud supplied the leadership. He was born in Embrun, Dauphine, France in 1641 or 1643 to a Huguenot father, Francis Arnaud, and Margierite Gos, a daughter of the Vaudois valleys. In about 1650, Arnaud's family, fleeing persecution in France, returned to the Valley of Lucerna, where Henri was educated at La Tour and later studied theology at the college in Basel (1662 and 1668) and the Geneva Academy (1666). Before entering the ministry, he enjoyed a brief military career, serving with his mentor, the Protestant prince, William of Orange, where he rose to the rank of Colonel[360] (some say Captain). He is said to have distinguished himself especially in military tactics.[361] He served as pastor in various valley parishes (in the Valley of San Martin as early as 1670 and in the Valley of Perosa in 1678) until finally being posted to the Vaudois capital city, Le Tour, were he was pastor as the expulsion began in 1686.[362]

Suffering with his parishioners under the dragoneers,[33] in October Arnaud removed his family to the friendly Swiss cantons and returned to join his flock in resisting the duke. During the Swiss exile Arnaud revisited the Dutch Republic and England, assessed the international situation and consulted with William III from whom he secured encouragement, funding and military supplies. Said Arnaud, "Without the assistance which he gave us, the return of the Vaudois to their own country would have been impos-

---

33 As a prelude to armed conflict, 17th century sovereigns bent on the extermination of heretics in their realms, commonly followed a practice of quartered troops (dragoneers or dragoons – horsed infantry) in the homes of the heretics, where the undisciplined soldiers were free to make life as miserable as possible for their hosts.

terminates two mountain chains running in diverse directions, but which meet at this point. Two rivers, flowing from the two valleys which they form, flow into each other at the foot of this peaked rock, and thence united form the rapid river Germanesco. The rock rears itself with wood covered terraces, as it were, three or four stories high, decreasing in size upward and terminating in the form of a cone.[383]

They had assembled in the wildest of the valleys, at the Fort of the Four Teeth (les Quatre Dents) otherwise known as Balsille. This place of defense is of a kind of promontory with precipitous sides, which juts out between two steep ravines, like a tongue of the mountain, all rugged behind, with points of rock which overhand and protect one another. It cannot be reached otherwise than by ascending the face of the precipice.[384]

European armies of the 17th century generally did not engage in battle in wintertime, partly by gentlemen's agreement, but also for the more practical reason that they would be unable to obtain fodder for their horses.[385] This, together with the impressive fortress location occupied by the Vaudois at Balsille, sent the Savoyard and French forces into winter quarters in October. Winters were tougher then at the absolute coldest point of the Little Ice Age.[386] Relieved of the sible.³⁶³ By this means the Vaudois secured the friendship and largess of the Dutch Republic and Great Britain, "the leading industrial nation[s] of Europe.³⁶⁴ Upon his return, he then met with the would-be insurgents and set in motion the plan to recover the Vaudois homeland.

Throughout much of August 1689, Vaudois recruits throughout Switzerland and the German states, quietly disengaged and left their posts, bade farewell to their loved ones and made their way south to an appointed rendezvous. Silently and discreetly, in the darkness of eventide on August 16, 1689, between 800 and 1000 volunteers, assembled, armed and made ready on the northern shore of Lake Geneva. Taking passage on a variety of water craft, they rendezvoused on the southern shore ready to begin their march as an armed religious camp, an adventure which became known as the "Glorious Return."

Who actually organized and commanded the camp from the beginning is not entirely clear, although it appears that Henri Arnaud was the chief instigator and initially acted as one of three minister-leaders accompanying the camp. Interestingly, for military leadership, the Vaudois turned to proven soldier-leaders not of their people. The original choice was Captain Bourgeois of Neuchatel in Switzerland. However as he failed to appear at the rendezvous point, General Turrel, a refugee of Die, France, was given the honor as he was known to the camp as one "in whose courage and experience the people had sufficient confidence to declare him commander-in-chief."³⁶⁵ Perhaps the skill of General Turrel was needed to see them through until their own men gained experience. But in the short time of three weeks, General Turrel deserted his post, was captured by the French, broken on the wheel at Grenoble and hanged. In his stead, near the end of the campaign, Peter Odin, one of the Vaudois' own, was appointed to command with the designation of major-general. The two brethren with whom Arnaud shared his ministerial duties as the camp began, were captured by the enemy, the first, Cyrus Chyon in the first day of the march, the second Montoux sometime later. Arnaud gradually assumed the role of minister-soldier, spiritual and military leader of the corps and in time he also became its principal historian and chronicler.

What was the motivation of these desperate men? First of all, they carried with them the *Instructions* provided by the Vaudois elder statesman and hero of previous battles, Jose Janavel, which became a sort of manifesto for their trek. Janavel's *Instructions* taught:

> It is not enough to be great soldiers and have a great strategy. Rather, as the soldiers of the Vaudois Camp constituted the army of the Lord's church and as such must trust in Him for deliverance. They must seek each day for forgiveness of their sins, and let daily prayer become the lifes-rhythm of their march. They are to seek more than the recovery of their homeland, but also the restoration of the true church in its rightful home.[366]

According to the farmer-soldier Daniele Rivoire's journal[367], supplemental to their desire for the recovery of their homes, they came at the command of William of Orange and were part of a Europe-wide military action, opening up a southern front against the French king and his puppet, the duke. They viewed themselves as fighting in alliance with their Protestant brethren from England, the States General (Netherlands) and the German Protestant states. In fact, the emergence of a new armed Protestant force on the Grand Alliance side permitted the waging of war against France on five separate fronts.[368] The journal of a participating theology student, Paul Reynaudin describes the march as one of the people of God, sharing a common prayer and a common worship, much as ancient Israel led by Jehovah contended against the anti-Christ. Some viewed the unfolding events as the fulfillment of the prophecy of John as recorded in the 11th chapter of Revelation concerning two witnesses, struck down and rising again after three-and-a-half days. The camp, though mostly Vaudois, included a few Huguenots (two witnesses) who were returning to their homeland after a three-and-a-half year exile.[369]

Arnaud declared the grounds for their action as four: 1. to recover their estimated 2000 children who had been kidnapped by Savoyard authorities to be raised Catholic[370], 2. To fulfill a sacred duty as keepers of the true religion of Christ (which had existed intact since apostolic times) to restore the church to its ancient home[371], 3. to battle the beast of the Apocalypse in fulfillment of Revelation, and 4. to join the Grand Design of allied forces marshaled against the French king. [372]

They were simple mountain men, not trained soldiers, yet with a long history of armed resistance to persecution, they were not unfamiliar with armed conflict. They set out to recover their homelands, in defiance of their prince, the Duke of Savoy and his crack army, as well as the vast military might of King Louis XIV, one of the most powerful and ruthless monarchs of history. Their march would take them across French and Savoyard territory from the southern shore of Lake Geneva in a southerly direction 227 kilometers to the north-western tip of their valleys near the summit of Mt. Pis. It was rugged country, with mountains, steep valleys and rivers to cross, thinly populated in widely separated villages. They had scant chance for the success of their venture really, and yet their advantages were several: They were acquainted with hardship and deprivation in a harsh and unforgiving environment, they knew the territory and its natural defenses; they were fighting for their homeland, their families and their religion; they had the moral high ground; and they had a strategy.

Thanks to the largesse of their English and Dutch benefactors the little troop was well-equipped and adequately financed. Their strategy derived from the *Instructions* of Janavel. "When you come into the country of the enemy, seize two or three men of the place where you happen to be. These are to serve as hostages, and to open a way to places into which you will afterwards pass. You will treat them with all the tenderness possible. Abstain from all disorder, pay for all you demand, and make prayer morning and evening."³⁷³ In addition they were to have in each valley a place fixed beforehand, "a place of sure retreat, which shall be in the valley of St, Martin, La Balciglia [or Balsille]."³⁷⁴ It was to be a strategy they followed routinely and with success on their march: they approached a village, made a show of force and, if not opposed, marched through, never foraging for supplies, in the typical ruthless military fashion of the time, but purchasing what they needed. If the village resisted, they took hostages and bargained their way ahead, threatening, cajoling and persuading – always avoiding combat if possible, "determined that the Vaudois would commit no breach of humanity, so long as resistance was not offered."³⁷⁵

The day-to-day march of the Vaudois camp is detailed in an account published under the sole authorship of Henri Arnaud entitled, *Glorieuse Rentree*.³⁷⁶³⁴ At first they passed near or through several villages without opposition. Seizure of hostages followed by negotiations eased their passage to the first major river crossing at Sallanches. There the wooden bridge over the river Avre was contested by a force of 600 armed militia. As neither side sought a battle, free passage was ultimately negotiated and the Vaudois camp rested at the village of Ceblou at the end of their second day.

The bulk of the next two days was consumed labori-

---

34 The most prominent account of the return march was that attributed to H. Arnaud, but actually written by Paul Reynaudin and published 20 years after the event. Additional details were obtained from two journals kept by participants, Paul Reynaudin and Daniele Rivoire, both of which accounts were cut short before the conclusion of the march, and so not tainted by the outcome. (Reference to these journals is found in De Lange and Schwinger.)

ously traversing mountain passes at Haute Luce and Mt. Bon Homme. Guides who purposely misled and knee-deep snows substantially slowed their progress. They attributed the unguarded state of the fortifications they encountered atop Mt. Bon Homme to the protection of Divine providence. Days five and six were spent in the valley of the Isére River, crossing and recrossing the stream, where they met little opposition and sometimes even freely received support from the local villagers. Hastening on in forced marches to avoid organized resistance, they covered an average of 27 kilometers per day. On day seven, they crossed the pass near Mt. Cénis, the modern-day boundary between France and Italy.

At length, they encountered a French fortified position at the bridge over the Dora at Salabertano. Troops for this resistance had been hastily drawn from the nearby French fortress at Exilles. In this first real test of strength, the Vaudois stormed the bridge and routed the defending forces (numbering an estimated 2500 soldiers), suffering losses of less than thirty dead and wounded, as against an estimated 700 of the enemy killed.[377] The victorious troops then destroyed the bridge and took possession of all the French supplies they could carry and set fire to the rest. It was a remarkable victory, yet as their further success depended on speed, stealth and avoidance, so, Arnaud recounts: "Though, after such action repose was more necessary than ever, especially when it is remembered that three days and nights had been occupied in heavy marches, with insufficient food, yet it was thought right to advance, lest the enemy should receive a reinforcement. The remainder of so glorious a night was therefore employed in climbing Mt. Sci by the light of the moon." [378]

On the eleventh day of the march they arrived at the village of Balsille, marking their arrival in the Vaudois valleys. They had passed through the French controlled lands and now found themselves under the jurisdiction of the Duke of Savoy and thus came into confrontation with Savoyard troops rather than French. Somehow there is a marked harshness that seemed to descend upon them, engaged as they were with former comrades in arms, for captured Savoyard soldiers were typically put to death. This practice is not mentioned before and it seems new, although it is in accord with the Janavel *Instruction*: "On the field of battle, give quarter to no one; for how will you keep prisoners. You can neither employ your men to guard them, nor your provisions to feed them; and upon leaving you, they will make known your position to the enemy."[379] Nonetheless, the initial instance of this practice called forth an explanation from Arnaud:

> Let not the reader be surprised that the Vaudois should thus put to death those who fell into their hands. We had no prisons to confine them; our numbers were too small, and the warfare too desultory to admit the possibility of guarding them; and to have released them, would have been to publish our plans, our weakness, and everything on which depended the success of

our enterprise.[380]

On September 1, 1689, sixteen days into the march, having scattered the opposing forces and taken control of the Valley of Lucerna, the Vaudois camp "assembled at the hill of Sibaud, whence there is a view of the whole basin of Bobbi (Valley of Lucerna). It was the Sabbath, and after a sermon, these pious and valiant patriots entered into a solemn covenant renewing the ancient path of union of the valleys."[381]

> God having happily brought us back to the heritage of our fathers, to re-establish here the pure service of our holy religion . . . we swear and promise before the living God on the life of our souls, to keep union and order among ourselves not to separate or disunite ourselves from one another . . . if we should be reduced even to three or four in number. The officers swear fidelity to the soldiers and the soldiers to the officers, all together promising to our Lord and Savior Jesus Christ to rescue, as far as is possible for us, the dispersed remnants of our brethren from the yoke which oppresses them, that among them we may re-establish and maintain in these valleys the kingdom of the gospel even unto death.[382]

As the nimble Vaudois corps surged throughout the valleys and inspected their villages, now abandoned for nearly four years and occupied by others, they seemed to have had no particular purpose in mind. Over a five-week period they took control of various villages, lost them again, advanced and retreated, engaging Savoyard and French troops in growing numbers as armies were hastily recalled to the valleys to confront them. Gradually the Vaudois forces, depleted by desertion and casualties to a mere 400 men, were compelled to assume a defensive posture and make their places of resort higher and higher into the mountains for safety. It became increasingly difficult to secure supplies. There is evidence that a measure of despair overtook the intrepid combatants as week after week their ranks were depleted and no sign of reprieve or reinforcement appeared. By October French and Savoyard forces had reoccupied all significant fortresses and strategic passes throughout the valleys.

Finally, the Vaudois forces were compelled to seek a refuge where they could regroup and fortify themselves against the vastly superior force which hounded them. On the previously written advice of their retired champion, Janavel, they repaired to Balsille– a natural fortress and citadel, located in the upper reaches of the Valley of San Martin, the north-westernmost outpost of their valleys. There they assembled the remnants of the Vaudois camp to make their last stand.

> In the valley of San Martino lies a rock which is called La Basiglia.[35] It is a peaked rock which

---

35 La Balsiglia and Balsille are the same.

need to defend themselves, the Vaudois Camp turned their attention to survival and then to strengthening their fortifications. Fortunately they discovered fields of unharvested grain in the nearby hamlets of Pral and Rodoret, buried beneath early snows. They repaired the mill on the banks of the Germanesque River, recovering the crucial millstone which they had cached in the sand four years earlier.[387] This, together with periodic foraging expeditions into the valleys below for supplies as needed, provided adequately for their needs through the winter. Adding to the natural fortifications, the Vaudois felled trees and moved rocks to further strengthen their defensive positions in a series of barricades up the mountainside. In this manner they outlasted the season until the spring of 1690 when the opposition forces again took to the field.

On May 1, 1690, the French and Savoyard armed forces returned in earnest under the command of de Catinat, and encircled the fortress to begin their siege. With a reported allied force of 10,000 French troops and 12,000 Piedmontese[36], Catinat commenced a series of assaults on the fortifications.[388] (Like most estimates in wartime, the reported numbers of the troops involved are likely seriously inflated. Boeri[389] reports that the entire army of the Duke of Savoy in the 1690s, including infantry and cavalry, consisted of fewer than 10,000 men.)

---

36 In this context, the designations of Piedmontese and Savoyard are synonymous.

The allied forces found the various levels of barricades virtually impregnable and fell back many a time over a two-week period with hundreds of casualties among the besiegers as opposed to very few of the Vaudois. Two weeks into the siege, Catinat brought forth his artillery and established it upon the shoulder of Mt. Gunivert which commands the Balsille. "Having unmasked his battery, he again hoisted a white flag and then a red flag, to signify to the besieged that if they did not surrender they were no longer to look for any quarter. It had, indeed, already been publicly announced in Pignerol that all the Vaudois who were not killed amongst the rocks, would be hanged in the city the next day." Arnaud, the religious leader, and Odin the military commander, responded that "the rocks, which were accustomed to the noise of thunder, would not be shaken by that of cannon."[390]

The use of artillery soon proved successful in reducing the fortifications. Muston reports:

> The Vaudois, seeing themselves so closely beset, considered that the hand of God alone could save them. They invoked his aid, continued their resistance until the night of May 14, 1690; and then profiting by the mists, which on rainy days arise in the deep glens . . . they issued from their retreat, and under the guidance of Captain Poulat, who was a native of these mountains . . . enveloped in these dark and humid clouds . . . on icy and moist slopes of almost perpendicular

rocks... they held their way one after another, in single file across the gaping crevasses above the deep chasms of the Germanesque [River] dragging themselves along on their bellies, clinging to the asperities of the mountain, or to bushes or roots hanging from the rocks, resting from time to time.. After all this they digged steps into the hardened snow to climb by, they gained the northern slope of Mt. Gunivert, where they turned the posts of the enemy, some of whom challenged them as they passed, and then, panting and exhausted, and half dead from fatigue, but blessing the Lord for such a miraculous deliverance, they arrived at the base of the glaciers of Le Pelvoux.[391]

Having escaped, the troop of 400 Vaudois took their flight further over mountain passes and arrived on May 17 at the village of Pramollo, where they engaged the French force posted to defend the inhabitants whom the duke had permitted to settle there. The Vaudois attacked vigorously, killing 57 of the French forces and seizing their commander, Mons. Vignaux. Then in an astounding turn of events,

> the victors were informed by their captive, Vignaux, that Victor Amadeus had only to the following Tuesday (May 20) to decide between Germany and France. If he should decide for France the Vaudois could expect nothing more

than to be destroyed or expelled from the valleys. If, on the contrary, the court of Savoy should pronounce in favor of the enemies of France, the Vaudois would be received again into favor by the sovereign. They would acquire, moreover, a real importance, from their position on the frontiers of the two states, and from the assistance which their troops, habituated with war, familiar with the Alps, and full of ardor against the king of France, might be able to afford to the cause of Savoy."[392]

Victor Amadeus II, the Duke of Savoy, was an amazing political chameleon, and a proficient potentate of the period – opportunistic, clever and duplicitous. He had emerged at the meridian of the 1000-year reign of the House of Savoy as the most striking and successful of his line, displaying a "Machiavellian shrewdness and enduring strength of will,"[393] equal to his times. Apparently a man of few convictions, the duke changed sides whenever it served his interests, which was often. At this propitious moment in Vaudois history, the Duke transferred his allegiance and his forces to the Protestant side.

"Next day the Vaudois received information that Victor Amadeus II had decided in favor of Austria [Germany], that he had declared war against France, restored peace to their exhausted tribes, gladly accepted the assistance of their arms and opened to them again the gates of their native land." [394] His fortuitous reversal at this moment was seen by the beneficiaries as the divine rescue of a doomed camp.

As Victor Amadeus II joined the Grand Alliance against his erstwhile ally, France, he immediately revoked the edict of January 31, 1686 against the Vaudois and restored their right to practice their religion in his realms.[395] "A messenger soon came to them from Chevalier de Vercellis, commandant of the fort of La Tour [which the Vaudois were resolved to attack] who, on the part of the duke, offered them provisions and arms and invited them to range themselves under the banner of their own legitimate sovereign."[396] This decree was promptly published in Switzerland, Brandenburg and Württemberg, where the displaced Vaudois had taken refuge. There the local Protestant princes assisted in organizing the stream of refugees that soon began to flow back to their homeland. From among the returning masses, soon emerged a fighting force, a regiment of Vaudois 1000 strong, "which the Prince of Orange, now become King of England and an ally of Victor Amadeus, had taken into his pay, and placed at the service of the latter, for the common interest of the powers confederated against France."[397]

Among the motivations for the duke's decision was the news that "The Grand Alliance was preparing, in the spring of 1690, an expedition of Protestant irregulars who would cross the duke's territory (with or without his consent) relieve the remnant of the [the camp of Vaudois] and enter France."[398] Further, should the duke join the Grand Alliance, there were promises of assistance in achieving control of the long-coveted French fortress at Pinerolo.

This particular duke of Savoy was skilled and successful

at retaining his small duchy which stood at the crossroads between the great powers of the age as events ebbed and flowed around him.

His action in this instance was not to further the Protestant cause nor to salvage the Vaudois, but to save his duchy. Like many of his actions, this new commitment to the Vaudois was opportunistic and fleeting. In five short years he would switch sides again, joining the French against the Grand Alliance, only to return to the Alliance fold again five years later. However mercenary it may have been, this particular action, permitted the embattled Vaudois to regain their ancient homeland, nevermore to be dislodged. And here, again, as so many times in their history, they had the duke to thank for their survival.

The years ahead would bring to the Vaudois many additional persecutions, some even at the hands of Victor Amadeus II and his successors. Genuine and lasting religious tolerance would have to wait another 158 years, "when on the 17th of February 1848 the royal decree of [Victor Amadeus II's distant cousin] Charles Albert, King of Sardinia and Piedmont was issued, giving freedom to the valleys.[399]

CHAPTER V.
Free at Last (1690-1848 AD)

Blind must be he who does not discern the finger of God in the preservation of the Vaudois. There is nothing like it in the history of man.[400]

In the bend of the great chain of the Alps, where the Cottian Range terminates and the Maritime Range begins, and where the mountains sweep round to the southwest to reach the Mediterranean lie those lovely valleys which the Lord of Hosts hath vouchsafed to the Waldenses. Here from a venerable antiquity, that remarkable people have maintained unswervingly their pure spiritual faith, and kept alive the lamp of the gospel, despite persecutions and woes innumerable. Led by the hand of God into this place of liberty and security, they have dwelt around the Ark, and though the gates of hell have, times without number, mustered on this plain and warred against this ark, they have not prevailed.[401]

Beginning with the 18th century, by some twist of fate, there was a confluence of European liberal thought and expression that historians later termed *The Enlightenment*. The writings of the French philosophers Voltaire and Rousseau and the German Kant perhaps best define the movement, which combined philosophical reasoning and political awareness to lead an entire continent into a better era. Over a period of 150 years the peoples of Europe were largely liberated from agrarian feudalism in social structure, absolutism in government, oppression in religion and rigidity in economy. It was a marvelous and unprecedented century-and-a-half of progress for the human condition with an ultimate world-wide impact. Although there were troops deployed and battles waged, the principal impetus for this transformation was not military, but rational thought and effective communication. One might question the ability of ideas alone to change the world of the 18th century, but Tholfsen claims that, "The enlightenment was a constituent that was as essential to the existence of the [French] Revolution as an atom of oxygen is to a molecule of water."[402]

The era rose in crescendo to its breath-taking conclusion in that great revolutionary year of 1848 of which Hobsbawm writes. "There has never been anything closer to the world-revolution of which the insurrectionaries of the period dreamed than this spontaneous and general conflagration. What had been in 1789 the rising of a single nation was now, it seemed, 'this springtime of peoples' of an entire continent."[403] One of the great outcomes of the springtime of the peoples was that, whereas the religious freedom the Vaudois had earnestly desired and perpetually sought was not possible in 1700, it was freely handed to them and to many others in perpetuity after 1848.

1. THE TIMES.

Throughout much of the 18th century, famine was the constant specter that haunted and often decimated the populace of Europe. Inefficient agricultural practices at the tail end of the New Ice Age made the life of all but the very wealthy a perpetual game of chance. "For the early modern household, by far the greatest single item of expenditure was food, and by far the greatest source of anxiety was fear that the harvest would fail."[404] The era of revolution was preceded by a series of food riots reflecting the simmering fear of starvation that hovered near the surface. Such riots erupted sporadically in Europe during the Middle Ages, but largely due to a burgeoning population without a commensurate increase in food production, they peaked in intensity and sophistication in 18th century western Europe, most commonly in France. The French recorded over four hundred food riots in the 1770s, over 200 in the period just preceding the French Revolution of 1788-1796.

Sometime after mid-18th century, the curve of humanity began to bend upward and Europe experienced "a decline in mortality, [because of] the diminution of the three great killers of the 17th century: famine, war and plague."[405] Amazingly, in spite of wretched living conditions commonly surrounded by filth, and subjected to rudimentary and often counterproductive medical practices, the population of European countries is estimated to have soared in this period from 110 million in 1700 to 190 million a century later. The principal determining elements of this improvement were

1. The plague had ceased to make its periodic visits,
2. More efficient agricultural methods were introduced, specifically crop rotation and fertilizers,
3. Roadways and hence movement of food and goods, improved,
4. Wars became less destructive.

These conditions meant that "the second half of the 18th century saw the beginning of that startling and henceforward unbroken rise in population so characteristic of the modern world."[406]

The spiritual and intellectual transformation of Europe

cannot easily be separated from the material, for in parallel with the Enlightenment an explosion occurred with perhaps even greater impact on mankind known as the Industrial Revolution. By secular reckoning, the Industrial Revolution may be viewed as the greatest event in world history. At its commencement European life was overwhelmingly agrarian, employing agricultural techniques that were woefully inefficient yet largely unchanged for centuries. The vast majority of the 180 million Europeans were either serfs, beholden to if not owned by their feudal lords, or free-holding peasants barely self-sufficient on their own land. They seldom, if ever, traveled outside the community of their birth. In just a few short decades much of that changed.

Writes Hobsbawm:

> Sometime in the 1780s, and for the first time in human history, the shackles were taken off the productive power of human societies, which henceforth became capable of constant, rapid and limitless multiplication of men, goods and services . . . then it was that all the relevant statistical indices took their sudden sharp, almost vertical turn upwards marking the take-off. The economy became, as it were, airborne.[407]

In contrast, the sweeping changes that characterized much else in this period came lately and only reluctantly to institutions and methods of governing. There were enlightened monarchs, but governmental leaders in the 18th century were mostly "Hereditary monarchs by the grace of God who headed hierarchies of nobles, and they, however modernist and innovatory, found it impossible – and indeed showed few signs of wanting – to achieve, the root and branch social and economic transformations which the progress of the economy required and the rising social groups called for."[408] Monarchs, though often knowledgeable of social issues and advised by enlightened counselors, only came to effect real change toward the end of the period, when insurrection made change inevitable.

The period under discussion cannot be properly understood without reference to the French Revolution of 1789 and the timeless hero who rode its crest to fame, Napoleon Bonaparte. The great central achievement of the French, the one that best characterizes the age of revolution, was when the delegates of the Third Estate (the non-privileged citizens) meeting amid the revolution's early convulsive stages, declared the "tennis court oath": They would not disperse until they could produce a constitution that, "proclaimed the principle of national sovereignty and claimed for themselves the right to exercise that right."[409] The oath was both a revolutionary act and an assertion that political authority derived from the people and their representatives rather than from the monarch himself.

In spite of the thousands who died at Napoleon's command (a quarter of a million Frenchmen alone) the French-Napoleonic legacy spread to all of continental Europe and beyond, with lasting impact on governments and societies. Invading and occupying troops, schooled in the attractive concepts of the French Revolution, carried with them an irresistible hope and enthusiasm for freedom from the bondages of the times. A leading Greek patriot of the period, wrote:

> The French revolution and the doings of Napoleon opened the eyes of the world. The nations knew nothing before, and the people thought that kings were gods upon the earth and that they were bound to say that whatever they did was well done. Through this present change it is more difficult to rule the people."[410]

Hobsbawm writes that:

> It was now known that revolution in a single country could be a European phenomenon; that its doctrines could spread across frontiers, and what was worse, its invading armies could blow the political systems of a continent. It was now known that social revolution was possible; that nations existed as something independent of states, peoples as something independent of their rulers, and even that the poor existed as something independent of the ruling classes."[411]

And wherever his conquests took him, Napoleon established the rule of law as he understood it. Because of its imposition on all conquered lands, some consider the Napoleonic Code to have been the most important single legal document of modern European history for it altered domestic institutions and transformed the political atmosphere. [412]

Emerging as a parallel phenomenon, the Romantic movement gave a human face to the revolution in progress by zeroing in on and seeking to elevate the lowest class of society. This focus found voice in the German philosopher, Herder:

> True value in any nation resides not with the elite's classical culture, but with the common people, especially in the countryside, where roots were firmly planted in the native soil and history."[413]

Rousseau, arguing the case of freedom and equality, established and popularized the principles of fairness and human liberty and laid the intellectual foundation for the revolutions that followed. Rousseau's novel, *Julie, or the New Heloise*, was probably the record best-seller of the whole 18th century. In it the peasant was presented as "the most useful and indeed the only truly necessary class in society, whose natural state of happiness could only be spoiled if the other classes tyrannize it with acts of violence or corrupt it with examples of vice."[414] Enlightenment extended to the masses as well, as the expansion of literacy produced a reading revolution. Whereas previously only the patrons of the royal courts and the clergy had access to education, schools now became state-sponsored, achieving much wider coverage.

It was a long drawn-out process, but in this era, the little person, ranging near the bottom of society's ladder, for the first time began to be more than a cypher. Wrote Goethe, "One thing is for certain, happy and great alone is the man who needs neither to command nor to obey to amount to something."[415]

A remarkable feature of this period was the manner in which the political influence of the church receded as a natural victim of the exclusive nature of sovereignty. "As the essence of sovereignty is its self-sufficiency, by virtue of its definition as 'ultimate authority from which there is no appeal,' no state can tolerate the interference of an international authority such as the papacy."[416] De Toqueville suggests one reason for this decline was that the church was in a self-destruct mode. "The universal discredit into which all religious belief fell at the end of the 18th century exercised without doubt the greatest influence upon the causes of revolution."[417] Yet the church did not expire, but rather fell back on the strength of its monastic structure, discovering its real power in an army of clergy and possession of choice lands and the peasants who worked them. Unusual was the famine whose sufferers did not turn for relief to the monastic granaries. The proliferation of monasteries in Europe reached its peak in the mid-18th century with at least 15,000 monasteries for men and 10,000 for women engaging a total population in excess of a quarter of a million.

As a myriad of factors of this period raised the hopes of its peoples, so it reduced the expectations of its hereditary monarchs and their progeny. The decline of monarchical power was accompanied by the emergence of nation states, made up of citizens who were, for the first time, feeling some measure of ownership and began to have a sense of national identity. Through a combination of international intrigue and power struggles, the dwarf states of central Europe disappeared in the only period of history where we can recall the names of the foreign ministers (Talleyrand, and Metternich for example) but we only vaguely remember who the heads of state were.

The political power structure in Europe was considerably altered as the Holy Roman Empire of the German nation faded from 243 weak German states, into less than forty and vacated the continental European power stage leaving in their place the empires of France, Spain, Prussia-Brandenburg and Austro-Hungary.

In short, the period 1700-1848 in European history was one of unprecedented expansion of freedom – individual, political, economic and spiritual. Hobsbawm writes that "Never in European history and rarely anywhere else, had revolutionism been so endemic, so general, so likely to spread by spontaneous contagion as well as by deliberate propaganda."[418] In the years that lay ahead, there were temporary reversals, but the positive advances could not be undone because the causes were systemic and because the times had awakened what Rousseau described as the great fundamental human desire – freedom. "Man is born free and everywhere he is in chains."[419] The modern age had arrived and there was to be no turning back.

2. THE VAUDOIS HOMELANDS.

At the dawn of the 18th century, the Vaudois, returning from exile, had reacquired their ancestral lands astride the Cottian Alps at the crossroads of southern Europe. The ordeal of exile had reduced the numbers of those initially returning to an estimated 4-6000. They settled again into the Alpine portion of Piedmont in the Duchy of Savoy, overlapping into the neighboring province of Dauphine in the French Empire. Reliable census numbers are scarce, but it is apparent that the beacon of the Glorious Return drew to its signal a large number of the scattered Vaudois from their exile in Germany and Switzerland, in time expanding the population in the valleys to upwards of 20,000 of the faithful. As an added welcome to these returnees, the Duchy of Savoy became one of a very small number of select European political entities to abolish serfdom and peasant dependence.[420]

For a time, the fate of the Vaudois had seemed to be inextricably connected with that of the Sun King, Louis XIV, the greatest king of the greatest nation of the period. Reigning from 1643 until his death in 1715, Louis achieved his apogee around 1688 when it was said of him, "Not a dog barks in Europe unless the king says he may."[421] It was his domineering influence on the Savoyard Duke Victor Amadeus II that had led to the total expulsion of the Vaudois from their ancestral home in 1686. It was Louis' ruthless military exploits that alienated all of France's neighbors, leading in 1686 to the "Grand Alliance," and giving Victor Amadeus II an excuse to reverse his allegiance just in time save the last gasp of the Vaudois as they sought to reenter their valleys.

Reflecting the duke's renewed commitment to the Protestant cause was the Edict of Pacification he issued in May 1694, restoring the Vaudois to the land of their ancestors, revoking the harsh edict of 1664, securing amnesty for the returning Vaudois and a promise of the prince's favor going forward. Three months later, Innocent XII issued a papal bull declaring the Edict of Pacification null and void. However, as a sign of how far the Vaudois interests had advanced, the senate of Turin, governing body of Savoy, in an unprecedented gesture, voted to defy the pope and prohibit publication of the papal bull throughout the duchy.

Following a flurry of military engagements with France, sometimes fighting beside and sometimes against, the Duchy of Savoy was saved from absorption into the French Empire of Louis XIV by the timely arrival of the famous Eugen of Savoy, one of the most powerful military commanders of European history. Eugen had earned his reputation defending the Holy Roman and Hapsburg Empires against the incursion of the Ottoman Turks, culminating in the decisive Battle of Zenta in 1697. Returning to the aid of his Savoyard cousin, Victor Amadeus II, Eugen's troops interrupted the French siege of Turin in 1706, frustrating the French intentions in Piedmont for a hundred years.

In 1713 the Duchy of Savoy, through the curious political machinations of the period, expanded momentarily to include the improbable additions of Sicily and Utrecht, only to disgorge them five years later to make room for the island of Sardinia and the city-state of Genoa. The boundary shuffling of this period was agreed to by powerful neighbors to provide a more effective buffer between two great powers of the region, the French and the Austro-Hungarian empires. What emerged in 1718 was the Kingdom of Sardinia ruled by the House of Savoy, where for the first time the Vaudois valleys were contained under a single jurisdiction.

As the 18th century proceeded, the House of Savoy (previously duke but now King of Sardinia) oscillation between allegiance to Catholic France and Protestant England continued. Beginning in 1700, Victor Amadeus II lurched back in the Catholic direction and issued a series of restrictive edicts against the Vaudois of escalating severity. First was the expulsion of all French-born from the region, which included three thousand Vaudois, seven of thirteen pastors and the leader of the Glorious Return, Henri Arnaud. The decree of 1716 forbade Vaudois assemblies of more than ten participants. That of 1724 required all babies to be baptized Catholic; that of 1730 required all inhabitants to confess the Catholic faith.[422]

The leaders of the House of Savoy were never ideologues. Their allegiance was seldom from religious conviction and their ready ambivalence was a key to their endurance. Unencumbered by dogma, they knew how to act for survival, which often meant that they readily, almost whimsically, transferred their allegiance. But also it meant that though they issued severe edicts, their hearts generally weren't in the implementation. Hence these onerous decrees were only loosely enforced, allowing the Vaudois to thrive during the first half of the 18th century.

The restrictive ordinances were soon followed by a surge of international generosity. Growing out of the horrific massacres of 1655, there had evolved an acute awareness among the Protestant states of Europe of the plight of the Vaudois, and "the European Protestants began to view the Vaudois as their legacy and tradition, a beloved forerunner."[423] It was painful to them to see their weakened and valiant spiritual forebears surrounded by ravenous enemies in a Roman Catholic land with only the protection of a capricious prince. The result was a flurry of diplomatic activity, but also the beginning of a decades-long outpouring of economic aid, principally from the English and the Dutch. The arrival of foreign funding launched an era of education, supported the construction of schools, the publication of books and the issuing of scholarships for studies abroad. This period of light and dark prompted one observer to write, "Even though Savoyard law restricted attendance at a Vaudois funeral to six, at least those six could read."[424]

In 1792 Savoy was overrun by French Revolutionary forces bent on exportation of the revolution throughout their international neighborhood and the region was annexed to the French Republic for the duration of French domination in European affairs. As the French Revolution spilled over into the Piedmont region, the Vaudois eagerly welcomed, along with its hopeful principles, a new measure of freedom. For the first time they had a voice in governing circles, as their moderator[37] joined a provisional government in Tu-

---
37 The appointed religious leader of the Vaudois in this period was desig-

rin. As an offshoot of the Napoleonic Era (1804-1815) the shackles of the Vaudois ghetto, both as a legal and a social entity, were theoretically dissipated. On paper, the Vaudois found themselves free to profess and practice their religion, free to purchase land and to join in commerce outside their previously restricted area. In reality, though it sounded good, the Napoleonic influence was fleeting. Following the Napoleonic wars, the Congress of Vienna of 1814-1815 returned Piedmont and Savoy to the Kingdom of Sardinia, where after 1815, the de-facto ghetto status was reinstated and continued virtually unchanged for another forty years.

Under a series of conservative monarchs after 1815, Sardinia adopted a reactionary policy, gradually restricting the people's freedoms and returning power to the nobility and the church. Victor Emmanuel I (1802-1821) disbanded the entire Code Napoléon and initiated a policy designed to unite the kingdom religiously. In the expanded, predominantly Catholic kingdom, the Vaudois again found themselves a Protestant minority whose continued presence was an embarrassment to the leaders. As a result, over much of the first half of the 19th century, a series of increasingly onerous restrictions were applied exclusively to the Vaudois who were smothered with rules and prohibitions even as the physical limits of their valleys were contracted. The Vaudois could not own property or practice any industry beyond their own boundaries. They were not permitted to erect a tombstone above their dead, nor even enclose their burial grounds with a wall. They were shut out from all learned pro-

---

nated the Moderator.

fessions. They could not be bankers, lawyers or physicians. There were no printing presses in their valleys, they were forbidden to have one. The few books they possessed, mostly Bibles, catechisms or hymn books, were printed abroad. They were forbidden to evangelize or make converts, but the priests had full liberty to enter their valleys and proselytize. They could not erect a sanctuary except on their soil. They could take no degrees in any colleges of Piedmont. Partially due to these and other onerous restrictions, the Vaudois experienced a severe economic depression, and they were reduced as nearly as practical to a simple existence, with one great exception – namely the liberty of Protestant worship within their territorial limits.[425]

3. THE BENEFACTORS.

The 19th century for the Vaudois was an exhilarating experience, even giddy - a soaring ride as they became, not only the recipients of compassionate and international largess of unprecedented generosity, but the beneficiaries of powerful friends and advocates who came to live among them. Prominent among these were Count Wallburg Truchsess, the Prussian ambassador, Stephen Gilly, an Anglican minister, and Colonel Charles Beckwith a retired British veteran of Waterloo. Their intervention produced enormous benefits to the impoverished and beleaguered Vaudois

Count Truchsess led the diplomatic intervention effort with timely reminders to the Sardinian king and his advisors that the friendship of powerful Protestant kingdoms such as Prussia, England and the Netherlands was in their best interest and could be easily damaged by ill treatment of the small Protestant contingent within their borders.

The observations and actions of Gilly and Beckwith provide an interesting description of the condition of the Vaudois as they approached the midpoint of the 19th century. Gilly was the first to come, arriving in 1823. Spurred by accounts of the valiant, oppressed Christian people of alleged ancient origin, he came as an Anglican minister to assess the situation and to judge the impact of monetary contributions which the Vaudois had now been receiving from their Protestant benefactors for over a hundred years. His first written account inspired Colonel Beckwith to join him. Almost from the moment of their arrival in the valleys, both Gilly and Beckwith became passionate and determined champions of the Vaudois as well as permanent residents among them.

What they found was a people oppressed - no longer suffering the severe persecutions of the past, yet confined in a de-facto ghetto, proscribed economically by a myriad of restrictive rules, surrounded and smothered in their worship and religious practice, and most of them living in abject poverty, "a people intimidated by suffering, cheated of its fancied liberty, caught in a network of cruel edicts that confined its movements."[426] But worrisome as were these conditions, more troublesome was that where Gilly and Beckwith expected to find a vibrant religious fervor, born of an ancient legacy, instead they discovered a people drifting in spiritual lethargy, seemingly unaware of the esteem in which they were held and of their unique place in the world or in the history of Christianity.

It was apparent to Gilly and Beckwith that much of the dependence and lethargy of the Vaudois could be attributed to their leaders being educated abroad, where they imbibed the doctrines and practices of others without adequate appreciation of conditions at home. But these officials were also under the watchful eye of the Sardinian government. "No Vaudois synod can be convoked without the king's permission, nor held but in the presence of the intendant of the province who represents the sovereign, and whose duty it is to take care that nothing illegal is done. When the acts of the synod have passed, without any veto on the part of the intendant, their validity and legality is tacitly acknowledged by the government."[427] Gilly and Beckwith described a people with schools in poor condition and available to only a few, with inadequate health care with only few church buildings and those dilapidated.

Secular and religious education were meshed together and both suffered due to serious impediments. "The vernacular tongue if the Vaudois was a barbarous dialect between Latin, French and Italian. The language of the state was Italian while that in which they received their instruction was French."[428] Gilly found it "astonishing that the population should be grounded and rooted in a faith, the knowledge of which is communicated to them under every possible impediment."[429] For years the Vaudois had been in a gradual transformation from their ancient Romaunt language into French, and now it was necessary to further adapt to Italian.

From the moment of his arrival, Beckwith became an

indefatigable personal benefactor and an effective fund raiser, doing much to transform education and health services from his arrival in the Valleys in 1827 until his death in 1853. Within a few short years Beckwith succeeded in establishing quarter (elementary) schools in every hamlet (169 in total), a Latin (secondary) school and the college of Holy Trinity at La Tour,[430] promoted the building of churches or temples in every commune, culminating finally with construction of a temple outside their restricted area near the site where many a Vaudois heretic had been burned in the capital city of Turin.

Wylie describes Beckwith's impact as follows:

> Beckwith felt himself drawn irresistibly to this people and from that hour (upon reading Gilly's book) his life was consecrated to them. He lived among them as a father – he devoted his fortune to them. He built schools and churches and parsonages. He provided improved school books and suggested better modes of teaching. He strove above all things to quicken their spiritual life. He taught them how to respond to the exigencies of modern times. He specially inculcated upon them that the field was wider than their valleys and that they would be called to arise and walk through Italy, the length of it and the breadth of it. He was their advocate at the court of Turin and when he obtained for

them the possession of a burial ground outside their valleys, he exclaimed, "Now they have got investment of Piedmont, as the patriarchs did of Canaan and soon all the land will be theirs."[431]

Both Gilly and Beckwith professed and demonstrated a deep love of the Vaudois people, but they admired them more for what they had been and what they wanted them to be than for what they actually were. "We understand your interests better than you do yourselves,"[432] they said. Deeply engaged, nonetheless Beckwith saw his Anglican experience and that of the Vaudois as worlds apart.

> In short, we are members of a monarchical church; based on the principle of authority, you, on the contrary, belong to a republican church founded on the will of the people. How can two such societies enter into natural relations without producing dissension, distrust and animosity? We are, in your eyes, tyrants and abettors of despotism. You are, in our eyes, anarchists and children of rebellion and schism. We wish to obtain obedience by obedience. To you our system appears only tyranny and slavery, yours appears to us as obstinacy and license.[433]

In particular, Beckwith looked beyond their humble circumstances to see a vision of the Vaudois as the vehicle for the evangelization of all of Italy.

> I lay it upon you always to . . . act like men specially charged with the interests of the Church of Christ in these countries; to discharge the debt contracted by you towards our Savior for the long years of preservation, of protection and encouragement and of blessing that have been accorded you, and towards the host of devoted friends who have assisted and sustained you in so many difficult circumstances. Henceforward, either you are missionaries or you are nothing.[434]

Curiously, as the Vaudois, at Beckwith's urging, established a mission in Turin, a first tentative step to proselytizing Italy, Catholic authorities established a mission in La Tour to recover the heretic Vaudois.[435]

Vaudois poverty was a more difficult issue. With growth in numbers, the proscribed domain in which they lived was increasingly unable to sustain the population. One eyewitness account reads:

> A majority of the people among these mountains are very ignorant, a great portion of them can neither read nor write, Many of their dwellings have no glass in the windows. Paper and sheepskins are used as a substitute for glass. In my travels I have often met women going into the fields to till the ground, carrying cradle and child with them, when overtaken by a storm,

> catch up cradle and child on their shoulder, and run to seek a place of shelter... It is heart sickening to see the great poverty that exists among these mountains. Last year there was a great falling short of cribs of grain, which together with the grape disease and potato rot, continues to largely augment the miseries of the laboring poor. The country is teeming with beggars. I never saw such miserable holes in my life as some of the people dwell in. The rough walls of most of the hovels are stuck up among the rocks, and in some cases the rock serves for one end and a side.[436]

There is some evidence that the years of dependence on funds from abroad (the first half of the 18th century) had done what the dole always does, rendered the recipient Vaudois weak-willed and dependent. However, when Beckwith sought to alter their leadership structure and rewrite their liturgy after the Anglican pattern, the Vaudois, to be firm without being ungrateful, simply ignored his repeated admonitions. Ruffled at first, Beckwith drew back, but being a man of compassion first and of dogma last, he overcame his disappointment and renewed his philanthropic enterprises until his passing in 1853.

4. FREE AT LAST.

King Charles Albert of Sardinia (of the House of Savoy),

inspired by the general rise of freedom throughout Europe but mostly to preempt insurrection in his own realms, issued a new constitution that became known as the Albertine Statute of 1848. The statute declared all citizens to be equal before the law, granted the right of habeas corpus, the sanctity of home and property and freedom of the press. Though Catholicism was identified as the sole state religion, freedom of religion was granted for all existing forms of worship. Albert's largesse was surely inspired by similar concessions granted earlier that year in Sicily and Tuscany, though his was the first to grant the kind of religious freedom that the Vaudois had sought and championed for centuries. With the unification of Italy, Piedmont and the eastern portion of Savoy, including the Vaudois valleys, became part of the Kingdom of Italy while the balance of the Duchy of Savoy reverted to French control. The endurance of Savoy was such that the House of Savoy quite logically and comfortably shifted their kingship of Sardinia to the whole of a united Italy in 1859 where their reign persisted until the formation of the Republic of Italy in 1949. The Albertine Statute, unlike most previous concessional decrees of the House of Savoy, had a longevity to it, for it prevailed and became the constitution of the united kingdom of Italy, remaining in force for a hundred years into the modern era.[437] Thus, "The Waldensian Church became the door by which freedom of conscience entered Italy."[438]

A telling climax to our story is a parade conducted in Turin in 1848 celebrating the emancipation inherent in the Albertine Statute in which 50,000 participants thrust the

Vaudois to the fore with the chant: "Vaudois! Until now you have been last. Today let justice be done, and march you at the head."[439]

The centuries have come and gone, religious denominations have arisen and collapsed, but the Vaudois remain. Formidable enemies have approached but their siege engines molder in decay. One of their themes comes to mind: "The hammers are broken but the anvil remains."

Stephen Gilly penned what might be their epitaph:

> The question naturally arises, how could half-armed and ignoble peasants surrounded on all sides by hosts of fighting men, renowned throughout Europe as the infantry of Piedmont, how could they maintain their ground against such fearful odds, and why is it that the church of the valleys has not long ago been blotted out from the face of the earth? The Vaudois had no fortresses into which they might retire when hard pressed; no magazine, no walled towns, no castles bristling with cannon; they had no military leaders who were men of war from their youth and schooled in the rules and stratagems of war; they had no nobles or feudal barons, under whose chieftainship they might be enrolled, and whose personal influence would keep them together, and direct their counsels. And yet these were they who jeopardized their lives unto the death in the high places of the field, and offered

themselves willingly for the people, Again and again did the fiat go forth for their utter destruction. It was no relenting nor want of inclination, nor tender mercy on the part of their enemies that they were not destroyed, witness the 68 enactments which were put in force against them between the years of 1561 and 1686, which were intended to exterminate, and which did waste and reduce them. It was the avowed object, the professional intention, the impious plot to eradicate them. "Wishing by every means within our power, to eradicate, to bury the heresy. In our zeal for the Holy Catholic, Apostolic and Roman faith, desiring to pluck up the tares." So ran the edicts and such was the intention.

Why then was it not carried into effect? How could a handful of mountaineers escape from the vengeance that threatened their total overthrow, and which achieved the downfall of their brethren in other parts? Because it was the will of God that they should be left as a remnant – because it was written in the counsels of heaven that they should continue as a miracle of Divine Grace and Providence.

There is nothing like it in the history of man. The tempest of persecution has raged against them for 700 years and yet it has not swept them away, but there they are in the land of their forefathers; because the Most High gave the people

of the valleys stout hearts and a resolute spirit – because he made them patient of hunger or thirst and nakedness, and all manner of affliction. Blind must be he who does not discern the finger of God in the preservation of the Vaudois.
440

BIBLIOGRAPHY

1. Allix, Pierre, *Some Remarks upon the Ecclesiastical History of the ancient Church of Piedmont*, Clarendon, New Edition, Oxford, 1821
2. Ames, Christine Caldwell, *Righteous Persecution, Inquisition, Dominicans, and Christianity in the Middle Ages*, U. of Pennsylvania Press, Philadelphia, 2009
3. Andrews, Frances, *The Early Humiliati*, Cambrdge University Press, 1999.
4. Arnaud, Henri, *The Glorious Return by the Vaudois to their Valleys,* translated by Acland, London, 1832
5. Audisio, Gabriel (1999), *The Waldensian Dissent, Persecution and Survival c.1170 – c.1270*, Cambridge University Press, Cambridge, 1999.
6. Audisio, Gabriel (2007), *Preachers by Night, The Waldensian Barbes (15th-16th Centuries)*, Studies

in Medieval and Reformation Traditions, Brill, Leiden-Boston, 2007.
7. Baigent, Michael and Leigh, Richard, *The Inquisition*, Penguin Books, NY, 2000.
8. Baird, Robert, *History of the Ancient Christians, Inhabiting the Valleys of the Alps*, Griffith and Simon, Philadelphia, 1847.
9. Bautz, F. W, *Biographisch-Bibliographisches Kirchenlexikon*, Band I, 1990
10. Beattie, William, *The Waldenses or Protestant Valleys of Piedmont and Dauphiny*, G. Virtue, London, 1838.
11. Bennett, A. F. "Triumph of the Alps," *The Instructor, Church of Jesus Christ of Latter-day Saints*, August, 1958
12. Bernier, Olivier, *Louis XIV, A Royal Life*, New York 1987
13. Biller, Peter, *The Waldenses, 1170-1530*, Ashgate, Burlington, 2001
14. Blair, Adam, *History of the Waldenses*, in 2 Volumes, reprint, Ulan Press, 2012
15. Blanning, Tim, *The Pursuit of Glory – Europe 1648-1815*, Penguin Group, NY, 2007.
16. Boeri, G. C., *The Army of the Duke of Savoy, 1688-1713*, pamphlet
17. Bossuet, James Benign, *The History of the Variations of the Protestant Churches*, Doyle, New York, 1842.
18. Bracebridge, Charles Holte and Brez, Jacques,

Authentic Details of the Valdenses, in Piedmont and other countries, Oxford 1827
19. Bremer, Fredrika , *Two Years in Switzerland and Italy*, London 1861
20. Bresse (or Brez), J., *Authentic Details of the Valdenses, including an Abridged Translation of the History of the Vaudois,* Hatchard, London, 1827
21. Brewer, Ebenezer Cobham, *Historic Note-Book: with an Appendix of Battles*, Philadelphia 1891
22. Cameron, Euan (1984), *The Reformation of the Heretics*, Clarendon, Oxford, 1984
23. Cameron, Euan (2000), *Waldenses: Rejections of the Holy Church in Medieval Europe,* Blackwell Publishers, Oxford, 2000.
24. Cardew, Lawrence G., *A Short History of the Inquisition*, Watts and Co., London, 1933.
25. Childs, John, *Warfare in the Seventeenth Century*, London 2001
26. Comba, Emilio, *History of the Waldenses of Italy from their Origin to the Reformation*, Truslove and Shirley, London, 1889
27. *The Crown or the Tiara? Considerations of the Present Condition of the Waldenses*, 1842.
28. Deanesly, Margaret, *The Lollard Bible and other Medieval Versions*, Cambridge University Press, 1920.
29. De Boer, Erik, *The Genevan School of the Prophets, The congregations of the Company of Pastors*

and their influence in 16th Century Europe, Librairie Droz, S.A., Geneva, 2012.
30. De Lange, Albert and Schwinger, Gerhard, *Pieter Valkenier und das Schicksal der Waldenser um1700*, 2004.
31. DiBella, B. I., *The Royal House of Savoy*, Regalis, 1998.
32. Dickens, A. G. and Tonkin, John, *The Reformation in Historical Thought*, Harvard University Press, Cambridge, 1985.
33. Durant, Will and Ariel, *The Story of Civilization, Vol. IV: The Reformation; Vol. VI., The Age of Faith; Vol. VIII: The Age of Louis XIV; Vol. X, Rousseau and Revolution;* Simon and Schuster, New York, 1963-67.
34. Esbenshade, Ann Augusta and Herbert, Roland, <u>An Annotated Reading List on the Waldenses: Selected Books and Articles in English</u>, The American Waldensian Aid Society, 1939.
35. Eusebius, *The Ecclesiastical History*, 4th Century AD, Harvard U. Press, Cambridge, 1965.
36. Faber, George S., *An Inquiry into the History and Theology of the Ancient Vallenses and Albigenses*, Seeley and Burnside, London 1838.
37. Fowler, William Chauncey, The English Review, Quarterly Journal of Ecclesiastical and General Literature, Vol. XI, London, 1845, pg. 215, *English Grammar: The English Language in its Elements and Forms with a history of its origins*, New

York, 1835.
38. Gell, Phillip, *The Revelations of Our Lord and Savior Jesus Christ*, Wertheim and Macintosh, London, 1854.
39. Gibbon, Edward, *The Decline and Fall of the Roman Empire in 3 Volumes*, Random House, New York, 1960, originally publ. 1910.
40. Gilly, William Stephen (1848), *The Romaunt version of the Gospel according to St John : from mss. preserved in Trinity College, Dublin, and the the Bibliothèque du Roi, Paris; with an introductory history of the version of the New Testament, anciently in use among the old Waldenses ; and Remarks on the texts of the Dublin, Paris, Grenoble, Zurich, and Lyons mss. of that version*, by, John Murray, London, 1848
41. Gilly, William Stephen (1831), *Waldensian Researches during a second visit to the Vaudois of Piemont*, London 1831.
42. Gilly, William Stephen (1826), *Narrative of the Excursion to the Mountains of Piemont, in the Year MDCCCXXIII, and Researches among the Vaudois, or Waldenses, Protestant Inhabitants of the Cottian Alps*, Rivington, London, 1826.
43. Gilly, William Stephen (1841), *Valdenses, Valdo, and Vigilantius*, Black, Edinburgh, 1841.
44. Grosek, Edward, *The Secret Treaties of History*, 2004
45. Grotke, K. L. and Putsch, M. J., editors, *Consti-*

tutionalism, Legitimacy and Power: Nineteenth Century Experiences, Oxford University Press, 2014, Section II: *The Albertine Statute and its Anti-revolutionary function in 1848*, by Anna Gianna Manca

46. Guy, Bernhard, *The inquisitor's guide: a Medieval manual on heretics*, Raventhal Books, 2006
47. Halsall, Paul, ed., *Internet Medieval Source Book*, Fordham University Center for Medieval Studies, 2006, *Twelfth Ecumenical Council, Lateran IV*, 121, Canon 3
48. Hartshorn, L. R., *Remarkable Stories from the Lives of Latter-Day Saint Women*, Deseret Book, Salt Lake City, 1973.
49. Hase, Karl August, *Kirchengeschichte*, Breitkopf and Haertel, Leipzig, 1877
50. Hobsbawm, Eric, *The Age of Revolution (1789-1848)*, Random House, NY, 1996.
51. Homer - Sunstone, M. W., *Voice of Joseph Tract*, as quoted in "The Italian Mission," Sunstone Magazine. .
52. Hritzu, J. N., *The Fathers of the Church*, Catholic University of America Press, 1965
53. Hughes, Philip Edgecumbe, *The Register of the Company of Pastors of Geneva in the Time of Calvin*, Eerdman Publishing, Grand Rapids, 1966
54. John, Eric, *The Popes, a Concise Biographical History, Hawthorne Books*, New York, 1964
55. Johnson, Paul, *A History of Christianity*, Athene-

um, 1976
56. Johnson, Lonnie R., *Central Europe, Enemies, Neighbors and Friends*, Oxford Press, NY 1996.
57. Jones, William, *The History of the Christian Church*, Cove, NY, 1824.
58. Keble, John transl., *Five Books of Ireneaus, Bishop of Lyon, Against Heresies*, Parker, London, 1872
59. Kieckenhefer, Richard, *Repression of Heresy in Medieval Germany*, University of Pennsylvania Press, 1979.
60. Knuth, Elizabeth T., *The Beguines*, posted to the Internet December 1992.
61. Krasinski, Valerian, *Historical Sketch of the Rise, Progress and Decline of the Reformation in Poland*, Murray, London, 1840.
62. Kurtz, Johann Heinrich, *Lehrbuch der Kirchengeschichte*, Neumann, Leipzig, 1899
63. Lambert, Malcolm, *Medieval Heresy, Popular Movements from the Gregorian Reform to the Reformation*, Blackwell, Malden MA, 2002
64. Lacosta, August, *Henri Arnaud und die Waldenser: der Kampf um die Rueckkehr in die hemlatlichen Taeler*, Lang, Bern, 1982.
65. Lawrence, Eugene, *Historical Studies, The Vaudois*, Harper Bros., NY, 1876.
66. Lea, Henry Charles, (1888), *The History of the Inquisition of the Middle Ages*, in 3 Volumes, Russell and Russell, New York, 1888

67. Lea, Henry Charles, (1961), *The History of the Inquisition of the Middle Ages*, abridged version, MacMillan, New York, 1961
68. Leger, Jean, *Histoire Generale des Eglises de Piemont ou Vaudoises*, originally published in 1669.
69. Luzzi, Giovanni, *The Struggle for Christian Truth in Italy*, Revell, New York, 1913
70. Manchester, William, *A World Lit only by Fire*, Little Brown and Co., Boston, 1992.
71. Marteilhe, Jean, *Galley Slave, an Autobiography*, ed. By Kenneth Fenwick, Folio Society, London, 1957.
72. McCracken, G. E. and Canabiss, A., *Early Medieval Theology*, Westminster Press, Philadelphia, 1957
73. M'Crie, Thomas, *History of the Progress and Suppression of the Reformation in Italy*, Blackwood, Edinburgh, 1833.
74. McDonnell, Ernest W., *The Beguines and Beghards in Medieval Culture*, New Brunswick, N.J. Rutgers University Press, 1954
75. McDonnell, Ernest W., *Vita Apostilica, Diversity or Dissent*, Church History Vol. 24, No. 1, Cambridge University Press, 1955.
76. McDuff, J. R, *The Exiles of Lucerna, or the Sufferings of the Waldenses during the Persecution of 1686*, Nisbet, London, 1871.
77. McGoldrick, James Edward, *Baptist Secession-*

isms, A crucial Question in Baptist History, The Scarecrow Press, London, 1994

78. Meille, Jean-Pierre, *General Beckwith, his Life and Labours among the Waldenses of Piedmont*, Nelson and Sons, London, 1873.

79. Melia, Pious, *The Origin, Persecutions and Doctrines of the Waldenses*, Toovey, London, 1870

80. Millennial Star, *The Latter-day Saints' Millennial Star*, the official publication of the Church of Jesus Christ of Latter-Day Saints in the British Isles from 1840 to 1970

81. Milner, Joseph, *The History of the Church of Christ in 6 Volumes*, Hogan and Thompson, Philadelphia, 1835

82. Monastier, Antoine, *The History of the Vaudois Church*, Lane-Scott, New York, 1849

83. Moore, R. I., *The Origins of European Dissent*, Blackwell, 1985.

84. Morland, Samuel, *History of the Evangelical Churches of the Valleys of Piemont*, Henry Hill, London, 1658

85. Morris, Colin, *The Papal Monarchy, The Western Church from 1050 to 1250*, Clarendon Press, Oxford, 1989.

86. Morris, Norval and Rohman, David J., *Oxford History of the Prison*, New York, 1995

87. Mosheim, John Lawrence, *An Ecclesiastical History, Ancient and Modern, from the Birth of Christ to the 18th Century, in 6 Volumes*, Baynes,

London, 1819
88. Moynahan, Brian, *The Faith, A History of Christianity*, Doubleday, New York, 2002
89. Muston, Alexis, *The Israel of the Alps, A History of the Persecution of the Waldenses*, Ingram-Cooke, London, 1852
90. Neander, August, *Allgemeine Geschichte der Christlichen Religion und Kirche*, 8 Volumes, Perthes, Hamburg, 1826
91. Orchard, G. H. and Graves, J. R., *A Concise History of the Baptists*, Ashland, Lexington, KY, 1956
92. Palacky, Franz, *Über die Beziehungen des Verhältnisses der Waldenser zu den Ehemaligen Secten in Böhmen*, Temsky, Prague, 1869.
93. Pastor, Ludwig, *History of the Popes*, 14 Volumes, St. Louis 1898, London 1910.
94. Patschovsky, Alexander and Selge, Kurt-Victor, *Quellen zur Geschichte der Waldenser*, Mohn, Guetersloh, 1973.
95. Perrin, Jean Paul, *History of the Old Waldenses, Anterior to the Reformation*, Griffith and Simon, Philadelphia, 1847, *Histoire des Vaudois et des Albigen*, originally published in 1618.
96. Perrin, Jean Paul, *History of the Ancient Christians, Waldenses, Albigenses, Vaudois*, Griffith and Simon, Philadelphia, 1847
97. Peters, Edward, editor, *Heresy and Authority in Medieval Europe. Documents in Translation*, University of Pennsylvania Press, Philadelphia, 1986.

98. Peyran, Jean Rodolphe, *An Historical Defence of the Waldenses or Vaudois*, Rivington, London, 1826
99. Reich, E. (ed.), *Select Documents*, London 1905 Robinson, J. H., *Readings in European History*, 2. vols., Boston, 1906,
100. Reuss, Eduard (Wilhelm Eugen), *History of the Sacred Scriptures if the New Testament*, Houghton, Mifflin, Boston, 1884.
101. Richards, D. B., *The Spiritual Allegory,* SLC Magazine Printing Cp., 1931, Pg. 297.
102. Robinson, Robert, *Ecclesiastical Researches*, 1792, republished by Church History and Archives, Gallatin, TN, 1984
103. Rule, W. H., *History of the Inquisition*, Hamilton-Adams, London, 1874.
104. Schaff, Phillip and Schaff, David F., *History of the Christian Church - in 6 Volumes*, Erdmans, Grand Rapids, 1910
105. Schaff, Phillip, *The History of Creeds,* Hodder and Stoughton, London, 1878.
106. Selge, Kurt-Victor, *Die Ersten Waldenser II, mit Edition des liber Antiheresis des Durandus von Osca*, Gruyter and Co., Berlin, 1967.
107. Shea, John Gilmary Ed, *The Catholic Educator: A Library of Catholic Devotion and Instruction*, New York, Thomas Kelly, 1888
108. Singer, S. F. and D. T. Avery, *Unstoppable Global Warming*, New York 2007

109. Snow, Eliza R., *Biography and Family Record of Lorenzo Snow*, Deseret News Co., 1884.
110. Sprout, J. Lamar, *The French Waldenses of Provence*, Masters Thesis, Seventh-Day Adventist Theological Seminary, Washington, D.C., 1957
111. Stalcup, Brenda, Ed., *The Inquisition*, Greenhaven Press, San Diego, 2001.
112. Stephens, Prescot, *The Waldensian Story: a study in faith, intolerance and survival*, Book Guild, Lewes, Sussex, 1998.
113. Storrs, Christopher, *War, Diplomacy and the Rise of Savoy 1690-1720*, Cambridge U. Press, 1999
114. Symcox, Geoffrey, *Victor Amadeus II: Absolutism in the Savoyard State*, U. of California Pres, Berkeley, 1983.
115. Taylor, Thomas, *The History of the Waldenses and Albigenses*, Bolton, London, 1793
116. Teissier, Antoine, *The History of the Negotiation of the Ambassadors sent to the Duke of Savoy by the Protestant Cantons of Switzerland concerning the Vaudois*, Richard Baldwin, London, 1690.
117. Thatcher, O. and McNeal, E., *Source Book of Medieval History*, NY, 1905.
118. Tholfsen, Trygve R., *Ideology and Revolution in Modern Europe, An Essay on the Role of Ideas in History*, Columbia University Press, NY, 1984.
119. Todd, James Henthorn, *The Waldensian Manuscripts preserved in the Library of Trinity College*, MacMillan, Dublin, 1865

120. Tourn, Giorgio, *You Are My Witnesses, The Waldenses Across 800 Years,* Claudiana, Torino, 1989.
121. Tuchman, Barbara, *A Distant Mirror – the Calamitous 14th Century*, Alfred Knopf, NY, 1978.
122. Vacanard, E., *The Inquisition*, NY, 1908.
123. Waddington, George, *The History of the Church from its Earliest Ages until the Reformation,* Baldwin and Cradick, London, 1835
124. Wakefield, Walter F., *Heresy, Crusade and Inquisition in Southern France*, UC Press, Berkeley, 1974
125. Worsfold, J. N., *The Vaudois of Piedmont*, Shaw, London, 1835
126. Wylie, James Aitken (1870), *The History of Protestantism*, Cassel, London, 1870.
127. Wylie, James Aitken (1858), *Wanderings and Musings in the Valleys of the Waldenses*, Edinburgh, 1858.
128. Zepp-LaRouche, Helga, *Alternatives to War and Depression,"* delivered to an Executive Intelligence Review (EIR) seminar in Washington, D.C. May 5, 1999

ACKNOWLEDGEMENTS

Thanks to our children, Heidi, Karl, Natasha, Elizabeth, Daniel and Jeremy all of whom inspired and encouraged me and many of whom provided detailed and helpful comments. Much is owed to Evan Stoddard for his eager support, careful and insightful review and helpful recommendations, and for generously sharing the resources of his publishing company. I express heartfelt gratitude to my beloved wife, Pat, whose ever-present love, patience and encouragement and occasional kindly suggestions saw me all the way through. Lastly I offer thanks to valiant ancestors whose commitment to the Savior, Jesus Christ was absolute, and whose incredible faith, courage and resourcefulness fortified them to meet every challenge.

REFERENCES

1. Attributed to John J. Zubly, quoted in a letter from John Adams to Abagail Adams, 1 October 1775, Adams Family Correspondence, I:290.
2. Biller, 237
3. Schaff, V:493
4. Mosheim, I, Century II, 177
5. Eusibius, II.iii,1-3, 115
6. Eusibius, IV.vii, 1, 313.
7. Milner, Century I:98
8. Gibbon, I:439,
9. Gibbon, I:409.
10. Hegesippus as cited by Eusebius. III:xxxii:7, 277
11. Milner, Century III, 233
12. Milner, Century III, 232
13. Cyprian as cited by Milner, Century III:8
14. Eusebius, I:Introduction, xxxiv
15. Schaff, III:607

16 Mosheim, I, Century I, 133
17 Mosheim I, Century II, 200
18 Mosheim, I, Introduction, 6
19 Neander I:528
20 Neander, I:532
21 Schaff, Phillip, Creeds of Christendom, with a History and Critical Notes, Volume 1
22 Muston, 1-2
23 Robinson, 302-303
24 Robinson, 303
25 Schaff, V:494
26 Waddington, 554-555
27 Neander, IV:605
28 *Nobla Leçon,* as given in Morland, 99. Blair, 473.
29 Comba, 9
30 Preger, *Der Tractat*, David von Augsburg, Munich, 1878, as cited in Comba, 7.
31 Kurtz, 170
32 Taylor, 57-63
33 *Nobla Leçon,* as given in Morland, 99.
34 Peyran, 457-466
35 Eusibius, III.xxv. 6, 257.
36 Mosheim, I: Century I, 215, Century III, 276
37 Neander, II:350, III:402
38 McCracken and Canabiss, 16.
39 P. Johnson, 293.
40 Mosheim III, Century XVIII:xxv
41 Milner, II:Century XII, 69.
42 Schaff, V: 502.

43 *Hieronymus ad Riparium*, contra Vigilantium, as cited in Monastier, 23.
44 Neander, II:605.
45 *Sacro-sancta Concilia*, studio Ph. Labbei t.v. col. 1519 as cited in Monastier, 2.
46 *Defense and Reply to Theodemir*, as given in McCracken and Canabiss, 241
47 McCracken and Canabiss, 217
48 Memoirs of M. A. Rorence, prior of St. Roc, printed in Turin, 1649, cited in Wylie (1870), Volume I, Book 1, Chpt. 6: 23
49 Wylie (1870), 23
50 Robinson, 405
51 Waddington, 290
52 Wakefield, 15:127.
53 Ibid.
54 Comba, 3-4.
55 Mosheim, III, Century XII; 123.
56 Jerome, *Letter to Riparium*, as cited in *St. Jerome Dogmatic and Polemical Works*, Hritzu
57 Mosheim, II: Century VIII, 266.
58 Wakefield, 19.
59 Schaff, V:463
60 Durant, VIII: 544.
61 Mosheim, II, Century VIII, 223-224.
62 Durant, VIII: 626.
63 Bryce, Jas., *Holy Roman Empire*, 158 as cited in Durant, VIII, 547.
64 Durant, VIII: 564.

65 Milner, I, Century XIII, 45
66 Canon 14 of the *Council of Toulouse, 1229* as cited in Allix, 213
67 Shea, 61
68 Durant, VIII:595, 612.
69 Schaff, V:330.
70 Lambert, 28-29.
71 Durant, VIII: 642, 645.
72 McDonnell, 15
73 Peters, 57-58.
74 Schaff, V:464.
75 Lambert, 55.
76 Lambert, 60.
77 Luzzi, 76.
78 Lambert, 31.
79 Schaff, V:462.
80 Waddington, 181
81 Martin, *History of France*, vi:b;xxiii. as cited in Comba, 16.
82 Milner, II, Century XII, 21
83 Allix, 163.
84 Milner, II, Century XII, 23.
85 Schaff, V:473
86 Kurtz, Abs. 2:254
87 Kurtz, Abs. 2: 254
88 Schaff, V: 468.
89 Doellinger, *Beiträge zur Sektengeschichte des Mittelalters*, Munich, 1890, III:300 as cited in Schaff, V: 468.
90 Kurtz, Abs 2: 255
91 Schaff, V: 469.

92 Migne 224:81 as cited in Schaff, V: 469. (The French priest, Jacques Paul Migne, published a compilation of church documents in 1845 AD entitled: *Patrologiae cursus completus,* as a universal library for the Catholic priesthood.)
93 Hase, 277.
94 Mosheim, III, Century XII:122.
95 Robinson, 300-310
96 Milner II, Century XII, 24
97 Biller, 222.
98 Kurtz, Abs. 2:265
99 Luzzi, 147
100 Hase 276
101 Orchard and Graves, Chpt. 2, Sect. 8, Para. 5
102 *Catholic Encyclopedia Online,* Arnold of Brescia, http://www.newadvent.org/cathen/01747b.htm
103 *John of Salisbury* as cited in Lambert, 53.
104 Peyran, 165
105 Cameron (1984), 12
106 Cameron (1984), 15
107 Gilly (1848), iv.
108 Gilly (1848), cv.
109 Wakefield, 32:204.
110 Wakefield, 32:210.
111 Lea (1961), 475
112 Wakefield, 32:208.
113 Migne 157:1050 as cited in Schaff, V: 466. (See Endnote 92)
114 Thatcher and McNeal, 209
115 Durant, VIII: 774.
116 Durant, IV: 779.

117 Wakefield, 140
118 Hase, 277.
119 Comba, 84.
120 Wakefield, 189
121 Comba, 94.
122 Morland, 3
123 Morland, 3
124 Muston, 4; Lawrence, 198
125 Bremer, 11
126 Bremer, 17
127 Hudry-Menos, *Israel of the Alps*, 1867, as cited in Comba, 87.
128 Robinson, 408, 420, 442
129 Comba, 101
130 Lea (1888), II:194
131 Lambert, 147.
132 Cardew, 11.
133 Manchester, 21.
134 Ibid. pg. 22
135 Tuchman, 141-2.
136 P. Johnson, 28.
137 Manchester, 21.
138 P. Johnson, 11
139 Schaff, VI:20
140 Schaff, VI:82-3.
141 Pastor, 143 (as quoted in Schaff VI:123.
142 Schaff, VI: 148, 164.
143 Gibbons, 3:2417.
144 Schaff, VI:178

145 Durant, IV:6.

146 Schaff, VI:307

147 St. Bernardino (1420), as quoted in Coulton, G. G., *Inquisition and Liberty*, London 1938, pg. 45.

148 Tuchman, 83.

149 Tuchman, 95.

150 Tuchman, 100-105.

151 Tuchman, 61-2.

152 Wakefield, 46/278; Comba, 73.

153 Cameron (1984), 48.

154 Cameron (1984), 85.

155 Gui, B. as quoted in Audisio (1999), 12.

156 Patschovski and Selge, as cited in Peters, 150.

157 Monastier, 106

158 Blair, 392, 397

159 Perrin, 118.

160 Camron (1848), 80-82,

161 Audisio (1999), 34-35.

162 Cameron (1984), 104-5.

163 Audisio (2007), 14.

164 Wylie (1870), 131.

165 Lambert, 149.

166 Cameron (1984), 97.

167 Palacky, 24.

168 Palacky, 27.

169 Comba, 101.

170 Lambert, 164.

171 Perrin, 96; Tuchman, 145.

172 Muston, 38.

173 Milner, 65; Schaff V:473.
174 Cameron (1984), 81.
175 Audisio (2007), 27.
176 Gell, 270.
177 Schaff, VI:514.
178 Audisio (1999), 29-30.
179 Audisio (1999), 35.
180 Audisio (1999), 38.
181 Audisio (1999), 68.
182 Ibid, 37.-
183 P. Johnson, 38.
184 Audisio (1999), 111.
185 Audisio (1999), 114.
186 Robinson, 313-314.
187 Audisio (1999), 116.
188 Ibid, 125.
189 Audisio (2007), 21.
190 Audisio (1999), 119.
191 Audisio (1999), 124.
192 Audisio (1999), 121.
193 Biller, Intro.
194 Biller, 211.
195 Biller, 213.
196 Ibid, 127.
197 Lambert, 159, 171.
198 Cardew, 32-38.
199 Kieckenhefer, 110.
200 Lea (1888), 169.
201 Lea (1888), 203

202 Lea (1888), 203
203 Lea (1888), 208.
204 Lea (1888), 211.
205 Stallcup, 20.
206 Augustine's *The City of God* as cited in Moynahan, 152, 154.
207 Vacanard, 68.
208 Wakefield, 16.
209 Cardew, 29-30.
210 Lea (1888), 252.
211 Ames, 184.
212 Stallcup, 21.
213 Cardew, 31.
214 Catholic Encyclopedia. online
215 Cardew, 75.
216 Cardew, 76.
217 Lawrence, 203.
218 Lea (1888), 389.
219 Comba, 52.
220 Gell, 281.
221 Schaff, VI:513.
222 Wylie (1870), 433.
223 Lea (1888), 400.
224 Lea (1888), 399.
225 Wylie (1870), 434; Lea (1888), 389.
226 Wylie (1870), 435, Monastier, 123.
227 Monastier, 124; Schaff, 513.
228 Lea (1888), 398.
229 Lea (1888), 401.

230 Tourn, 67.
231 Tourn, 68.
232 Audisio (2007), 206.
233 Milner, I:49.
234 Tourn, 66.
235 Wylie (1870), 446.
236 Monastier, 135.
237 Audisio (1999), 166.
238 As reported by Leger, *Hist. de Vaudois*, vol. 11, p. 27, as cited in Wylie (1870), 448.
239 Selge, xi.
240 Audisio (2007), 7.
241 Cameron (1984), 215.
242 Audisio (1999), 95.
243 Cameron (1984), 237.
244 Audisio (1999), 152.
245 Audisio (2007), 202.
246 Wylie (1870), 446.
247 Tourn, 67.
248 Cameron (1984), 237.
249 Schaff, VIII:243.
250 Muston, 43.
251 Vinay, *Confessioni de fede ...reformati*, as cited by Cameron (1984), 246-251.
252 Baird, 81.
253 Monastier, 140.
254 Gilles, 30, as cited in Monastier, 141.
255 Audisio (1999), 172-173.
256 Audisio as cited in Encyclopedia of Christian Theology,

Volume 1, by Jean-Yves Lacoste

 257 Melia, 100.

 258 Schaff, VIII:809.

 259 Wylie (1870), 448.

 260 Audisio (1999), 173.

 261 Cameron (1984), 253.

 262 Audisio (2007), 221.

 263 Audisio (2007), 177..

 264 Miton, John, Sonnett: *On the Late Massacre in Piedmont*, 1655.

 265 Pastor, as cited in Durrant VI, page 918.

 266 Papal commission of 1536 as cited in Durant, VI:897.

 267 Giovan Battista Caccia, treatise on reformation of the church as cited by Durant, VI:897.

 268 L. Johnson, 85.

 269 Durant, VI:932-3.

 270 Baigent and Leigh, 181.

 271 Ibid. 131.

 272 Pastor, XIV:277, as cited in Durant, VI:925-6.

 273 Audisio (1999), 186.

 274 Ibid. 182.

 275 Ibid. 180.

 276 De Boer, 38, 48.

 277 Hughes, 300-320.

 278 Tourn, 110-112; Monastier, 228.

 279 Monastier, 147.

 280 Cameron (2000), 286.

 281 Folio XII of Gretser's writings, *Polemic against the Lutherans and Waldenses*, Vol. VII of the Original Catholic

Encyclopedia, Appleton, 1912, 29.
282 Audisio (1999), 194.
283 Monastier, 149; Tourn, 84.
284 Tourn, 87.
285 Cameron (2000), 260.
286 Tourn, 88-89.
287 Cameron (2000), 275.
288 Wylie (1870), 71.
289 Leger, as cited in Wylie (1870), 73.
290 Wylie (1870), 73.
291 Muston, as cited by Wylie (1870), 91.
292 Tourn, 104-5.
293 Monastier, 188.
294 Tourn, 94-96.
295 Morland, 326.
296 Audisio (1999), 205
297 Tourn, 118.
298 Leger, ii:111; as cited in Wylie (1870), Cpt. 13; Morland, 319
299 Monastier, 261.
300 Wylie (1870), 161-162.
301 Monastier, 271.
302 Janavel, Joshua, Manual on Guerilla Warfare, Memorie ed avvisi denti alli Religionari, as cited in Tourn, 125-126.
303 Leger
304 Wylie (1870), 165.
305 Morland, 670-1.
306 Morland, 716.
307 The Crown or the Tiara.
308 Lawrence, 199

309 The Crown or the Tiara,14
310 Ibid. 18
311 Morland, 215
312 Durant, VIII:71
313 Reich, Peace of Augsburg, Articles 16, 17 and 20, 230-232
314 Reich, Edict of Nantes, Articles VI and XVII.
315 Reich, Peace of Westfalia, Article 28.
316 Zepp-LaRouche.
317 Reich, Peace of Westfalia, Article 49
318 Durant, VIII:3
319 Bernier, 114
320 Bernier, 214
321 Bernier, 114
322 Catholic Encyclopedia, *Louis XIV and the Heretics*, www.catholic.org
323 Robinson, 2:287-291
324 Ibid.
325 Reich, Revocation of the Edict of Nantes, October 22, 1685, Articles I through XII.
326 Muston, 416-417
327 Durant, VIII:690
328 by dispatch from Louis XIV, dated from Versailles, 17th January 1686, cited in Muston, 421.
329 Monastier 290
330 Jones, II:385
331 Muston, 433
332 Muston, II:438
333 Arnauld, Preface, xxiii
334 Monastier, 293

335 Muston, 436
336 Monastier, 295
337 Childs, 88
338 Boeri
339 Bernier, 47
340 Childs, 38
341 Childs, 208
342 Childs, 149-150
343 Monastier, 297
344 Monastier, 298
345 Muston, 2:21
346 Monastier, 299
347 Muston, 2:19
348 Dr. Burnett's letter written in 1678 and printed in 1688, cited in Jones II:415
349 Arnaud, xviii
350 Muston, 466-7
351 Muston, 469
352 Morris and Rohman, 79
353 Lawrence, 227
354 Salvejot, *Memoirs*, cited in Muston, 476
355 Monastier, 307
356 Durant, VIII:691
357 Muston, 2:11-17
358 Storrs, 24
359 History of the War of the Grand Alliance, historyworld.net.
360 Bresse, 30
361 Bremer, 18
362 Bautz, 220-221

363 Muston, II:28
364 Durant, VIII:166
365 Original manuscript of the Glorious Return by Arnaud, Royal Library in Berlin, cited by Muston, 38
366 De Lange and Schwinger, 249
367 De Lange and Schwinger, 246
368 History of the War of the Grand Alliance, historyworld.net.
369 De Lange and Schwingerr, 252
370 Arnaud, Henri, Letter to the minister Jacques Pineton de Chambrun in the Hague, December 25, 1688, cited in De Lange and Schwinge, 266
371 Arnaud, Henri, Letter to Jacques Gautier, March 1690, cited in De Lange and Schwinger, 266
372 De Lange and Schwinger, 267
373 Muston, 30
374 Muston, 31
375 Arnauld, 30
376 Reynaudin, H., original manuscript, Royal Library of Berlin, cited in Muston, II:40
377 Relation de ce qui s'est paise de pius remarquable dans le retour des Vaudois, The Hage, 1698, cited in Muston, 49.
378 Arnaud, 68
379 *Instructions* of Janavel as cited in Muston, 31
380 Arnaud, 82
381 Muston, 52
382 Muston, 53
383 Brewer, 22
384 Memoiresur les passages du val St. Martin (MS of Royal Library at Turin) cited by Muston 59

385 Bernier, 126
386 Singer and Avery, 24
387 Arnaud, 208, as cited in Muston, 60
388 Arnaud, 159.
389 Boeri
390 Arnaud, 342, 404, cited in Muston I::69
391 Muston 0-71
392 Muston, 73
393 DiBella, Introduction
394 Muston, II:73
395 Grosek, 78
396 Arnaud, 313
397 Muston, II:79
398 Storrs, 1
399 Lawrence, 242; Muston, II:391
400 Gilly (1831), 289.
401 Wylie (1870), 8.
402 Tholfsen, 28.
403 Hobsbawm, 112.
404 Blanning, 50.
405 Blanning, 50.
406 Hobsbawm, 18
407 Hobsbawm, 28.
408 Hobsbawm, 22
409 Blanning, 338.
410 Kolokotronis as cited in Hobsbawm, 92
411 Hobsbawm, 51.
412 Blanning, 349.
413 Herder, Johann Gottfried, as cited in Blanning, 336.

414 Rousseau, *Julie*, 1761...as cited in Blanning, 191.
415 Goethe, Goetz von Berchlingen, 1773 as cited in Blanning, 519.
416 Blanning, 362.
417 De Toqueville 1856 as cited in Durant, X:898.
418 Hobsbawm, 109.
419 Tholfsen, 50.
420 Hobsbawm, 23,
421 Blanning, 543.
422 Tourn, 146.
423 Tourn, 160.
424 Tourn, 150.
425 Wylie (1858), 209-210.
426 Meille, 207.
427 Gilly (1831), 58.
428 Gilly (1831), 200
429 Gilly (1831), 200.
430 Tourn, 161.
431 Wylie (1858), 217
432 Meille, 165
433 Beckwith Letter from England to the Vaudois, dated 21 August 1840, cited in Meille, 170
434 Beckwith Letter of 10 September 1855, as cited in Meille, 199 and 249.
435 Meille, 204
436 Elder G. D. Keaton, letters dated March and June 1854, *Millennial Star*, Vol. 16, pp. 204-20.
437 Grotke and Putsch, pg. 55
438 Wylie (1858) 210.

439 Meille, 204.
440 Gilly (1831), Chapter V:6.

ABOUT THE AUTHOR

Stephen G. Beus, was born in Idaho in 1939, received his undergraduate education at the University of Utah and earned his PhD in mechanical engineering at Carnegie Mellon University in 1968. He worked for the Bettis Atomic Power Laboratory in Pittsburgh, Pennsylvania for 36 years, specializing in thermal-hydraulics and retiring as a consulting engineer in 2004. Steve and his wife, Pat, are the parents of six children and now reside in Portland, Oregon. Steve's 2nd great grandparents, Michel and Marianne Beux were born among the Vaudois in Italy and immigrated with their family of eight children to the United States in 1856.

www.ingramcontent.com/pod-product-compliance
Lightning Source LLC
Chambersburg PA
CBHW030430010526
44118CB00011B/578